NE능률 영어교과서

대한민국 고등학생 **10**명 중 **4.7**명이 보는 교과서

영어 고등 교과서 점유율 1위

[7차, 2007 개정, 2009 개정, 2015 개정]

능률보카

그동안 판매된
능률VOCA 1,100만 부

대한민국 박스오피스
**천만명을 넘은 영화
단 28개**

리딩튜터

그동안 판매된
리딩튜터 1,900만 부
차곡차곡 쌓으면 19만 미터

**에베레스트
21 배 높이**

190,000m

에베레스트 8,848m

그래머존

그동안 판매된 450만 부의 그래머존을 바닥에 쭉 ~ 깔면

1000km 서울 - 부산 왕복가능

서울

부산

STARTER

지은이	NE능률 영어교육연구소
선임연구원	김지현
연구원	박효빈, 가민아
영문교열	Curtis Thompson, Angela Lan
디자인	민유화
맥편집	허문희

Let's grow together

NE능률이
미래를
창조합니다.

건강한 배움의 고객가치를 제공하겠다는 꿈을 실현하기 위해
40년이 넘는 시간 동안 열심히 달려왔습니다.

앞으로도 끊임없는 연구와 노력을 통해
당연한 것을 멈추지 않고

고객, 기업, 직원 모두가 함께 성장하는 NE능률이 되겠습니다.

GRAMMAR

Inside

STARTER

STRUCTURES

- I have a **sister**.
- Amy has two **sisters**.

A 명사

1 명사는 사람, 사물, 장소, 개념 등의 이름을 나타내는 말이다.
Amy, sister, book, TV, park, Korea, peace, help ...

2 명사는 '하나, 둘…'의 형태로 셀 수 있는 명사와 '하나, 둘…'의 형태로 셀 수 없는 명사로 나뉜다.
a **dog**, two **dogs**, three **dogs** ...
love (a love, two loves, three loves ...)

B 셀 수 있는 명사의 단수형

셀 수 있는 명사 하나를 나타낼 때는 명사의 원래 형태(단수형)를 쓰고 앞에 a/an을 붙인다.
a pen, **a** watch, **a** house, **an** apple, **an** umbrella, **an** idea ...

C 셀 수 있는 명사의 복수형

둘 이상의 셀 수 있는 명사를 나타낼 때는 보통 명사 뒤에 -(e)s를 붙인다.

대부분의 명사	명사 + -s	cars maps books chairs friends
-s, -x, -ch, -sh, -o 로 끝나는 명사	명사 + -es	buses classes boxes watches dishes tomatoes (예외: pianos, photos)
〈자음 + y〉로 끝나는 명사	y를 i로 고치고 + -es	baby → babies city → cities puppy → puppies
-f, -fe로 끝나는 명사	f, fe를 v로 고치고 + -es	leaf → leaves knife → knives (예외: roofs)
예외 불규칙변화	man → men woman → women child → children foot → feet tooth → teeth mouse → mice	
형태가 같은 경우	fish → fish sheep → sheep deer → deer	

We need two **chairs**.
The **puppies** are cute.
I brush my **teeth** every day.
The farmer has three **deer**.

PRACTICE

🔍 Answer Key p-2

STEP 1

밑줄 친 부분이 명사이면 O표, 명사가 아니면 X표 하시오.

0 She loves her cat. _____O_____
1 Andy is very kind. _____
2 I have an umbrella. _____
3 I need your help. _____
4 We go to school together. _____
5 There is a cup in the box. _____

STEP 2

주어진 명사의 복수형을 쓰시오.

0 a ball — two ___balls___
1 a rose — three _____
2 a dish — four _____
3 a foot — two _____
4 a boy — three _____
5 a leaf — five _____
6 a city — two _____
7 a woman — eight _____
8 a sheep — four _____

STEP 3

주어진 명사를 적절한 형태로 써서 문장을 완성하시오.

0 toy   a. There is a ___toy___ on the floor.
        b. There are three ___toys___ on the floor.
1 potato a. We need a _____.
        b. We need two _____.
2 child   a. He has a _____.
        b. He has four _____.
3 knife   a. There is a _____ on the table.
        b. There are three _____ on the table.
4 fish   a. We have a _____ in the fish tank.
        b. We have seven _____ in the fish tank.

GRAMMAR POINT

해당 Unit에서 배워야 할 핵심 문법들을
명확한 설명과 실용적인 예문으로 체계적으로 정리했습니다.

PRACTICE

Grammar Point에서 학습한 내용을 다양한 유형의
문제를 통해 자연스럽게 익힐 수 있습니다.

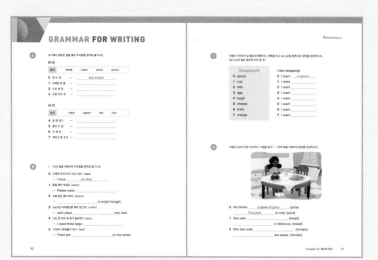

GRAMMAR FOR WRITING

다양한 형태의 쓰기 문제를 풀어봄으로써 Grammar Point를 반복 학습하며 sentence writing의 기초를 마련할 수 있습니다.

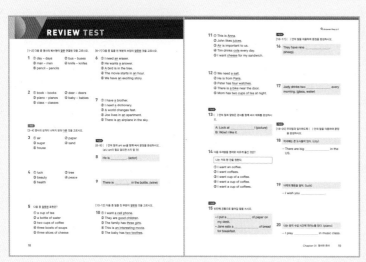

REVIEW TEST

실제 학교 시험과 가장 유사한 유형의 문제들로 구성하여 실전에 대비할 수 있습니다.
서술형 문제를 대폭 수록하여 학교 내신 시험의 서술형 주관식 문항에 완벽하게 대비할 수 있도록 하였습니다.

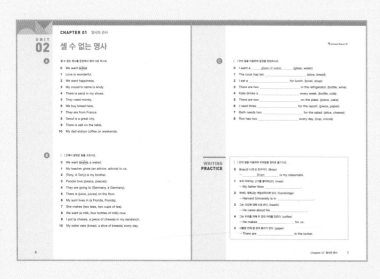

WORKBOOK

각 Unit별 연습문제와 쓰기 문제, Chapter별 Review Test를 수록하였습니다.
더 많은 문제를 풀어봄으로써 문법을 보다 완벽하게 익힐 수 있도록 하였습니다.

CONTENTS

01 단어의 종류

영어 단어에는 명사, 대명사, 동사, 형용사, 부사, 전치사, 접속사, 감탄사 등이 있다.

명사 명사는 사람, 사물, 장소 등의 이름을 나타내는 말이다.

Ella, Mr. Smith, father ...
table, book, window, TV ...
room, library, New York, China ...
time, health, love, war ...

I know **Brian**.

대명사 대명사는 명사를 대신하는 말로, '나, 너, 그, 우리, 이것, 저것…' 등을 나타낸다.

I, you, he, she, it, we, they ...
this, that ...

He is **my** friend.

동사 동사는 사람, 동물, 사물의 동작이나 상태를 나타내는 말이다.

am, are, is ...
have, like, hate, know, live ...
go, walk, run, eat, make, buy ...
will, can, may, must ...

He **likes** soccer.

형용사 형용사는 사람이나 사물의 형태, 성질, 상태 등을 묘사하는 말로 명사나 대명사를 꾸며준다.

tall, short, big, small ...
happy, sad, kind, interesting ...
handsome, pretty, young, old ...

He is a **tall** boy.

부사 부사는 방법, 시간, 횟수, 장소, 정도 등을 나타내는 말로
동사, 형용사, 다른 부사나 문장 전체를 꾸며준다.

slowly, fast, early, late ...
always, sometimes, often ...
here, there, very, much ...

He runs **fast**.

전치사 전치사는 명사 또는 대명사 앞에 쓰여 시간, 장소 등을
나타내는 말이다.

at, on, in ...
before, after ...
over, under, behind ...

He lives **in** Seoul.

접속사 접속사는 단어와 단어, 문장과 문장 등을 이어주는 말이다.

and, but, or ...
when, because ...

He is kind **and**
handsome.

감탄사 감탄사는 기쁨, 감탄, 놀람 등의 감정을 표현하는 말이다.

Bravo, Wow ...
Oh, Oops ...

Oh, he's there!

02 문장의 구성

문장을 이루는 구성 요소에는 주어, 동사, 목적어, 보어, 수식어가 있다.
영어 문장의 기본 뼈대는 주어와 동사이며, 동사 뒤에 어떤 구성 요소가 오느냐에 따라 문장의 종류가 달라진다.

주어 주어는 '누가 ~하다[이다]'에서 '누가'에 해당하는 말이다.
주어 자리에는 보통 명사나 대명사, 또는 명사 역할을 하는 말이 올 수 있다.

동사 동사는 '누가 ~하다[이다]'에서 '~하다', '~이다'에 해당하는 말로, 주어의 행동이나 상태를 나타낸다.
동사에는 be동사, 일반동사, 조동사가 있다.

Sarah	cooked.
주어	동사

목적어 목적어는 '누가 ~을 …하다'에서 '~을'에 해당하는 말로, 동사의 목적 또는 대상이 되는 말이다.
목적어 자리에는 주어와 마찬가지로 명사나 대명사, 또는 명사 역할을 하는 말이 올 수 있다.

Sarah	cooked	pasta.
주어	동사	목적어

동사에 따라 두 개의 목적어가 필요한 경우도 있는데, 이 목적어들은 각각 '~에게'와 '…을'의 의미를 나타낸다.

Sarah	cooked	us	pasta.
주어	동사	목적어 1	목적어 2

보어 보어는 주어나 목적어를 보충 설명해 주는 말로, 보어 자리에는 명사나 형용사 등이 올 수 있다.
주격 보어는 '누가 A이다'에서 A에 해당된다.

Sarah	is	a good cook.
주어	동사	주격 보어

목적어 뒤에 쓰이는 목적격 보어는 목적어의 성질, 상태 등을 보충 설명해 준다.

We	call	her	a good cook.
주어	동사	목적어	목적격 보어

수식어 수식어는 문장의 필수 요소는 아니지만 다른 문장 요소를 꾸며 문장의 뜻을 더 자세하게 해주는 말이다.
수식어의 위치는 다양하며 한 문장 안에 여러 개가 있을 수도 있다. 수식어로는 형용사나 부사 등을 쓸 수 있다.

Sarah	cooks	well.
주어	동사	수식어

ESSENTIAL RULES OF
ENGLISH GRAMMAR

CHAPTER
01

명사와 관사

셀 수 있는 명사

- I have a **sister**.
- Amy has two **sisters**.

A 명사

1 명사는 사람, 사물, 장소, 개념 등의 이름을 나타내는 말이다.

Amy, sister, book, TV, park, Korea, peace, help …

2 명사는 '하나, 둘…'의 형태로 셀 수 있는 명사와 '하나, 둘…'의 형태로 셀 수 없는 명사로 나뉜다.

a **dog**, two **dogs**, three **dogs** …
~~love (a love, two loves, three loves …)~~

B 셀 수 있는 명사의 단수형

셀 수 있는 명사 하나를 나타낼 때는 명사의 원래 형태(단수형)를 쓰고 앞에 a/an을 붙인다.

a pen, **a** watch, **a** house, **an** apple, **an** umbrella, **an** idea …

C 셀 수 있는 명사의 복수형

둘 이상의 셀 수 있는 명사를 나타낼 때는 보통 명사 뒤에 -(e)s를 붙인다.

대부분의 명사	명사 + -s	car**s** map**s** book**s** chair**s** friend**s**
-s, -x, -ch, -sh, -o 로 끝나는 명사	명사 + -es	bus**es** class**es** box**es** watch**es** dish**es** tomato**es** (예외: piano**s**, photo**s**)
〈자음 + y〉로 끝나는 명사	y를 i로 고치고 + -es	baby → bab**ies** city → cit**ies** puppy → pupp**ies**
-f, -fe로 끝나는 명사	f, fe를 v로 고치고 + -es	leaf → lea**ves** knife → kni**ves** (예외: roof**s**)
예외	불규칙변화	man → **men** woman → **women** child → **children** foot → **feet** tooth → **teeth** mouse → **mice**
	형태가 같은 경우	fish → **fish** sheep → **sheep** deer → **deer**

We need two **chairs**.
The **puppies** are cute.
I brush my **teeth** every day.
The farmer has three **deer**.

PRACTICE

🔍 Answer Key p.2

STEP 1

밑줄 친 부분이 명사이면 O표, 명사가 아니면 X표 하시오.

0 She loves her <u>cat</u>.　　　　　　　　　O

1 <u>Andy</u> is very kind.　　　　　_____

2 I have <u>an</u> umbrella.　　　　　_____

3 I need your <u>help</u>.　　　　　_____

4 We <u>go</u> to school together.　　　_____

5 There is a <u>cup</u> in the box.　　　_____

STEP 2

주어진 명사의 복수형을 쓰시오.

0 a ball　　–　two _____balls_____

1 a rose　　–　three _____

2 a dish　　–　four _____

3 a foot　　–　two _____

4 a boy　　–　three _____

5 a leaf　　–　five _____

6 a city　　–　two _____

7 a woman　–　eight _____

8 a sheep　–　four _____

STEP 3

주어진 명사를 적절한 형태로 써서 문장을 완성하시오.

0 toy　　　　a. There is a _____toy_____ on the floor.

　　　　　　　b. There are three _____toys_____ on the floor.

1 potato　　a. We need a _____.

　　　　　　　b. We need two _____.

2 child　　　a. He has a _____.

　　　　　　　b. He has four _____.

3 knife　　　a. There is a _____ on the table.

　　　　　　　b. There are three _____ on the table.

4 fish　　　　a. We have a _____ in the fish tank.

　　　　　　　b. We have seven _____ in the fish tank.

셀 수 없는 명사

• I drink **milk** in the morning.

A 셀 수 없는 명사의 종류

1 셀 수 없는 물질을 나타내는 명사

water, milk, juice, salt, sand, air, paper, money …
(a water, two waters …)

2 추상적인 개념을 나타내는 명사

love, peace, beauty, happiness, luck, health, friendship …
(a health, two healths …)

3 사람이나 지역 등의 이름을 나타내는 명사

Peter, Sarah, Mr. Jones, Seoul, Canada, Europe …
(a Seoul, two Seouls …)

B 셀 수 없는 명사의 수

1 셀 수 없는 명사는 항상 단수형으로 쓰고, 앞에 a나 an을 쓰지 않는다.

We need **salt**. (a salt)

2 셀 수 없는 물질을 나타내는 명사의 수는 단위 명사를 써서 나타내며, 복수형을 나타낼 때는 단위 명사에
-(e)s를 붙인다.

· a glass of milk/water/juice	· a cup of coffee/tea
· a piece of paper	· a slice[piece] of bread/cheese/cake
· a bowl of rice/soup	· a bottle of water/cola/wine

a glass of milk, **two glasses of** milk

a cup of coffee, **two cups of** coffee

a piece of paper, **two pieces of** paper

a slice of bread, **two slices of** bread

a bowl of rice, **two bowls of** rice

a bottle of water, **two bottles of** water

PRACTICE

🔍 Answer Key p.2

STEP 1

셀 수 없는 명사를 문장에서 찾아 O표 하시오.

0 We need (sugar).

1 Friendship is important.

2 My aunt lives in London.

3 I like cheese very much.

4 The air is fresh and clean.

5 They spend money every day.

STEP 2

( ) 안에서 알맞은 말을 고르시오.

0 He enjoys (tea, a tea) after lunch.

1 We want (peace, a peace).

2 I exercise for my (health, healths).

3 (New York / A New York) is a big city.

4 She buys (bread, two breads) in a bakery.

5 I want (two juice, two glasses of juice).

STEP 3

사진을 보고 ( ) 안의 말을 이용하여 빈칸을 완성하시오.

0 a _cup of coffee_
(coffee)

1 two _____
(bread)

2 three _____
(water)

3 two _____
(cake)

4 a _____
(soup)

5 four _____
(paper)

관사

• **A** bird is in **the** sky.

A 관사

관사는 명사 앞에 쓰여 명사의 성격에 대한 정보를 주는 말이다. 관사에는 부정관사 a/an과 정관사 the가 있다.

a pencil, **an** egg, **the** boy …

B 부정관사 a/an

부정관사 a/an은 셀 수 있는 명사의 단수형 앞에 쓴다. 발음이 자음으로 시작하는 단어 앞에는 a, 발음이 모음으로 시작하는 단어 앞에는 an을 쓴다.

a notebook, **a** mirror, **a** desk, **an** eraser, **an** umbrella, **an** hour …

1 특정하지 않은 하나를 나타낼 때

He is **a** student.
I know **a** funny story.

2 하나를 나타낼 때 (= one)

I have two shirts and **a** skirt.

C 정관사 the

정관사 the는 명사의 단수형과 복수형 앞에 모두 쓰인다.

1 앞에서 언급한 명사를 다시 가리킬 때

I have *a* bag. **The** bag is brown.
There is *an* orange in the basket. **The** orange is big.

2 서로 알고 있는 것을 가리킬 때

Look at **the** window.
Pass me **the** salt.

3 관용적으로 쓰이는 경우

1) 유일한 것: **the** sun, **the** moon, **the** earth, **the** sky, **the** world …
2) 악기 이름(연주의 대상): play **the** piano/violin/flute …

PRACTICE

🔍 Answer Key p-2

STEP 1

빈칸에 a나 an 중 알맞은 것을 쓰시오.

0 Mike has ____a____ cat.

1 She is _____ artist.

2 They have _____ daughter.

3 This is _____ old house.

4 There is _____ pen on the desk.

5 You need _____ umbrella today.

STEP 2

( ) 안에서 알맞은 말을 고르시오. (X는 필요 없음을 뜻함)

0 (A, (The)) sun shines in the morning.

1 I play (the, an) piano.

2 (A, The) girls are my friends.

3 Tom is my uncle. He is (a, X) teacher.

4 I have a bicycle. (A, The) bicycle is red.

5 My older brother is (a, the) high school student.

STEP 3

우리말과 일치하도록 빈칸에 알맞은 관사를 넣어 문장을 완성하시오.

0 아빠와 나는 매주 그 체육관에 간다.

→ Dad and I go to ____the____ gym every week.

1 Jenny는 우유와 달걀 하나가 필요하다.

→ Jenny needs milk and _____ egg.

2 지구는 태양 주위를 돈다.

→ _____ earth goes around the sun.

3 세계에는 많은 나라들이 있다.

→ There are many countries in _____ world.

4 새로운 공원이 문을 열었다. Sam과 Mina는 그 공원에 있다.

→ A new park is open. Sam and Mina are in _____ park.

GRAMMAR FOR WRITING

A 보기에서 알맞은 말을 골라 우리말을 영어로 옮기시오.

[0-3]

보기	book	class	email	photo

0 책 두 권 → <u>two books</u>

1 이메일 한 통 → _____

2 사진 세 장 → _____

3 수업 다섯 개 → _____

[4-7]

보기	cake	paper	tea	rice

4 밥 한 공기 → _____

5 종이 두 장 → _____

6 차 세 잔 → _____

7 케이크 한 조각 → _____

B ( ) 안의 말을 이용하여 우리말을 영어로 옮기시오.

0 나에게 아이디어가 하나 있다. (idea)

→ I have <u>an idea</u>.

1 문을 열어 주세요. (door)

→ Please open _____.

2 오늘 밤은 달이 밝다. (moon)

→ _____ is bright tonight.

3 Jack은 바이올린을 매우 잘 켠다. (violin)

→ Jack plays _____ very well.

4 나는 큰 상자 세 개가 필요하다. (box)

→ I need three large _____.

5 거리에 나뭇잎들이 있다. (leaf)

→ There are _____ on the street.

C 다음은 수진이가 살 물건의 목록이다. 목록을 보고 a나 an을 함께 써서 문장을 완성하시오.
(a나 an이 필요 없으면 쓰지 말 것)

Shopping List	I like shopping!
0 spoon	**0** I want ___a spoon___ .
1 cup	**1** I want _____ .
2 milk	**2** I want _____ .
3 egg	**3** I want _____ .
4 sugar	**4** I want _____ .
5 cheese	**5** I want _____ .
6 knife	**6** I want _____ .
7 orange	**7** I want _____ .

D 다음은 Iris의 아침 식사이다. 그림을 보고 ( ) 안의 말을 이용하여 문장을 완성하시오.

0 Iris drinks _____a glass of juice_____ . (juice)
  _____The juice_____ is cold. (juice)
1 She eats _____ . (bread)
  _____ is delicious. (bread)
2 She also eats _____ . (tomato)
  _____ are sweet. (tomato)

REVIEW TEST

[1-2] 다음 중 명사의 복수형이 <u>잘못</u> 연결된 것을 고르시오.

1　① day – days　　② bus – buses
　　③ man – men　　④ knife – knifes
　　⑤ pencil – pencils

2　① book – books　　② deer – deers
　　③ piano – pianos　　④ baby – babies
　　⑤ class – classes

〔빈출〕
[3-4] 명사의 성격이 나머지 넷과 <u>다른</u> 것을 고르시오.

3　① air　　　② paper
　　③ sugar　　④ sand
　　⑤ house

4　① luck　　② tree
　　③ beauty　④ peace
　　⑤ health

5　다음 중 <u>잘못된</u> 표현은?
　　① a cup of tea
　　② a bottle of water
　　③ two cups of coffee
　　④ three bowls of soups
　　⑤ three slices of cheese

[6-7] 다음 중 밑줄 친 부분의 쓰임이 <u>잘못된</u> 것을 고르시오.

6　① I need <u>an</u> eraser.
　　② He wants <u>a</u> answer.
　　③ <u>A</u> bird is in the tree.
　　④ The movie starts in <u>an</u> hour.
　　⑤ We have <u>an</u> exciting story.

7　① I have <u>a</u> brother.
　　② I need <u>a</u> dictionary.
　　③ <u>A</u> world changes fast.
　　④ Joe lives in <u>an</u> apartment.
　　⑤ There is <u>an</u> airplane in the sky.

〔서술형〕
[8-9] ( ) 안의 말과 a나 an을 함께 써서 문장을 완성하시오.
　　　(a나 an이 필요 없으면 쓰지 말 것)

8　He is _____ . (actor)

9　There is _____ in the bottle. (wine)

[10-12] 다음 중 밑줄 친 부분이 <u>잘못된</u> 것을 고르시오.

10　① I want <u>a cell phone</u>.
　　② They are <u>good children</u>.
　　③ The family has <u>three girls</u>.
　　④ This is <u>an interesting movie</u>.
　　⑤ The baby has <u>two toothes</u>.

11 ① This is <u>Anna</u>.
② John likes <u>juices</u>.
③ <u>Air</u> is important to us.
④ Tim drinks <u>cola</u> every day.
⑤ I want <u>cheese</u> for my sandwich.

12 ① We need <u>a salt</u>.
② He is from <u>Paris</u>.
③ Peter has <u>four watches</u>.
④ There is <u>a bike</u> near the door.
⑤ Mom has <u>two cups of tea</u> at night.

서술형

13 ( ) 안의 말과 알맞은 관사를 함께 써서 대화를 완성하시오.

A: Look at _____! (picture)
B: Wow! I like it.

14 다음 우리말을 영어로 바르게 옮긴 것은?

나는 커피 한 잔을 원한다.

① I want an coffee.
② I want coffees.
③ I want cup of a coffee.
④ I want a cup of coffee.
⑤ I want a cup of coffees.

서술형

15 빈칸에 공통으로 들어갈 말을 쓰시오.

• I put a _____ of paper on my desk.
• Jane eats a _____ of bread for breakfast.

서술형

[16-17] ( ) 안의 말을 이용하여 문장을 완성하시오.

16 They have nine _____.
(sheep)

17 Judy drinks two _____ every morning. (glass, water)

서술형

[18-20] 우리말과 일치하도록 ( ) 안의 말을 이용하여 문장을 완성하시오.

18 미국에는 큰 도시들이 있다. (city)

→ There are big _____ in the US.

19 너에게 행운을 빌어. (luck)

→ I wish you _____.

20 나는 음악 수업 시간에 피아노를 친다. (piano)

→ I play _____ in music class.

WORD LIST

- **park** 공원
- **peace** 평화
- **umbrella** 우산
- **idea** 아이디어
- **dish** 접시
- **city** 도시
- **puppy** 강아지
- **leaf** 잎
- **knife** 칼
- **woman** 여자
- **foot** 발
- **tooth** 치아
- **sheep** 양
- **deer** 사슴
- **need** 필요하다
- **floor** 바닥
- **fish tank** 어항
- **beauty** 아름다움
- **happiness** 행복
- **luck** 행운
- **health** 건강
- **friendship** 우정
- **bowl** 그릇
- **important** 중요한
- **want** 원하다
- **bright** 밝은
- **large** 큰
- **dictionary** 사전
- **apartment** 아파트
- **cell phone** 휴대 전화
- **interesting** 재미있는
- **put** 두다

ESSENTIAL RULES OF
ENGLISH GRAMMAR

CHAPTER
02

대명사

인칭대명사

• I love **my** family.

A 대명사

대명사는 명사를 대신해서 쓰는 말로, 같은 명사를 반복하여 쓰지 않기 위해 사용한다.

Mike is funny. **He** is popular at school.

B 인칭대명사

인칭대명사는 나(1인칭), 너(2인칭), 그/그녀/그것(3인칭) 등을 나타내는 대명사이다.

수	인칭	주격(~는, ~가)	소유격(~의)	목적격(~을)	소유대명사 (~의 것)
단수	1인칭	I	my	me	mine
	2인칭	you	your	you	yours
	3인칭	he	his	him	his
		she	her	her	hers
		it	its	it	–
복수	1인칭	we	our	us	ours
	2인칭	you	your	you	yours
	3인칭	they	their	them	theirs

C 인칭대명사의 격

1 주격(~는, ~가): 문장에서 주어 역할을 한다.

   I like Sue. **She** is smart.

2 소유격(~의): 명사 앞에 쓰여 소유 관계를 나타낸다.

   I know **his** *name*. He is **my** *friend*.

   cf. 고유명사의 소유격은 고유명사에 's를 붙여 나타낸다.
   Nora's *book*, **Peter's** *pen* …

3 목적격(~을): 문장에서 동사나 전치사의 목적어 역할을 한다.

   I *miss* **her** very much.
   Dave is angry *at* **me**.

4 소유대명사(~의 것): 「소유격+명사」를 나타낸다.

   The cell phone is **mine**.
   <u></u> = my cell phone

PRACTICE

🔍 Answer Key p.3

STEP 1

주어진 말을 가리키는 주격 대명사를 쓰시오.

0 Tom   →   he

1 a pen   → _____

2 my sister   → _____

3 you and I   → _____

4 Mr. Brown   → _____

5 Emily and Tim   → _____

6 you and Jessica   → _____

7 the buildings   → _____

STEP 2

( ) 안에서 알맞은 말을 고르시오.

0 (He, His) is friendly.

1 The jacket is (his, him).

2 Jay smiles at (my, me).

3 I like (her, hers) songs.

4 Paul helps (our, us) a lot.

5 He is (Mary, Mary's) brother.

6 The computer is (them, theirs).

STEP 3

( ) 안의 말을 적절한 형태로 써서 문장을 완성하시오.

0 I like _____your____ voice. (you)

1 I remember _____. (he)

2 This is _____ house. (we)

3 The wallet is _____. (I)

4 She is _____ cousin. (I)

5 The suitcase is _____. (she)

6 _____ are my best friends. (they)

7 The boy looks at _____. (she)

8 I like the T-shirt. _____ color is nice. (it)

UNIT 02

this, that, it

• **This** is a new jacket.

A this

1 가까이 있는 사물이나 사람을 가리킬 때 쓰며, '이것', '이 사람', '이 (~)'의 의미를 나타낸다.

This is a tennis ball.
This is my friend Susan.
This *street* is clean.

2 this의 복수형은 these이다.

These are my parents.
We need **these** *boxes*.

B that

1 멀리 떨어져 있는 사물이나 사람을 가리킬 때 쓰며, '저것', '저 사람', '저 (~)'의 의미를 나타낸다.

That is my locker.
That is Jason's uncle.
I want **that** *computer*.

2 that의 복수형은 those이다.

Those are nice pictures.
Those *shoes* are expensive.

C 비인칭 주어 it

시간, 요일, 날짜, 날씨, 거리, 명암, 계절 등을 나타낼 때 문장의 주어로 it을 쓰고 이 it을 비인칭 주어라고 부른다. 비인칭 주어 it은 특별한 의미가 없으므로, '그것'이라고 해석하지 않는다.

It is three o'clock now.
It is Saturday today.
It is November 10.
It is sunny this morning.
It is 2 km to the park.
It is dark outside.
It is spring again.

PRACTICE

🔍 Answer Key p-3

STEP 1

( ) 안에서 알맞은 말을 고르시오.

0 (That, Those) is Susan's bag.

1 (That, It) is Thursday today.

2 (That, Those) are his books.

3 (This, These) is a sad story.

4 I like (this, these) movie posters.

STEP 2

그림을 보고 보기에서 알맞은 말을 골라 문장을 완성하시오.

보기	this	that	these	those

0 ___That___ is a police car.

1 _____ is a new bike.

2 He works in _____ building.

3 _____ is my friend Philip.

4 _____ cookies are delicious.

5 _____ are nice clothes.

STEP 3

( ) 안의 말을 이용하여 문장을 완성하시오.

0 _____It is Monday_____ today. (Monday)

1 _____ outside. (rainy)

2 _____ now. (10:30 a.m.)

3 _____ today. (October 17)

4 _____ from here to my school. (1 km)

GRAMMAR FOR WRITING

A 보기에서 알맞은 말을 골라 우리말을 영어로 옮기시오.

[0-3]

보기	~~you~~	her	him	ours

0 너는 매우 친절하구나. → ___You___ are very kind.

1 Betty는 그를 좋아한다. → Betty likes _____.

2 그녀의 미소는 밝다. → _____ smile is bright.

3 파란색 차가 우리 것이다. → The blue car is _____.

[4-7]

보기	this	that	these	those

4 저 타워는 높다. → _____ tower is high.

5 이 케이크는 달콤하다. → _____ cake is sweet.

6 저 사람들은 축구 선수들이다. → _____ are soccer players.

7 이것들은 Jack에게서 온 편지들이다. → _____ are the letters from Jack.

B 알맞은 대명사를 이용하여 우리말을 영어로 옮기시오.

0 이것은 공포 영화이다.

→ ___This___ is a horror movie.

1 나는 너희들의 도움이 필요하다.

→ I need _____ help.

2 그 검은색 코트는 그의 것이다.

→ The black coat is _____.

3 그 목걸이는 그녀를 위한 것이다.

→ The necklace is for _____.

4 오늘은 5월 23일이다.

→ _____ is May 23 today.

5 이분들은 나의 이웃인 Parker 부부이다.

→ _____ are my neighbors, Mr. and Mrs. Parker.

C 빈칸에 알맞은 대명사를 써서 문장을 완성하시오.

0 Julie is my cousin. ___She___ is lovely.

1 Tony has a watch. This is _____ watch.

2 I know _____. She is Tim's sister.

3 The garden is wonderful. I like _____.

4 They are twins. _____ names are Sue and Lucy.

5 My brother and I share a room. This is _____ room.

6 Nick is my friend. I often play basketball with _____.

7 Brian and I are classmates. _____ go to school together.

8 A: Is this your textbook?
   B: Yes, it is _____.

D 그림을 보고 보기에서 알맞은 말을 골라 문장을 완성하시오. (단, 한 번씩만 쓸 것)

보기	~~this~~
	that
	we
	he
	them
	these

0 ___This___ is my family.

1 _____ are my parents. I love _____ very much.

2 _____ is our puppy Toby. _____ is very smart.

3 _____ are happy together.

REVIEW TEST

[1-3] 빈칸에 들어갈 알맞은 말을 고르시오.

1

_____ tomatoes are fresh.

① This   ② That   ③ These
④ It   ⑤ Theirs

2

I have a candle. _____ smell is sweet.

① My   ② His   ③ It
④ Its   ⑤ Our

3

_____ is windy outside.

① This   ② That   ③ It
④ These   ⑤ Those

서술형

[4-6] ( ) 안의 말을 적절한 형태로 써서 문장을 완성하시오.

4

This is _____ photo. (she)

5

We visit _____ every Sunday. (they)

6

The ball is _____. (we)

7 빈칸에 들어갈 말로 알맞지 <u>않은</u> 것은?

It is _____ camera.

① hers   ② your   ③ his
④ their   ⑤ Sam's

[8-9] 다음 중 밑줄 친 부분이 잘못된 것을 고르시오.

8 ① The bag is <u>mine</u>.
② <u>Your</u> advice is helpful.
③ The presents are for <u>they</u>.
④ That lady is <u>Linda's</u> mom.
⑤ <u>We</u> live in an apartment.

9 ① I love <u>your</u> idea.
② <u>It's</u> color is beautiful.
③ The wallet is <u>hers</u>.
④ My friends are angry at <u>me</u>.
⑤ <u>Larry's</u> dad is a pilot.

빈출

10 다음 중 밑줄 친 부분을 가리키는 대명사가 잘못된 것은?

① This is <u>my book</u>. → mine
② I know <u>Kevin's address</u>. → his
③ <u>Emily</u> is my best friend. → She
④ I need <u>a notebook and a pen</u>. → them
⑤ <u>Tom and I</u> are at the mall now. → They

[11-12] 빈칸에 들어갈 말이 바르게 짝지어진 것을 고르시오.

11
| • The concert ticket is ___(A)___ . |
| • ___(B)___ shoes are big for me. |

	(A)		(B)
①	its	......	This
②	your	......	This
③	your	......	These
④	yours	......	That
⑤	yours	......	These

12
| A: Hi, Kelly. ___(A)___ is Mark. |
| B: Hi, Mark. Nice to meet ___(B)___ . |

	(A)		(B)
①	This	......	him
②	This	......	you
③	That	......	he
④	That	......	him
⑤	That	......	me

[13-14] 밑줄 친 부분의 쓰임이 나머지 넷과 다른 것을 고르시오.

13 ① This is <u>her</u> key.
② I borrow <u>her</u> pencils.
③ Wendy enjoys <u>her</u> job.
④ <u>Her</u> family is from India.
⑤ We visit <u>her</u> every weekend.

14 ① <u>It</u> is cloudy today.
② <u>It</u> is ten o'clock in Seoul.
③ <u>It</u> is summer in Australia.
④ <u>It</u> is my favorite chocolate.
⑤ <u>It</u> is two kilometers to the beach.

서술형

[15-16] 빈칸에 알맞은 대명사를 써서 문장을 다시 쓰시오.

15 Ben and Joe have the same shirt.

→ _____ have the same shirt.

16 These are her earphones.

→ These earphones are _____ .

서술형

[17-18] 우리말과 일치하도록 ( ) 안의 말을 이용하여 문장을 완성하시오.

17 그의 눈은 갈색이다. (eyes)

→ _____ are brown.

18 지금은 오후 5시 30분이다. (5:30 p.m.)

→ _____ now.

WORD LIST

- **funny** 재미있는
- **popular** 인기 있는
- **miss** 그리워하다
- **friendly** 친절한
- **smile** 미소 짓다, 미소
- **help** 돕다, 도움
- **voice** 목소리
- **remember** 기억하다
- **wallet** 지갑
- **cousin** 사촌
- **suitcase** 여행 가방
- **uncle** 삼촌
- **expensive** 비싼
- **outside** 바깥에
- **building** 건물
- **delicious** 맛있는
- **clothes** 옷, 의복
- **sweet** 달콤한
- **soccer player** 축구 선수
- **letter** 편지
- **horror movie** 공포 영화
- **neighbor** 이웃
- **twins** 쌍둥이
- **share** 같이 쓰다
- **textbook** 교과서
- **candle** 양초
- **windy** 바람이 부는
- **visit** 방문하다
- **pilot** 조종사
- **address** 주소
- **Australia** 호주
- **brown** 갈색의

ESSENTIAL RULES OF
ENGLISH GRAMMAR

CHAPTER
03

be동사

UNIT 01 be동사의 현재형 1

- She **is** a reporter.

A be동사

be동사는 주어 뒤에 쓰여 '~이다', '(~에) 있다'의 의미를 나타낸다.

I **am** a middle school student.
You **are** very kind.

Peter **is** in his room.
They **are** at home.

B be동사의 현재형

	주어		be동사 현재형	줄임말
단수	1인칭	I	am	I'm
	2인칭	You	are	You're
	3인칭	He	is	He's
		She		She's
		It		It's
복수	1인칭	We	are	We're
	2인칭	You		You're
	3인칭	They		They're

1 be동사의 현재형은 주어에 따라 am, are, is 중 하나를 쓴다.

I **am** thirsty.
He **is** an actor.
My mother **is** at work.
We **are** on the train now.

2 일상 대화에서는 주로 줄임말을 쓴다.

I'm thirteen years old.
She's my sister.
A: **You're** a great dancer.
B: Thank you.

PRACTICE

🔍 Answer Key p-3

STEP 1

주어진 주어에 맞게 빈칸에 알맞은 be동사와 줄임말을 각각 쓰시오.

0 She ____is____ → ____She's____

1 I _____ → _____

2 They _____ → _____

3 We _____ → _____

4 You _____ → _____

5 It _____ → _____

6 He _____ → _____

STEP 2

( ) 안에서 알맞은 말을 고르시오.

0 It (am, is) Sally's blog.

1 I (am, are) busy now.

2 Brian (are, is) in the library.

3 You (are, is) a wonderful friend.

4 My parents (are, is) at the mall.

STEP 3

그림을 보고 알맞은 be동사를 써서 문장을 완성하시오.

0 We ____are____ brothers.

1 I _____ sleepy.

2 The bird _____ in the cage.

3 The man _____ a singer.

4 They _____ at the bookstore.

5 Her name _____ Chloe.

UNIT 02

be동사의 현재형 2

- **I'm not** cold.
- **Are you** cold?

A be동사 현재형의 부정문

be동사 현재형의 부정문(~가 아니다, (~에) 있지 않다): be동사 현재형 + not

주어			be동사 + not	줄임말	
단수	1인칭	I	am not	I'm not	
	2인칭	You	are not	You're not	You aren't
	3인칭	He	is not	He's not	He isn't
		She		She's not	She isn't
		It		It's not	It isn't
복수	1인칭	We	are not	We're not	We aren't
	2인칭	You		You're not	You aren't
	3인칭	They		They're not	They aren't

I **am not** at the airport. / We **are not** at the airport.
She's not a baker. = **She isn't** a baker.

cf. am not은 줄여 쓰지 않는다.
   I'm not sure. (I amn't)

B be동사 현재형의 의문문

be동사 현재형의 의문문(~입니까, (~에) 있습니까?): be동사 현재형 + 주어 ~?

		be동사 + 주어 ~?	긍정의 대답	부정의 대답
단수	1인칭	Am I ~?	Yes, you are.	No, you aren't.
	2인칭	Are you ~?	Yes, I am.	No, I'm not.
	3인칭	Is he ~?	Yes, he is.	No, he isn't.
		Is she ~?	Yes, she is.	No, she isn't.
		Is it ~?	Yes, it is.	No, it isn't.
복수	1인칭	Are we ~?	Yes, you/we are.	No, you/we aren't.
	2인칭	Are you ~?	Yes, we are.	No, we aren't.
	3인칭	Are they ~?	Yes, they are.	No, they aren't.

A: **Are you** angry? B: **Yes, I am. / No, I'm not.**

cf. 긍정의 대답을 할 때는 주어와 be동사를 줄여 쓰지 않는다.
   Yes, I'm.

PRACTICE

Answer Key p.4

STEP 1

( ) 안에서 알맞은 말을 고르시오.

0 (I'm not, I amn't) tall.

1 (Am, Are) you in the park?

2 Amy (am not, is not) shy.

3 (Is, Are) they your friends?

4 We (aren't, isn't) from France.

5 Mr. Brown (not is, is not) a soldier.

6 A: Is she your neighbor?
　 B: No, she (is, isn't).

STEP 2

빈칸에 be동사 현재형의 부정형과 그 줄임말을 각각 쓰시오.

0 She ___is not___ at school.　　→　She ___isn't___ at school.

1 I _____ wrong.　　　　　→　_____ wrong.

2 He _____ a baby.　　　　→　He _____ a baby.

3 We _____ ready.　　　　→　We _____ ready.

4 Anna _____ American.　　→　Anna _____ American.

5 They _____ in the pool.　→　They _____ in the pool.

6 Tom and Mike _____ here.　→　Tom and Mike _____ here.

STEP 3

( ) 안의 말과 be동사를 이용하여 현재형 의문문과 대답을 완성하시오.

0 A: _____Is he_____ popular? (he)
　 B: Yes, _____he is_____ .

1 A: _____ too loud? (I)
　 B: No, _____ .

2 A: _____ a hairdresser? (you)
　 B: No, _____ .

3 A: _____ twins? (you and Kate)
　 B: Yes, _____ .

4 A: _____ your favorite song? (it)
　 B: No, _____ .

UNIT
03　be동사의 과거형

• It **was** sunny yesterday.

A　be동사의 과거형

1　be동사의 과거형은 '~였다', '(~에) 있었다'의 의미로, 과거의 일을 나타낸다.

Kelly *is* in Seoul now.
She **was** in Busan yesterday.

2　be동사의 과거형은 주어에 따라 was 또는 were를 쓴다.

주어	be동사 과거형
I/He/She/It	was
We/You/They	were

I **was** tired yesterday.
We **were** at the concert last night.

B　be동사 과거형의 부정문

be동사 과거형의 부정문(~이지 않았다, (~에) 있지 않았다): be동사 과거형 + not

주어	be동사 과거형 + not	줄임말
I/He/She/It	was not	wasn't
We/You/They	were not	weren't

He **was not** happy. / The movie **wasn't** great.
The kids **were not** in the hospital. / They **weren't** sick.

C　be동사 과거형의 의문문

be동사 과거형의 의문문(~이었습니까, (~에) 있었습니까?): be동사 과거형 + 주어 ~?

be동사 과거형 + 주어 ~?	긍정의 대답	부정의 대답
Was + 주어 ~?	Yes, 주어 + was.	No, 주어 + wasn't.
Were + 주어 ~?	Yes, 주어 + were.	No, 주어 + weren't.

A: **Was it** a nice trip?
B: **Yes, it was. / No, it wasn't.**

PRACTICE

🔍 Answer Key p.4

STEP 1

( ) 안에서 알맞은 말을 고르시오.

0 I (am, ⓦas) in Spain last year.

1 I (not was, was not) hungry.

2 It (wasn't, weren't) hot yesterday.

3 (Was, Were) you at the gym this morning?

4 We (was, were) at the beach last weekend.

5 Mr. Jones (was, were) my teacher two years ago.

6 A: Was she at the party last night?
　 B: Yes, she (was, were).

STEP 2

보기에서 알맞은 말을 골라 문장을 완성하시오.

보기	was	were	wasn't	weren't

0 I ____was____ in Taiwan last spring. It was great.

1 John _____ in class yesterday. He was at home.

2 The weather _____ nice. It was a beautiful day.

3 Lily _____ in the office. She was on vacation.

4 They are new players. They _____ on the team last year.

5 The traffic was bad this morning. We _____ late for the meeting.

STEP 3

( ) 안의 말과 be동사를 이용하여 과거형 의문문과 대답을 완성하시오.

0 A: _____Was it_____ windy yesterday? (it)
　 B: No, _____it wasn't_____.

1 A: _____ at the post office? (he)
　 B: Yes, _____.

2 A: _____ busy yesterday? (you)
　 B: Yes, _____.

3 A: _____ open last Sunday? (the shop)
　 B: No, _____.

4 A: _____ happy with your present? (they)
　 B: Yes, _____.

There is/are

• **There is** a clock on the wall.

A **There is/are의 의미**

There is/are는 '~가 있다'의 의미이며, there를 '거기에'라고 해석하지 않는다.

There is a boy in the garden.
There are five people in my family.

B **There is/are의 형태**

「There is/are + 주어」 형태로 쓰며, be동사는 뒤에 나오는 명사의 수에 따라 is 또는 are를 쓴다.

There + be동사	주어
There is	단수명사, 셀 수 없는 명사
There are	복수명사

There is *a bag* on the chair.
There is *money* in my pocket.
There are *three elephants* at the zoo.

C **There is/are의 부정문과 의문문**

1 There is/are의 부정문(~가 있지 않다): There is/are + not ~

There isn't[is not] enough food for us.
There aren't[are not] many people in the park.

2 There is/are의 의문문(~가 있습니까?): Is/Are there ~?

A: **Is there** a library near here?
B: **Yes, there is. / No, there isn't.**

D **There is/are의 과거형**

There is/are의 과거형(~가 있었다): There was/were ~

There was a soccer game yesterday.
There were tomatoes in the refrigerator.

PRACTICE

🔍 Answer Key p.4

STEP 1

( ) 안에서 알맞은 말을 고르시오.

0 There (⟨is⟩, are) tea in the cup.

1 There (was, were) people at the door.

2 There (is, are) a computer in my room.

3 There (isn't, aren't) many clouds in the sky.

4 There (was, were) a truck here yesterday.

5 (Is, Are) there children on the playground?

6 (Is, Are) there a French restaurant on this street?

STEP 2

사진을 보고 There is 또는 There are를 넣어 문장을 완성하시오.

0	1	2	3

0 _____There is_____ a dog in the yard.

1 _____ water in the pool.

2 _____ four eggs in the basket.

3 _____ a glass on the table.

STEP 3

보기에서 알맞은 말을 골라 문장을 완성하시오. (단, 한 번씩만 쓸 것)

보기	There is	~~There are~~	There was	There were

0 _____There are_____ two girls on the bench.

1 _____ a cell phone on the floor.

2 _____ a festival in our town yesterday.

3 _____ many visitors in the museum last Sunday.

GRAMMAR FOR WRITING

A be동사를 이용하여 우리말을 영어로 옮기시오.

[0-6]

0 나는 한국인이다.

→ I _____am_____ Korean.

1 Rachel은 키가 크다.

→ Rachel _____ tall.

2 그녀는 지금 일본에 있지 않다.

→ She _____ in Japan now.

3 이것들은 우리의 우산이 아니다.

→ These _____ our umbrellas.

4 그들은 내 조부모님이시다.

→ They _____ my grandparents.

5 거실에 소파가 한 개 있다.

→ There _____ a sofa in the living room.

6 우리 반에는 30명의 학생들이 있다.

→ There _____ thirty students in my class.

[7-12]

7 그는 어제 운이 좋았다.

→ He _____ lucky yesterday.

8 그 경기는 재미있지 않았다.

→ The game _____ interesting.

9 지난주는 날씨가 따뜻했다.

→ It _____ warm last week.

10 너는 어제 집에 있었니?

→ _____ you at home yesterday?

11 탁자 위에 쿠키 네 개가 있었다.

→ There _____ four cookies on the table.

12 그들은 이번 주에 학교에 지각하지 않았다.

→ They _____ late for school this week.

B be동사를 이용하여 대화를 완성하시오.

0 A: _____Is_____ she American?

B: No, ___she isn't___. She's Canadian.

1 A: _____ it July 10 today?

B: Yes, _____.

2 A: _____ Jim in Hawaii last month?

B: No, _____. He was in Guam.

3 A: _____ they at the mall this morning?

B: No, _____. They were at the gym.

4 A: _____ you in the sixth grade now?

B: No, _____. I'm in the fifth grade.

C 그림을 보고 There is 또는 There are를 이용하여 대화를 완성하시오. (필요하면 형태를 바꿀 것)

Mom: Dan, **0** _____are there_____ apples in the refrigerator?

Dan: No, **1** _____.

Mom: Are there lemons?

Dan: Yes, **2** _____ three lemons.

Mom: Great. **3** _____ milk, too?

Dan: Yes, there is!

REVIEW TEST

[1-2] 빈칸에 들어갈 알맞은 말을 고르시오.

1

> A man _____ on the boat now.

① am   ② are   ③ is

④ was   ⑤ were

2

> _____ you excited now?

① Am   ② Are   ③ Is

④ Was   ⑤ Were

`서술형`

[3-4] 빈칸에 There is 또는 There are를 넣어 문장을 완성하시오.

3

> _____ a big tree in her garden.

4

> _____ four people in the elevator.

`빈출`

[5-7] 다음 중 밑줄 친 부분이 <u>잘못된</u> 것을 고르시오.

5

① You <u>are</u> beautiful.

② They <u>are</u> Jessica's toys.

③ He and I <u>am</u> best friends.

④ My sister <u>is</u> eight years old.

⑤ Thomas and Bill <u>are</u> in the car.

6

① The cat <u>is</u> on my bed now.

② She <u>is</u> at work yesterday.

③ The kids <u>are</u> in the pool now.

④ We <u>were</u> classmates last year.

⑤ Brian <u>was</u> late for school this morning.

7

① I'm <u>not</u> a singer.

② He <u>wasn't</u> a TV reporter.

③ We <u>aren't</u> in Tokyo now.

④ Sam and Jason <u>isn't</u> busy.

⑤ They <u>weren't</u> in the kitchen.

`서술형`

[8-10] 빈칸에 알맞은 be동사를 써서 문장을 완성하시오.

8

> The sun _____ hot.

9

> I _____ in Italy two years ago.

10

> Mary and Julie _____ at the movie theater last night.

42

11 다음 중 대화가 자연스럽지 <u>않은</u> 것은?

① A: Is Susan in her room?
B: Yes, she is.

② A: Are you Amy's brother?
B: No, I'm not.

③ A: Was it warm yesterday?
B: Yes, it was.

④ A: Are you and Tim cousins?
B: Yes, you are.

⑤ A: Were they with you last night?
B: No, they weren't.

12 다음 중 밑줄 친 부분의 줄임말이 <u>잘못된</u> 것은?

① I <u>am not</u> tired. → I amn't
② <u>It is</u> Monday today. → It's
③ <u>She is</u> sick today. → She's
④ <u>They are not</u> doctors. → They aren't
⑤ <u>We were not</u> at school yesterday.
→ We weren't

[13-14] 빈칸에 들어갈 말이 바르게 짝지어진 것을 고르시오.

13
A: ____(A)____ these your shoes?
B: No, ____(B)____ .

(A)		(B)
① Is	……	it is
② Is	……	it isn't
③ Are	……	it isn't
④ Are	……	they are
⑤ Are	……	they aren't

14
- ____(A)____ buses on the street now.
- ____(B)____ a math test last Thursday.

(A)		(B)
① There is	……	There is
② There is	……	There was
③ There are	……	There is
④ There are	……	There was
⑤ There were	……	There are

[15-17] 우리말과 일치하도록 ( ) 안의 말을 이용하여 문장을 완성하시오.

15 그 문제들은 쉽지 않았다. (easy)

→ The questions _____ .

16 Liam과 Jamie는 어제 너의 집에 있었니?
(Liam and Jamie)

→ _____ at your house yesterday?

17 그릇 안에 밥이 있었다. (rice)

→ _____ in the bowl.

WORD LIST

- **reporter** 기자 _____
- **thirsty** 목마른 _____
- **work** 일, 직장 _____
- **blog** 블로그 _____
- **library** 도서관 _____
- **sleepy** 졸린 _____
- **cage** (짐승의) 우리 _____
- **bookstore** 서점 _____
- **cold** 추운 _____
- **shy** 수줍어하는 _____
- **wrong** 틀린 _____
- **ready** 준비가 된 _____
- **pool** 수영장 _____
- **favorite** 가장 좋아하는 _____
- **tired** 피곤한 _____
- **trip** 여행 _____
- **on vacation** 휴가 중인 _____
- **traffic** 교통 _____
- **pocket** 주머니 _____
- **elephant** 코끼리 _____
- **enough** 충분한 _____
- **refrigerator** 냉장고 _____
- **playground** 운동장 _____
- **yard** 마당 _____
- **festival** 축제 _____
- **visitor** 방문객 _____
- **museum** 박물관 _____
- **Canadian** 캐나다 사람 _____
- **grade** 학년 _____
- **movie theater** 영화관 _____
- **easy** 쉬운 _____

ESSENTIAL RULES OF
ENGLISH GRAMMAR

CHAPTER
04

일반동사 1

UNIT 01 일반동사의 현재형 1

- I **like** vegetables.

A 일반동사

일반동사는 주어의 동작이나 상태를 나타낸다.

eat, sleep, speak, play, walk, run, have, like, know ...

B 일반동사의 현재형

일반동사의 현재형은 현재의 사실이나 반복적인 습관을 나타낸다.

I **have** two brothers.
Peter **watches** the news every evening.

C 일반동사 현재형의 형태

1 주어가 1인칭, 2인칭, 복수일 때는 동사원형을 쓰고, 3인칭 단수일 때는 주로 「동사원형 + -(e)s」 형태로 쓴다.

1인칭/2인칭/복수 주어	동사원형		3인칭 단수 주어	동사원형 + -(e)s

I **speak** Korean. / Jack **speaks** English.

2 일반동사의 3인칭 단수 현재형 만드는 법

대부분의 동사	동사원형 + -s	comes eats reads likes
-o, -s, -ch, -sh, -x로 끝나는 동사	동사원형 + -es	does goes passes teaches watches washes brushes fixes
〈자음 + y〉로 끝나는 동사	y를 i로 고치고 + -es	cry → cries study → studies fly → flies try → tries
예외	have → **has**	

This dog **hates** the rain.
She **goes** to school by bus.
An airplane **flies** in the sky.
Zoe **has** three cats.

PRACTICE

🔍 Answer Key p.5

STEP 1

주어진 동사의 3인칭 단수 현재형을 쓰시오.

0 go → _goes_   **1** get → _____

2 fly → _____   **3** watch → _____

4 like → _____ **5** say → _____

6 teach → _____ **7** cry → _____

8 fix → _____   **9** pass → _____

10 carry → _____ **11** run → _____

STEP 2

사진을 보고 (   ) 안에 주어진 동사의 현재형을 써서 문장을 완성하시오.

0  **1**  **2**  **3**

0 She _____drives_____ a taxi. (drive)

1 Jenny _____ hard. (study)

2 Alex _____ baseball on Saturdays. (play)

3 My dad _____ the dishes after dinner. (wash)

STEP 3

주어진 동사의 현재형을 써서 문장을 완성하시오.

0 walk   a. I _____walk_____ home.

           b. Brenda _____walks_____ home.

1 have   a. We _____ music class today.

           b. Tommy _____ music class today.

2 brush   a. Olivia _____ her teeth after meals.

           b. They _____ their teeth after meals.

3 do   a. I _____ my homework after school.

           b. My sister _____ her homework after school.

일반동사의 현재형 2

- I **don't eat** breakfast.
- **Do you eat** breakfast?

A 일반동사 현재형의 부정문

1인칭/2인칭/복수 주어	don't + 동사원형 (= do not + 동사원형)	3인칭 단수 주어	doesn't + 동사원형 (= does not + 동사원형)

I **do not have** classes on Sundays.
The man **does not smoke**.

일상 대화에서는 주로 줄임말을 쓴다.

We **don't like** sad movies.
Sam **doesn't wear** glasses.

B 일반동사 현재형의 의문문

Do/Does + 주어 + 동사원형?			긍정의 대답	부정의 대답
Do	1인칭/2인칭/복수 주어	동사원형?	Yes, 주어 + do.	No, 주어 + don't.
Does	3인칭 단수 주어		Yes, 주어 + does.	No, 주어 + doesn't.

A: **Do you read** the newspaper?
B: **Yes, I do. / No, I don't.**

A: **Do they understand** Chinese?
B: **Yes, they do. / No, they don't.**

A: **Does Alice play** the guitar?
B: **Yes, she does. / No, she doesn't.**

PRACTICE

🔍 Answer Key p.5

STEP 1

( ) 안에서 알맞은 말을 고르시오.

0 David (don't, ⓓoesn't) live here.

1 I (don't, doesn't) remember his name.

2 Does he (have, has) a child?

3 (Do, Does) you study Spanish?

4 (Do, Does) Nora keep a diary every day?

5 Jesse and Anne (don't, doesn't) work on Saturdays.

6 My brother doesn't (play, plays) soccer after school.

STEP 2

( ) 안의 말을 이용하여 현재형 부정문을 완성하시오. (줄임말로 쓸 것)

0 I _____ don't tell _____ lies. (tell)

1 We _____ coffee. (drink)

2 Sandra _____ yoga. (do)

3 They _____ my address. (know)

4 Brian _____ names. (forget)

5 My sister _____ her room. (clean)

6 The building _____ an elevator. (have)

STEP 3

( ) 안의 말을 이용하여 현재형 의문문을 완성하시오.

0 A: _____ Does _____ Jane _____ cook _____ well? (cook)
B: Yes, she does.

1 A: _____ you _____ roses? (like)
B: Yes, I do.

2 A: _____ this bus _____ downtown? (go)
B: No, it doesn't.

3 A: _____ your parents _____ English? (speak)
B: Yes, they do.

4 A: _____ Bill _____ this computer? (use)
B: No, he doesn't.

일반동사의 과거형 1

- We **watched** a movie yesterday.

A 일반동사의 과거형

1 일반동사의 과거형은 과거에 일어난 일을 나타낸다.

I *visit* my grandparents every week.
I **visited** my grandparents yesterday.

2 주로 yesterday, last night/week/month/year, ~ ago 등 과거를 나타내는 표현과 함께 쓴다.

I **called** you *last night*.

B 일반동사 과거형의 형태

1 주어의 수와 인칭에 관계없이 보통 「동사원형 + -(e)d」 형태로 쓴다.

We **walked** in the park. / She **walked** in the park.

2 일반동사의 과거형 만드는 법

1) 규칙 변화

대부분의 동사	동사원형 + -ed	watch**ed** talk**ed** walk**ed** start**ed**
〈자음 + e〉로 끝나는 동사	동사원형 + -d	liv**ed** mov**ed** lik**ed** lov**ed**
〈자음 + y〉로 끝나는 동사	y를 i로 고치고 + -ed	cry → cr**ied** study → stud**ied** try → tr**ied** carry → carr**ied**
〈단모음 + 단자음〉으로 끝나는 동사	자음을 한 번 더 쓰고 + -ed	stop → stop**ped** plan → plan**ned** drop → drop**ped** chat → chat**ted**

Sam **lived** in London two years ago.
They **studied** in the library.

2) 불규칙 변화

현재형과 과거형이 같은 동사	put → **put**	cut → **cut**	hit → **hit**	read → **read**
현재형과 과거형이 다른 동사	do → **did** eat → **ate** hear → **heard** make → **made** drink → **drank** write → **wrote**	have → **had** lose → **lost** tell → **told** take → **took** meet → **met** sing → **sang**	come → **came** sleep → **slept** swim → **swam** give → **gave** find → **found** sit → **sat**	go → **went** see → **saw** run → **ran** buy → **bought** teach → **taught** break → **broke**

Ted **read** the bestseller last week.
I **slept** for eight hours yesterday.

PRACTICE

🔍 Answer Key p.5

STEP 1

주어진 동사의 과거형을 쓰시오.

0 ask → ___asked___
1 eat → _____
2 do → _____
3 have → _____
4 run → _____
5 try → _____
6 buy → _____
7 chat → _____
8 make → _____
9 like → _____
10 play → _____
11 carry → _____

STEP 2

밑줄 친 부분을 적절한 형태로 바꾸어 문장을 완성하시오.

0 I go to bed late every night. → I ___went___ to bed late last night.

1 They live in Jeju now. → They _____ in Jeju last year.

2 We drink tea every morning. → We _____ tea an hour ago.

3 Eva listens to music every day. → Eva _____ to music last night.

4 He comes to my house on Mondays. → He _____ to my house yesterday.

5 She cuts her finger on paper often. → She _____ her finger on paper yesterday.

STEP 3

그림을 보고 ( ) 안에 주어진 동사의 과거형을 써서 문장을 완성하시오.

0 I ___cried___ after the movie. (cry)

1 Liam _____ his smartphone on the ground. (drop)

2 We _____ our teacher on the street. (meet)

3 My father _____ his coat in the closet. (put)

일반동사의 과거형 2

- I **didn't finish** my homework.
- **Did you finish** your homework?

A 일반동사 과거형의 부정문

주어의 수와 인칭에 관계없이 「didn't + 동사원형」 형태로 쓴다.

주어	didn't + 동사원형 (= did not + 동사원형)

I **did not have** lunch.
He **did not take** the train last night.

일상 대화에서는 주로 줄임말을 쓴다.

We **didn't enjoy** the movie.
They **didn't bring** their wallets.
Nicole **didn't order** a salad.

B 일반동사 과거형의 의문문

주어의 수와 인칭에 관계없이 「Did + 주어 + 동사원형?」 형태로 쓴다.

의문문	긍정의 대답	부정의 대답
Did + 주어 + 동사원형?	Yes, 주어 + did.	No, 주어 + didn't.

A: **Did you lose** your umbrella?
B: **Yes, I did. / No, I didn't.**

A: **Did they meet** last Sunday?
B: **Yes, they did. / No, they didn't.**

A: **Did Olivia solve** the problem?
B: **Yes, she did. / No, she didn't.**

PRACTICE

🔍 Answer Key p.5

STEP 1

( ) 안에서 알맞은 말을 고르시오.

0 I (don't, ⓓidn't) see Joan last week.

1 Did Tom (break, broke) his arm?

2 (Do, Did) you fight with Bill yesterday?

3 Julie didn't (know, knew) the answer.

4 Did the train (leave, leaves) the station?

5 I (don't, didn't) live with my grandparents now.

6 Paul (doesn't, didn't) wash his hair last night.

STEP 2

( ) 안의 말을 이용하여 과거형 부정문을 완성하시오. (줄임말로 쓸 것)

0 I _____didn't sleep_____ well last night. (sleep)

1 We _____ pizza yesterday. (eat)

2 Sophia _____ much this morning. (talk)

3 They _____ tennis last Sunday. (play)

4 He _____ a shower this morning. (take)

5 Ben _____ to school yesterday. (come)

6 My father _____ TV this morning. (watch)

STEP 3

( ) 안의 말을 이용하여 과거형 의문문을 완성하시오.

0 A: ___Did___ Amy ___go___ to the waterpark yesterday? (go)
   B: Yes, she did.

1 A: _____ you _____ this wall last week? (paint)
   B: No, we didn't.

2 A: _____ you _____ your bike this morning? (ride)
   B: Yes, I did.

3 A: _____ Mark _____ early yesterday? (get up)
   B: No, he didn't.

4 A: _____ the children _____ in the field? (run)
   B: Yes, they did.

GRAMMAR FOR WRITING

A 보기에서 알맞은 말을 골라 적절한 형태로 바꾸어 우리말을 영어로 옮기시오.

[0-5]

보기	go	~~like~~	drive	play	read	watch

0 Jenny는 아이스크림을 좋아한다.

→ Jenny _____ likes _____ ice cream.

1 우리 아빠는 골프를 치지 않으신다.

→ My dad _____ golf.

2 너는 매일 밤 책을 읽니?

→ _____ books every night?

3 Andy는 오전 8시에 학교에 간다.

→ Andy _____ to school at 8:00 a.m.

4 Sandra는 토요일마다 토크쇼를 본다.

→ Sandra _____ talk shows on Saturdays.

5 그녀는 사무실에 운전해서 가니?

→ _____ to her office?

[6-10]

보기	buy	join	have	hear	see

6 Henry는 배드민턴 동아리에 가입했다.

→ Henry _____ a badminton club.

7 나는 어젯밤에 엄마로부터 그 소식을 들었다.

→ I _____ the news from my mom last night.

8 우리는 어제 숙제가 없었다.

→ We _____ homework yesterday.

9 너는 오늘 아침에 그 새로운 학생을 봤니?

→ _____ the new student this morning?

10 Alex는 지난달에 시계를 샀다.

→ Alex _____ a watch last month.

B   ( ) 안의 말을 이용하여 대화를 완성하시오.

0   A: _____Do_____ you ___know___ Jason? (know)
   B: Yes, I do. He's my friend.

1   A: Do you want some chicken?
   B: No, thanks. I _____ meat. (eat)

2   A: Does Matt like baseball?
   B: No, he doesn't. He _____ sports. (like)

3   A: Does your aunt live in Daegu?
   B: No, she doesn't. She _____ in Daejeon. (live)

4   A: Did she travel to India?
   B: No, she didn't. She _____ to China. (travel)

5   A: _____ he _____ a goal yesterday? (score)
   B: Yes, he did.

C   그림을 보고 ( ) 안의 말을 이용하여 문장을 완성하시오.

0   Last weekend, my family _____went on vacation_____. (go on vacation)

1   Dad and I _____ in the sea. (swim)

2   My brother _____. (make a sandcastle)

3   Mom _____ of us at the beach. (take a picture)

4   We _____! (have a good time)

REVIEW TEST

1 다음 중 동사의 3인칭 단수 현재형이 <u>잘못</u> 연결된 것은?

① do – does　　② fix – fixes
③ have – has　　④ cry – cries
⑤ teach – teachs

2 다음 중 동사의 과거형이 <u>잘못</u> 연결된 것은?

① see – saw　　② read – read
③ like – liked　　④ meet – meeted
⑤ stop – stopped

[3-4] 빈칸에 들어갈 알맞은 말을 고르시오.

3

Cindy _____ history.

① study　　　　② studies
③ don't study　　④ don't studies
⑤ doesn't studies

4

I visited the museum _____.

① now　　　　　② tomorrow
③ tomorrow night　④ next week
⑤ two months ago

5 빈칸에 공통으로 들어갈 말은?

• My dad _____ not smoke. • _____ Jessy play the violin?

① is[Is]　　② are[Are]　　③ be[Be]
④ do[Do]　　⑤ does[Does]

서술형
[6-7] ( ) 안의 말을 이용하여 문장을 완성하시오.

6

Sarah _____ long hair now. (not / have)

7

It _____ last Sunday. (not / rain)

서술형
[8-9] 빈칸에 알맞은 말을 써서 대화를 완성하시오.

8

A: Does Steve speak Korean? B: Yes, _____ _____.

9

A: Did you take a walk last night? B: No, _____ _____. I was 　　too tired.

[10-12] 다음 중 밑줄 친 부분이 <u>잘못된</u> 것을 고르시오.

10 ① The store <u>opened</u> yesterday.
② He <u>went</u> to Mexico last year.
③ I <u>run</u> in the park every morning.
④ Lisa <u>watches</u> TV every day.
⑤ We <u>play</u> soccer last weekend.

11 ① Bill <u>don't eat</u> breakfast.
② She <u>doesn't like</u> carrots.
③ We <u>didn't close</u> the window.
④ They <u>didn't enjoy</u> the music.
⑤ I <u>don't download</u> movies for free.

12 ① <u>Did the dog bark</u> at night?
② <u>Does Mary have</u> a brother?
③ <u>Did you found</u> your key?
④ <u>Did he meet</u> Susan yesterday?
⑤ <u>Do you understand</u> my question?

13 다음 질문에 대한 대답으로 알맞은 것은?

> A: Do the boys play basketball after
>   school?
> B: _____

① Yes, they do.
② Yes, they did.
③ Yes, they does.
④ No, they didn't.
⑤ No, they doesn't.

서술형 빈출
[14-16] 우리말과 일치하도록 ( ) 안의 말을 이용하여
문장을 완성하시오.

14 수진이는 유명한 노래를 많이 안다. (know)

→ Sujin _____ many famous
songs.

15 나는 너의 비밀을 말하지 않았다. (tell)

→ I _____ your
secret.

16 너는 손을 씻었니? (wash)

→ _____ you _____
your hands?

서술형
[17-18] 우리말과 일치하도록 ( ) 안에 주어진 말을 바르게
배열하시오.

17 Sally는 매일 태권도를 연습하니?
(Sally, does, taekwondo, practice)

→ _____
every day?

18 우리는 수업 시간에 휴대 전화를 사용하지 않는다.
(use, we, cell phones, don't)

→ _____
in class.

WORD LIST

- **airplane** 비행기
- **play baseball** 야구를 하다
- **wash the dishes** 설거지를 하다
- **brush one's teeth** 이를 닦다
- **do one's homework** 숙제를 하다
- **smoke** 담배를 피우다
- **glasses** 안경
- **understand** 이해하다
- **guitar** 기타
- **keep a diary** 일기를 쓰다
- **tell a lie** 거짓말하다
- **forget** 잊다
- **elevator** 엘리베이터
- **cook** 요리하다
- **downtown** 시내에[로], 중심가에[로]
- **grandparents** 조부모
- **drop** 떨어뜨리다
- **go to bed** 잠자리에 들다
- **cut one's finger** 손가락을 베다
- **closet** 옷장
- **enjoy** 즐기다
- **order** 주문하다
- **bring** 가져오다
- **wallet** 지갑
- **answer** 대답, 답
- **leave** 떠나다
- **take a shower** 샤워를 하다
- **join** 가입하다
- **score** 득점을 올리다
- **take a walk** 산책하다
- **famous** 유명한
- **secret** 비밀

ESSENTIAL RULES OF
ENGLISH GRAMMAR

CHAPTER
05

형용사와 부사

형용사

- I drink **warm** tea.

A 형용사의 쓰임

1 명사 앞에 쓰여 명사를 꾸며준다.

Sydney is a **big** *city*.
I have **good** *friends*.

> *cf.* -thing으로 끝나는 말은 형용사가 뒤에서 꾸며준다.
> I want *something* **spicy** for lunch.

2 동사 뒤에 쓰여 주어를 보충 설명해 준다.

Julie is **honest**.
My brother is **tall**.

> *cf.* 형용사와 함께 쓰이는 동사: be, become, look, feel, sound, smell, taste 등
> He *became* **famous**.
> You *look* **tired**.

B **some, any**

1 some

1) 긍정문에 쓰여 '조금의', '몇 개의'의 의미를 나타낸다.

I need **some** help.
I bought **some** bananas at the market.

2) 권유를 나타내는 의문문에 쓰인다.

Do you want **some** cookies?

2 any

1) 부정문에 쓰여 '조금의 (~도 없다)'의 의미를 나타낸다.

I don't have **any** time now.
Sam doesn't eat **any** meat.

2) 의문문에 쓰여 '조금의', '몇 개의'의 의미를 나타낸다.

Do you have **any** questions?
Do we have **any** juice in the refrigerator?

PRACTICE

🔍 Answer Key p.6

 STEP 1

( ) 안에서 알맞은 말을 고르시오.

0 Dolphins (are smart, smart are).

1 It is a (large house, house large).

2 I don't have (some, any) money now.

3 That sounds (interest, interesting).

4 I heard (strange something, something strange) outside.

STEP 2

사진을 보고 보기에서 알맞은 말을 골라 문장을 완성하시오. (단, 한 번씩만 쓸 것)

보기	fast	~~big~~	young	angry	tall	black

0 He wears ___big___ glasses.　**1** It's a _____ cat.　**2** The girl is _____.

3 Lily looks _____.　**4** The car is _____.　**5** This is a _____ building.

STEP 3

빈칸에 some 또는 any를 넣어 문장을 완성하시오.

0 Did you make _____any_____ friends?

1 I have _____ pictures.

2 He didn't buy _____ books.

3 Do you want _____ pizza?

4 We don't have _____ plans for the weekend.

UNIT
02 부사

• He swims **well**.

A 부사의 쓰임

1 동사를 꾸며준다.

My father *drives* **carefully**.

2 형용사를 꾸며준다.

She is **very** *popular*.

3 다른 부사나 문장 전체를 꾸며준다.

Mark runs **quite** *fast*.
Sadly, *we lost the game*.

B 부사의 형태

대부분의 부사	형용사 + -ly	sad**ly** slow**ly** loud**ly** kind**ly**
-y로 끝나는 형용사로 만드는 부사	y를 i로 고치고 + -ly	easy → eas**ily** happy → happ**ily** lucky → luck**ily** heavy → heav**ily**
형용사와 형태가 같은 부사	fast(빠른) → **fast**(빠르게)　　　early(이른) → **early**(일찍) late(늦은) → **late**(늦게)　　　high(높은) → **high**(높게) hard(어려운, 열심히 하는) → **hard**(열심히)	
예외	good → **well**	

The dog barks **loudly**.
Thomas practices the piano **hard**.

cf. -ly로 끝나지만 부사가 아니라 형용사인 단어: friendly, lovely, lonely 등
She is a **friendly** girl.

C 빈도부사

1 어떤 일이 얼마나 자주 일어나는지를 나타내는 부사이다.

(0%) never　→　sometimes　→　often　→　usually　→　always (100%)
(결코 ~ 않다)　　(가끔)　　(자주)　　(보통, 대개)　　(항상)

2 문장에서 be동사나 조동사의 뒤, 일반동사의 앞에 쓰인다.

Lisa *is* **always** polite.
We **often** *take* a walk in the evening.

62

PRACTICE

🔍 Answer Key p.6

STEP 1

주어진 형용사의 부사형을 쓰시오.

0 sad → <u>   sadly   </u>

1 new → <u>   </u>

2 kind → <u>   </u>

3 easy → <u>   </u>

4 fast → <u>   </u>

5 soft → <u>   </u>

6 quick → <u>   </u>

7 careful → <u>   </u>

STEP 2

( ) 안에서 알맞은 말을 고르시오.

0 They lived (happy, (happily)) ever after.

1 Jessica speaks French (good, well).

2 (Lucky, Luckily), I found my wallet.

3 The library is (very quiet, quiet very).

4 I get up (early, earlily) in the morning.

5 The kite flew (high, highly) in the sky.

6 Dave worked (late, lately) yesterday.

STEP 3

( ) 안의 말을 알맞은 곳에 넣어 문장을 완성하시오.

0 Kate buys shoes on the internet. (sometimes)

→ Kate <u>   sometimes buys shoes   </u> on the internet.

1 She is kind to everyone. (always)

→ She <u>   </u>.

2 It rains in July. (often)

→ <u>   </u> in July.

3 I am bored with action movies. (never)

→ I <u>   </u>.

4 Andrew goes to bed at eleven. (usually)

→ Andrew <u>   </u> at eleven.

GRAMMAR FOR WRITING

A 보기에서 알맞은 말을 골라 우리말을 영어로 옮기시오.

[0-3]

보기	expensive	new	~~warm~~	fresh

0 봄에는 따뜻하다. → It is _____warm_____ in the spring.

1 그 차는 비싸 보인다. → The car looks _____.

2 나는 신선한 주스를 원한다. → I want _____ juice.

3 그들은 새 탁자를 샀다. → They bought a _____ table.

[4-7]

보기	very	some	any	quietly

4 Judy는 조용하게 말한다. → Judy speaks _____.

5 나는 어떤 운동도 좋아하지 않는다. → I don't like _____ sports.

6 버스에 몇몇 사람들이 있다. → There are _____ people on the bus.

7 그 4D 영화는 매우 신이 났다. → The 4D movie was _____ exciting.

B ( ) 안의 말을 이용하여 우리말을 영어로 옮기시오. (필요하면 형태를 바꿀 것)

0 너 오늘 멋져 보인다. (look, nice)

→ You _____look nice_____ today.

1 전화가 갑자기 울렸다. (sudden)

→ The telephone rang _____.

2 그 개는 항상 배가 고프다. (always, hungry)

→ The dog _____.

3 James는 조심스럽게 문을 열었다. (careful)

→ James opened the door _____.

4 Tom은 가끔 자전거를 탄다. (sometimes, ride)

→ Tom _____ a bike.

5 나는 후식으로 달콤한 것을 원한다. (sweet, something)

→ I want _____ for dessert.

C 주어진 단어를 적절한 형태로 써서 문장을 완성하시오.

0 slow   a. My computer is _____slow_____ .

                   b. Jack walks _____slowly_____ .

1 hard   a. Nora studies _____ .

                   b. They are _____ workers.

2 good   a. She is a _____ cook.

                   b. Peter plays tennis _____ .

3 easy   a. It was an _____ question.

                   b. He solved the puzzle _____ .

4 surprising   a. _____ , everyone was safe.

                   b. _____ events sometimes happen.

D 그림을 보고 보기에서 알맞은 말을 골라 ( ) 안의 말과 함께 써서 문장을 완성하시오. (과거형으로 쓸 것)

0   **1**   **2**   **3**

보기	~~heavily~~	late	high	fast

0 It _____snowed heavily_____ at night. (snow)

1 She _____ to the train. (run)

2 The boy _____ to class. (come)

3 We _____ into the mountains. (climb)

REVIEW TEST

[1-3] 빈칸에 들어갈 알맞은 말을 고르시오.

1

Sarah is a _____ girl.

① very   ② well   ③ lovely
④ happily   ⑤ carefully

2

He explains the rules _____.

① well   ② nice   ③ good
④ perfect   ⑤ wonderful

3

The story was _____.

① very   ② really   ③ greatly
④ funny   ⑤ suddenly

[4-5] 밑줄 친 부분의 성격이 나머지 넷과 <u>다른</u> 것을 고르시오.

4
① He is a <u>strong</u> boy.
② They feel <u>happy</u> now.
③ Jack is <u>good</u> at sports.
④ I had lunch <u>late</u> today.
⑤ These are <u>nice</u> shoes.

5
① You did the job <u>well</u>.
② Amy is very <u>lonely</u>.
③ She came home <u>early</u>.
④ I passed the test <u>easily</u>.
⑤ The kangaroos jump <u>high</u>.

6 다음 중 밑줄 친 부분이 <u>잘못된</u> 것은?

① I ate <u>some</u> bread.
② I sent <u>any</u> emails to her.
③ I don't need <u>any</u> money.
④ Do you want <u>some</u> syrup?
⑤ Do you have <u>any</u> sisters?

빈출
[7-9] ( ) 안의 말이 들어갈 위치를 고르시오.

7

(new) ① We ② want ③ something ④ for ⑤ dinner.

8

(often) Dan and ① Mia ② are ③ late ④ for ⑤ school.

9

(never) ① It ② snows ③ in ④ this desert ⑤.

서술형
[10-11] 빈칸에 some 또는 any를 넣어 문장을 완성하시오.

10

Cathy brought _____ snacks for her brother.

11 We didn't buy _____ fruit.

[12-13] 빈칸에 들어갈 말이 바르게 짝지어진 것을 고르시오.

12
• Today was a ___(A)___ day.
• ___(B)___, our team won the game.

　　　(A)　　　　　(B)
① luck ……… Lucky
② luck ……… Luckily
③ lucky ……… Lucky
④ lucky ……… Luckily
⑤ luckily ……… Luckily

13
• Do you want ___(A)___ popcorn?
• Is there ___(B)___ ice in the refrigerator?

　　　(A)　　　　　(B)
① some ……… some
② some ……… any
③ any ……… some
④ any ……… any
⑤ any ……… something

14 다음 우리말을 영어로 바르게 옮긴 것은?

그는 항상 숙제를 빠르게 끝낸다.

① He finishes his homework always quick.
② He finishes always his homework quickly.
③ He finishes always his homework quick.
④ He always finishes his homework quick.
⑤ He always finishes his homework quickly.

서술형

[15-17] 우리말과 일치하도록 ( ) 안의 말을 이용하여 문장을 완성하시오.

15 이 수프는 냄새가 좋다. (smell, good)

→ This soup _____.

16 슬프게도, 그녀는 나를 사랑하지 않는다. (sad)

→ _____, she doesn't love me.

17 그는 지하철에서 보통 음악을 듣는다. (usually, listen to)

→ He _____ music on the subway.

서술형

[18-19] 우리말과 일치하도록 ( ) 안에 주어진 말을 바르게 배열하시오.

18 우리는 큰 가위가 필요하다. (big, need, we, scissors)

→ _____.

19 이번 여름은 아주 덥다. (is, this summer, hot, quite)

→ _____.

WORD LIST

- **spicy** 양념 맛이 강한, 매운 _____
- **honest** 정직한 _____
- **question** 질문 _____
- **dolphin** 돌고래 _____
- **smart** 영리한 _____
- **strange** 이상한 _____
- **outside** 밖에서 _____
- **plan** 계획 _____
- **weekend** 주말 _____
- **carefully** 조심스럽게 _____
- **quite** 아주, 꽤 _____
- **sadly** 슬프게(도) _____
- **lose** 지다, 패배하다 _____
- **easily** 쉽게 _____
- **luckily** 운 좋게(도) _____
- **heavily** 심하게 _____
- **polite** 예의 바른 _____
- **fly** 날다 _____
- **be bored with** ~에 싫증이 나다 _____
- **ring** (전화가) 울리다 _____
- **dessert** 디저트, 후식 _____
- **worker** 근로자, 일하는 사람 _____
- **solve** (문제 등을) 풀다 _____
- **puzzle** 퍼즐 _____
- **surprising** 놀라운 _____
- **safe** 안전한 _____
- **happen** 발생하다 _____
- **climb** 오르다 _____
- **explain** 설명하다 _____
- **rule** 규칙 _____
- **be good at** ~을 잘하다 _____
- **win** 이기다 _____

ESSENTIAL RULES OF
ENGLISH GRAMMAR

CHAPTER
06

전치사

UNIT 01 장소를 나타내는 전치사

• The Eiffel Tower is **in** Paris.

A 전치사

1 전치사는 명사나 대명사의 앞에 쓰여 장소나 시간 등을 나타낸다.

on the grass, **at** the concert, **in** February ...

2 전치사 뒤에 대명사가 올 때는 목적격을 쓴다.

Matt sat **behind me**. (behind I)

B in(~에, ~ 안에), at(~에)

in + 공간의 내부, 도시, 국가	**in** a box, **in** a room **in** London, **in** China
at + 장소의 한 지점	**at** home, **at** school **at** the store, **at** the bus stop

There is a table **in** the kitchen.
My uncle lives **in** LA.

Jane stayed **at** home yesterday.
I saw Mr. Simpson **at** the store.

C on(~ 위에), under(~ 아래에)

on은 표면과 맞닿은 바로 위를 나타낸다.

There are toys **on** the floor.
My cat was **under** the bed.

D in front of(~ 앞에), behind(~ 뒤에), next to(~ 옆에)

I met my boyfriend **in front of** the library.
The thief hid **behind** the door.
The bank is **next to** the supermarket.

PRACTICE

🔍 Answer Key p.7

STEP 1

( ) 안에서 알맞은 말을 고르시오.

0 Ted was (in, at) France last year.

1 I walked behind (he, him).

2 The train arrived (at, on) the station.

3 My brother hung a calendar (in, on) the wall.

4 The boat passed (on, under) the bridge.

5 A handsome boy sat (next, next to) me.

6 There are twenty rooms (in, behind) the hotel.

7 Chris put the TV (in front, in front of) the sofa.

STEP 2

빈칸에 in과 at 중 알맞은 전치사를 넣어 문장을 완성하시오.

0 I met Jake ____at____ the party.

1 Joan lives _____ Boston.

2 The children are _____ the store.

3 He left his wallet _____ home.

4 I put some flowers _____ the vase.

5 We waited for Emily _____ the bus stop.

6 I have an umbrella _____ my bag.

7 There are many countries _____ the world.

STEP 3

그림을 보고 보기에서 알맞은 말을 골라 문장을 완성하시오. (단, 한 번씩만 쓸 것)

보기	on	under	~~in front of~~	behind	next to

0 A girl is ___in front of___ the table.

1 There is a bed _____ the table.

2 Some books are _____ the table.

3 There are slippers _____ the table.

4 There is a dog _____ the table.

UNIT 02

시간을 나타내는 전치사

• The show begins **at** 6:30 p.m.

A in, at, on(~에)

in + 오전, 오후, 월, 계절, 연도	in the morning/afternoon/evening in May, in summer, in 2021
at + 구체적인 시각, 하루의 때	at seven o'clock, at 4:30 p.m. at noon, at night
on + 날짜, 요일, 특정한 날	on April 13, on Tuesday on his birthday, on Christmas Day

I eat fruit **in** the morning.
Jack went to Russia **in** September.

Susan gets up **at** 6:00 a.m.
The city is beautiful **at** night.

She has a meeting **on** March 23.
I have a math test **on** Monday.

B before(~ 전에), after(~ 후에)

I wash my hair **before** breakfast.
Spring comes **after** winter.

C for, during(~ 동안)

for 뒤에는 숫자를 포함한 구체적인 기간이 오고, during 뒤에는 특정한 때를 나타내는 명사가 온다.

for *a week*, **for** *three months*, **for** *two years* …
during *the movie*, **during** *the vacation*, **during** *the winter* …

I watched TV **for** an hour.
Joe traveled in Europe **during** his vacation.

PRACTICE

🔍 Answer Key p.7

STEP 1

( ) 안에서 알맞은 말을 고르시오.

0 I called Ned (in, (at)) noon.

1 The bus left (in, at) eight o'clock.

2 I cleaned the kitchen (in, after) lunch.

3 Grace cried (for, during) the movie.

4 They moved to Greece (in, at) 2020.

5 There is a concert (in, on) April 27.

6 We swam in the pool (for, during) an hour.

7 I studied hard (at, before) the exam.

STEP 2

빈칸에 in, at, on 중 알맞은 전치사를 넣어 문장을 완성하시오.

0 Leaves fall down _____in_____ autumn.

1 The class starts _____ 9:10 a.m.

2 We had dinner _____ Christmas Day.

3 Cinderella left the party _____ midnight.

4 Summer vacation begins _____ July.

5 My dad washes his car _____ Sundays.

6 I visited my grandmother _____ her birthday.

7 Bill and I played tennis _____ the afternoon.

STEP 3

보기에서 알맞은 말을 골라 대화를 완성하시오. (단, 한 번씩만 쓸 것)

보기	before	~~after~~	for	during

0 A: Do you take a shower ____after____ dinner?
B: No, I don't. I usually take a shower before dinner.

1 A: Do you keep a diary?
B: Yes, I write in my diary _____ bedtime every night.

2 A: Tim was sick. He was in the hospital _____ two weeks.
B: Oh, is he okay now?

3 A: Did you go to Daejeon _____ the holidays?
B: Yes, I visited my uncle.

GRAMMAR FOR WRITING

A 보기에서 알맞은 말을 골라 ( ) 안의 말과 함께 써서 우리말을 영어로 옮기시오.

[0-4]

보기	in	at	~~on~~	behind	next to

0 그들은 잔디 위에 누웠다. (the grass)

→ They lay _____on the grass_____ .

1 내 자리는 창문 옆이다. (the window)

→ My seat is _____ .

2 Kevin은 뉴욕에 산다. (New York)

→ Kevin lives _____ .

3 나는 공항에서 여권을 잃어버렸다. (the airport)

→ I lost my passport _____ .

4 언덕 뒤에는 호수가 있다. (the hill)

→ There is a lake _____ .

[5-10]

보기	in	during	on	before	after	for

5 그는 자정 전에 집에 왔다. (midnight)

→ He came home _____ .

6 우리는 방과 후에 영화를 보러 갔다. (school)

→ We went to the movies _____ .

7 Sandra는 3주 동안 캐나다를 여행했다. (three weeks)

→ Sandra traveled in Canada _____ .

8 토요일에 야구 경기가 있다. (Saturday)

→ There is a baseball game _____ .

9 나는 방학 동안 바이올린 레슨을 받았다. (the vacation)

→ I took violin lessons _____ .

10 한국에서는 12월에 자주 눈이 온다. (December)

→ In Korea, it often snows _____ .

B ( ) 안의 말과 전치사를 함께 써서 대화를 완성하시오.

0 A: Is Robert married?
B: Yes, he married Ann _____ in 2020 _____. (2020)

1 A: Is the restaurant open today?
B: No, it doesn't open _____. (Mondays)

2 A: Did he leave the gym _____? (noon)
B: Yes, he left there at twelve o'clock.

3 A: Do you know London well?
B: Yes, I lived there _____. (two years)

4 A: Does she work _____? (the evening)
B: No, she finishes work at 4:00 p.m.

C 그림을 보고 보기에서 알맞은 말을 골라 문장을 완성하시오. (단, 한 번씩만 쓸 것)

보기	under	on	behind	~~at~~	in

0 Today Lina and Henry played badminton _____ at _____ school.
1 A bicycle was _____ a window.
2 There were balls _____ a box.
3 Henry's bottle was _____ a bench.
4 A cat was _____ Lina's bag.

REVIEW TEST

[1-2] 빈칸에 들어갈 알맞은 말을 고르시오.

1

There are many mountains _____ Korea.

① in   ② at   ③ on
④ under   ⑤ after

2

We have a school festival _____ June 12.

① in   ② at   ③ on
④ for   ⑤ during

3 빈칸에 들어갈 말로 알맞지 <u>않은</u> 것은?

Mike was in front of _____.

① me   ② she   ③ you
④ Jack   ⑤ the door

[4-5] 빈칸에 공통으로 들어갈 말을 고르시오.

4

• I put coins _____ my pocket.
• They enjoy hot chocolate _____ winter.

① in   ② at   ③ on
④ under   ⑤ during

5

• Mary is _____ home now.
• The TV show starts _____ six o'clock.

① in   ② at   ③ on
④ before   ⑤ next to

[6-7] 빈칸에 들어갈 말이 나머지 넷과 <u>다른</u> 것을 고르시오.

6 ① We eat lunch _____ noon.
② Ted met Lisa _____ 3:00 p.m.
③ The train arrived _____ 7:30 a.m.
④ I go to bed late _____ night.
⑤ They worked _____ Sunday.

7 ① They study _____ Tokyo.
② The key was _____ my room.
③ I saw him _____ the party.
④ We were _____ Italy last year.
⑤ There is a zoo _____ this town.

[8-10] 우리말과 일치하도록 빈칸에 알맞은 전치사를 쓰시오.

8   나는 30분 동안 친구와 이야기를 나눴다.

→ I chatted with my friend _____ thirty minutes.

9   우리의 휴가 동안 비가 많이 왔다.

→ It rained a lot _____ our holidays.

10   우리 학교 앞에는 우체국이 있다.

→ There is a post office _____ my school.

서술형 빈출

[11-13] Brian의 일과표를 보고 빈칸에 알맞은 전치사를 쓰시오.

7:00 a.m.	have breakfast
7:30 a.m.	go to school
5:00 p.m.	play basketball
6:00 p.m.	have dinner

11 Brian has breakfast _____ 7:00 a.m.

12 Brian goes to school _____ breakfast.

13 Brian plays basketball _____ dinner.

[14-15] 다음 중 밑줄 친 부분이 잘못된 것을 고르시오.

14 ① Gangnam is in Seoul.
② Julie sat next the door.
③ It is dark after sunset.
④ I bought a book at the bookstore.
⑤ They sang in front of many people.

15 ① School starts in March.
② I get presents on Christmas Day.
③ I met John at six o'clock yesterday.
④ We stayed in Paris during three days.
⑤ Jack finished his homework before 10:00 p.m.

서술형

[16-18] 우리말과 일치하도록 보기에서 알맞은 말을 골라 전치사와 함께 써서 문장을 완성하시오.

보기	the afternoon the building
	Saturdays

16 건물 뒤에는 정원이 하나 있다.

→ There is a garden _____.

17 그들은 토요일마다 소풍을 간다.

→ They go on a picnic _____.

18 나는 오후에 피자를 먹었다.

→ I ate pizza _____.

WORD LIST

- **grass** 잔디
- **concert** 콘서트
- **hide** 숨다, 감추다
- **supermarket** 슈퍼마켓
- **arrive** 도착하다
- **station** 역
- **hang** 걸다, 매달다
- **calendar** 달력
- **pass** 지나가다, (시험에) 합격하다
- **bridge** 다리
- **put** 놓다, 넣다
- **vase** 꽃병
- **wait for** ~을 기다리다
- **country** 국가, 나라
- **slipper** 슬리퍼
- **noon** 정오
- **vacation** 방학, 휴가
- **travel** 여행하다
- **autumn** 가을
- **midnight** 자정
- **lie** 눕다
- **marry** 결혼하다
- **gym** 체육관
- **badminton** 배드민턴
- **festival** 축제
- **chat** 이야기를 나누다
- **post office** 우체국
- **present** 선물
- **finish** 끝내다
- **picnic** 소풍

CHAPTER

07

동사의 종류

동사의 종류 1

- I **have** red shoes.
- Dad **bought** me shoes.

A 목적어나 보어가 필요 없는 동사

목적어나 보어 없이 동사만으로 완전한 의미를 나타내는 동사로, 「주어 + 동사」 형태의 문장을 이룬다. 주로 수식어를 함께 써서 더 자세한 의미를 나타낸다.

주어	smile, cry, walk, run, come, go, sing, study, live, sleep …

I **smiled**.
Amy **runs** fast.
Howard **came** alone.

B 목적어가 필요한 동사

목적어(~을)가 필요한 동사로, 「주어 + 동사 + 목적어」 형태의 문장을 이룬다.

주어	like, want, have, eat, watch, read, meet, know …	목적어

Mom **likes** *comedy shows*.
Chris **has** *a sister*.

C 목적어가 두 개 필요한 동사

간접목적어(~에게)와 직접목적어(…을)가 모두 필요한 동사로, 「주어 + 동사 + 간접목적어 + 직접목적어」 형태의 문장을 이룬다. 간접목적어가 대명사일 경우 목적격을 쓴다.

주어	**give**(~에게 …을 주다) **send**(~에게 …을 보내주다) **lend**(~에게 …을 빌려주다) **show**(~에게 …을 보여주다) **tell**(~에게 …을 말해주다) **teach**(~에게 …을 가르쳐주다) **make**(~에게 …을 만들어주다) **buy**(~에게 …을 사주다)	간접목적어 (~에게)	직접목적어 (…을)

Brian **showed** *me his album*.
She **made** *us a sandwich*.

PRACTICE

🔍 Answer Key p-7

STEP 1 주어진 문장의 형태를 보기에서 고르시오.

보기	ⓐ 주어 + 동사 ⓑ 주어 + 동사 + 목적어 ⓒ 주어 + 동사 + 간접목적어 + 직접목적어

0 Andy studies hard.   _____ⓐ_____

1 They walked slowly.   _____

2 He knows the answer.   _____

3 We told Ally a secret.   _____

4 I met her yesterday.   _____

5 Sandra lent me $20.   _____

6 Paul sent her a package.   _____

STEP 2 보기에서 알맞은 말을 골라 문장을 완성하시오. (현재형으로 쓸 것)

보기	help	play	~~check~~	speak	want

0 I _____check_____ the weather every day.

1 Nicole _____ English well.

2 Daniel always _____ his friends.

3 My sister _____ a new watch.

4 The boys _____ baseball on Saturdays.

STEP 3 ( ) 안에 주어진 말을 바르게 배열하여 문장을 완성하시오.

0 I _____sent him a Christmas card_____. (sent, a Christmas card, him)

1 Henry _____. (them, an amazing story, told)

2 He _____. (me, made, some coffee)

3 Ms. Brown _____. (us, science, taught)

4 I _____. (some books, bought, Jessica)

5 Julie _____. (her new shoes, showed, us)

6 Andrew _____. (a tip, gave, the waiter)

동사의 종류 2

- I **feel** sleepy.
- The book **makes** me sleepy.

A 주격 보어가 필요한 동사

주어의 상태를 보충 설명하는 주격 보어가 필요한 동사로, 「주어 + 동사 + 주격 보어」 형태의 문장을 이룬다.
주격 보어로는 명사, 형용사 등을 쓴다.

특히 look, feel, sound, smell, taste와 같이 감각을 나타내는 동사는 보어로 형용사를 쓴다.

주어	**be**(~이다) **become**(~해지다, ~이 되다) **look**(~해 보이다) **feel**(~하게 느끼다) **sound**(~하게 들리다) **smell**(~한 냄새가 나다) **taste**(~한 맛이 나다)	주격 보어

He **is** *a bus driver*.
The restaurant **became** *popular*.
The dress **looks** *nice*.
The soup **tastes** *good*.

B 목적격 보어가 필요한 동사

목적어와 목적어를 보충 설명하는 목적격 보어가 필요한 동사로, 「주어 + 동사 + 목적어 + 목적격 보어」
형태의 문장을 이룬다. 목적격 보어로는 명사, 형용사 등을 쓴다.

주어	**call**(~을 …라고 부르다) **make**(~을 …하게 만들다) **keep**(~을 …하게 유지하다) **find**(~이 …한 것을 알다)	목적어	목적격 보어

People **call** *him a liar*.
The news **made** *us sad*.
Mom **kept** *the window open*.
They **found** *the box empty*.

PRACTICE

🔍 Answer Key p.7

STEP 1

( ) 안에서 알맞은 말을 고르시오.

0 The room was (warm, warmly).

1 He made me (angry, angrily).

2 We (call, look) our dog Leo.

3 The milk smells (bad, badness).

4 This salad tastes (fresh, freshly).

5 I (sounded, found) his joke funny.

6 You (look, see) great in that shirt.

7 My sister always keeps her room (clean, cleanly).

STEP 2

보기에서 알맞은 말을 골라 문장을 완성하시오. (단, 한 번씩만 쓸 것)

보기	~~became~~	feels	sounded	tastes

0 Mike _____became_____ a soccer player.

1 This curry _____ spicy.

2 The music _____ beautiful.

3 The towel _____ very soft.

STEP 3

그림을 보고 보기에서 알맞은 말을 골라 적절한 형태로 써서 문장을 완성하시오. (단, 한 번씩만 쓸 것)

보기	~~call~~	find	keep	make

0 Jack is very smart. His friends _____call_____ him a genius.

1 Robin sang a popular song. The song _____ him famous.

2 I go to the gym every day. Exercise _____ me healthy.

3 We _____ the movie boring. We fell asleep during the movie.

GRAMMAR FOR WRITING

 보기에서 알맞은 말을 골라 ( ) 안의 말과 함께 써서 우리말을 영어로 옮기시오. (필요하면 형태를 바꿀 것)

[0-5]

보기	give	lend	sleep	meet	show	~~visit~~

0 우리는 그 박물관을 방문했다. (the museum)

→ We _____ visited the museum _____ .

1 나는 어젯밤에 잘 잤다. (well)

→ I _____ last night.

2 나는 Tom에게 내 자전거를 빌려주었다. (my bike)

→ I _____ .

3 Keira는 그녀의 아버지께 편지를 드렸다. (her father, a letter)

→ Keira _____ .

4 Peter는 반 친구를 길에서 만났다. (a classmate)

→ Peter _____ on the street.

5 나는 그에게 내 그림을 보여주었다. (my picture)

→ I _____ .

[6-10]

보기	become	find	make	sound	taste

6 우리는 여행하는 동안 피곤해졌다. (tired)

→ We _____ during the trip.

7 그 이야기는 재미있게 들렸다. (interesting)

→ The story _____ .

8 그 오디션 프로그램은 그녀를 스타로 만들었다. (a star)

→ The audition program _____ .

9 이 오렌지는 신맛이 난다. (sour)

→ This orange _____ .

10 우리는 그 소년이 무례하다는 것을 알게 되었다. (the boy, rude)

→ We _____ .

B 보기에서 알맞은 말을 골라 문장을 완성하시오. (과거형으로 쓸 것)

[0-3]

보기	~~be~~	watch	keep	hear

0 Yesterday _____was_____ Mother's Day.

1 The ice _____ my juice cold.

2 Sarah _____ a familiar voice.

3 We _____ a baseball game together.

[4-7]

보기	look	become	call	buy

4 People _____ him a hero.

5 Harry and I _____ best friends.

6 Her new hairstyle _____ nice.

7 My parents _____ me a school uniform.

C 그림을 보고 보기에서 알맞은 말을 골라 ( ) 안의 말과 함께 써서 문장을 완성하시오. (과거형으로 쓸 것)

0   1   2   3

보기	~~tell~~	teach	make	find

0 She _____told us a funny story_____. (us, a funny story)

1 Cold milk _____. (him, sick)

2 He _____ at school. (us, English)

3 We _____. (the hotel, old)

REVIEW TEST

1 빈칸에 들어갈 말로 알맞은 것은?

> The girl looks _____.

① happy ② happily ③ happiness
④ be happy ⑤ is happy

[2-4] 빈칸에 들어갈 말로 알맞지 <u>않은</u> 것을 고르시오.

2
> I usually walk _____.

① fast ② slowly ③ a park
④ to school ⑤ in the morning

3
> The pasta _____ delicious.

① is ② makes ③ looks
④ tastes ⑤ smells

4
> Tim showed _____ his family photo.

① me ② us ③ she
④ Linda ⑤ the boy

서술형

[5-7] 보기에서 알맞은 말을 골라 문장을 완성하시오. (과거형으로 쓸 것)

| 보기 | be | invite | give |

5
> Alice _____ kind to us.

6
> He _____ me a birthday gift.

7
> I _____ my neighbors for dinner.

빈출

[8-9] 다음 중 보기와 문장의 형태가 같은 것을 고르시오.

8
> 보기 I feel cold now.

① She came to my house.
② His idea sounded great.
③ Nora passed the test.
④ My uncle bought me lunch.
⑤ The strong wind made us cold.

9
> 보기 I found the book useful.

① Today is my birthday.
② Sally told us a scary story.
③ Tony lent me his book.
④ Mary became a scientist.
⑤ Mom kept the soup warm.

[10-11] 밑줄 친 부분의 쓰임이 나머지 넷과 다른 것을 고르시오.

10 ① Mom bought me a jacket.
② We bought Steve movie tickets.
③ I bought my sister emoticons.
④ He bought us some ice cream.
⑤ Sandra bought a new camera.

11 ① She made her baby a hat.
② Alex made me a bookshelf.
③ My father made me dinner.
④ The goal made him a winner.
⑤ Jennifer made us some pancakes.

[12-13] 다음 중 밑줄 친 부분이 잘못된 것을 고르시오.

12 ① She looks friendly.
② Emily felt lonely.
③ The soap smells good.
④ The juice tastes an orange.
⑤ Your plan sounds wonderful.

13 ① He often cries.
② We ate some fruit.
③ The rain stopped suddenly.
④ The boots keep my feet warm.
⑤ Mrs. Wilson teaches music us.

[14-16] 우리말과 일치하도록 ( ) 안의 말을 이용하여 문장을 완성하시오.

14 그 수학 숙제는 쉬워 보인다. (easy)

→ The math homework _____.

15 우리 할아버지는 밝게 웃으신다. (smile)

→ My grandfather _____ brightly.

16 Susan은 동물을 사랑한다. (love, animals)

→ Susan _____.

[17-18] 우리말과 일치하도록 ( ) 안에 주어진 말을 바르게 배열하시오.

17 나는 Andy에게 내 운동화를 빌려주었다.
(lent, my running shoes, Andy)

→ I _____.

18 우리는 방이 지저분하다는 것을 알게 되었다.
(the room, found, dirty)

→ We _____.

WORD LIST

- **alone** 혼자
- **show** 보여주다
- **package** 소포
- **amazing** 놀라운
- **tip** 팁, 봉사료
- **waiter** 종업원, 웨이터
- **sound** ~하게 들리다
- **keep** 유지하다
- **liar** 거짓말쟁이
- **empty** 비어 있는
- **warm** 따뜻한
- **joke** 농담
- **funny** 재미있는
- **curry** 카레 (요리)
- **towel** 수건
- **genius** 천재
- **gym** 체육관
- **healthy** 건강한, 건강에 좋은
- **fall asleep** 잠들다
- **sour** (맛이) 신
- **rude** 무례한
- **school uniform** 교복
- **strong** 강한
- **useful** 유용한
- **scary** 무서운
- **scientist** 과학자
- **bookshelf** 책꽂이
- **goal** 골, 득점
- **pancake** 팬케이크
- **running shoes** 운동화
- **dirty** 더러운

ESSENTIAL RULES OF
ENGLISH GRAMMAR

CHAPTER

08

조동사

UNIT
01 can, may

- The robot **can** clean the house.
- You **may** take a rest.

A 조동사

조동사는 동사 앞에 쓰여 동사에 능력, 허가, 의무 등의 의미를 더해주는 말이다. 조동사 뒤에는 항상 동사원형을 쓴다.

Jacob **can** *ride* a bike.

B can

1 ~할 수 있다(능력, 가능)

1) can: ~할 수 있다

Birds **can** fly.
John **can** pass the exam.
They **can** swim in the sea.

cf. can의 과거형은 could(~할 수 있었다)이다.
We **could** finish our work early.

2) can't[cannot]: ~할 수 없다

Peter **can't[cannot]** play the piano.
I **can't[cannot]** talk to you now.

3) Can + 주어 + 동사원형?: ~할 수 있니?

Can *he drive* a car?

2 ~해도 좋다(허가)

You **can** go home now.
You **can** take my umbrella.
Can I borrow your book?

C may

may는 허가를 나타내는 can(~해도 좋다)과 바꾸어 쓸 수 있지만, can보다 좀 더 정중한 표현이다.

You **may** stay with us.
= can

You **may** use my computer.
= can

May I sit here?
= Can

PRACTICE

🔍 Answer Key p-8

STEP 1

( ) 안에서 알맞은 말을 고르시오.

0 He can (⟨run⟩, runs) fast.

1 Jack (can, cans) lift heavy boxes.

2 (May, Can) you play the guitar?

3 May (have I, I have) your student ID card?

4 I (cannot fix, can fix not) my computer.

5 Emily could (answer, answered) the question.

STEP 2

사진을 보고 can 또는 can't를 넣어 문장을 완성하시오.

0 **1** **2** **3**

0 I _____can_____ solve these problems. They're easy.

1 The baby _____ talk. He is too young.

2 Jane _____ go to school today. She is sick.

3 Jackson is a chef. He _____ make delicious food.

STEP 3

보기에서 알맞은 말을 골라 ( ) 안의 말과 함께 써서 대화를 완성하시오. (단, 한 번씩만 쓸 것)

보기	ask	~~play~~	go	open

0 A: _____Can you play_____ golf? (can)
   B: No, I can't.

1 A: _____ your name? (may)
   B: Yes. My name is Alice.

2 A: _____ the present? (can)
   B: Of course you can.

3 A: _____ to the restroom now? (may)
   B: No. You can go after class.

UNIT
02 must, have to

- I **must** leave now.
- You **have to** lock the door.

A must

1 must: ~해야 한다(의무)

I **must** arrive on time.
You **must** follow the rules.
Drivers **must** wear seat belts.

2 must not: ~해서는 안 된다(강한 금지)

You **must not** tell lies.
You **must not** hit others.
You **must not** cross the road at a red light.

B have to

1 must(~해야 한다)와 같은 의미로, 주어가 3인칭 단수일 때는 has to를 쓴다.

You **have to** listen to his advice.
    = must

We **have to** get up early tomorrow.
    = must

Tom **has to** do his homework now.
    = must

2 don't/doesn't have to: ~할 필요가 없다

You **don't have to** worry about me.
He **doesn't have to** work on Sundays.

cf. must not과 don't have to가 서로 다른 의미를 나타낸다는 것에 유의한다.
    You **must not** stay here. (~해서는 안 된다)
    You **don't have to** stay here. (~할 필요가 없다)

PRACTICE

🔍 Answer Key p.8

 STEP 1

( ) 안에서 알맞은 말을 고르시오.

0 The kids must ((get), gets) enough sleep.

1 You (must, have) to drive slowly.

2 He must (eat not, not eat) too much.

3 You must (bring, to bring) your passport.

4 Nora (have to, has to) wash the dishes now.

5 Kate must (come, comes) home by ten o'clock.

6 Jack (don't has to, doesn't have to) pay for his lunch.

7 You (must not, doesn't have to) be late for class again.

STEP 2

빈칸에 must 또는 must not을 넣어 문장을 완성하시오.

0 You _____ must not _____ walk on the grass.

1 You _____ fight with your classmates.

2 You _____ wear a swimsuit in the pool.

3 You _____ touch that dog. It is a wild dog.

4 You _____ wash your hands before dinner.

5 You _____ stay at home. The weather is bad outside.

STEP 3

have to 또는 don't have to와 ( ) 안의 말을 함께 써서 문장을 완성하시오. (필요하면 형태를 바꿀 것)

0 You _____ have to be _____ quiet in the library. (be)

1 You _____. I can hear you. (shout)

2 Brian is sick. He _____ a doctor. (see)

3 You _____ a coat. It is warm today. (wear)

4 He _____ late into the night. He is very busy. (work)

5 Josh _____ a ticket. I already bought his ticket. (buy)

6 There isn't an elevator here. We _____ the stairs. (take)

GRAMMAR FOR WRITING

A   보기에서 알맞은 말을 골라 조동사와 함께 써서 우리말을 영어로 옮기시오.

[0-4]

보기	close	have	~~ride~~	remember	win

0 그 배우는 말을 탈 수 있다.

→ The actor _____can ride_____ a horse.

1 제가 창문을 닫아도 될까요?

→ _____ the window?

2 나는 그의 이름을 기억할 수가 없다.

→ I _____ his name.

3 우리는 그 경기를 이길 수 있다.

→ We _____ the game.

4 너는 이 사과를 먹어도 좋다.

→ You _____ this apple.

[5-10]

보기	speak	wait	go	play	take	waste

5 우리는 버스를 탈 필요가 없다.

→ We _____ a bus.

6 나는 시간을 낭비해서는 안 된다.

→ I _____ time.

7 너는 기차에서 조용히 말해야 한다.

→ You _____ quietly on the train.

8 그녀는 줄을 서서 기다려야 한다.

→ She _____ in line.

9 아이들은 불을 가지고 놀면 안 된다.

→ Kids _____ with fire.

10 Shawn은 내일 학교에 갈 필요가 없다.

→ Shawn _____ to school tomorrow.

B 보기에서 알맞은 말을 골라 대화를 완성하시오. (단, 한 번씩만 쓸 것)

보기	can	may	must	~~have to~~

0 A: You _____have to_____ return the book by Friday.
B: Okay. Don't worry.

1 A: _____ you play chess?
B: Yes. I learned it from my father.

2 A: Is this coffee free?
B: No, you _____ pay for it.

3 A: _____ I borrow your pen?
B: Sure. Here you are.

C 그림을 보고 보기에서 알맞은 말을 골라 (   ) 안에 주어진 조동사의 부정형과 함께 써서 문장을 완성하시오.

0   **1**   **2**   **3**

보기	hurry	~~wear~~	park	answer

0 I ____can't[cannot] wear____ this shirt. It is too small. (can)
1 We _____. We have enough time. (have to)
2 You _____ in this area. (must)
3 He _____ the phone now. He is too busy. (can)

REVIEW TEST

[1-2] 다음 밑줄 친 부분과 의미가 같은 것을 고르시오.

1

> A: <u>May</u> I come in?
> B: Sure.

① Am   ② Do   ③ Have
④ Can   ⑤ Must

2

> You <u>must</u> keep your promise.

① are   ② do   ③ can
④ may   ⑤ have to

[3-5] 빈칸에 들어갈 알맞은 말을 고르시오.

3

> I _____ read my book. It is too dark here.

① am not   ② can   ③ can't
④ may   ⑤ don't have to

4

> You _____ tell this to anyone. It's a secret.

① aren't   ② must   ③ must not
④ can   ⑤ have to

5

> Danny _____ the violin beautifully.

① can play ② can plays ③ can played
④ cans play ⑤ can't plays

6 밑줄 친 부분의 쓰임이 나머지 넷과 <u>다른</u> 것은?

① <u>Can</u> I use the oven?
② I <u>can</u> understand you.
③ They <u>can</u> speak French.
④ I <u>can</u> see your face well.
⑤ You <u>can</u> spell well.

[7-9] 보기에서 알맞은 말을 골라 대화를 완성하시오.

보기	can't	may	don't have to

7

> A: Jack _____ play soccer. He broke his leg.
> B: Oh, I feel sorry for him.

8

> A: _____ I have some ice cream?
> B: No. You have a cold!

9

> A: I'm worried about my grades.
> B: You _____ worry. You studied hard.

[10-11] 다음 중 밑줄 친 부분이 잘못된 것을 고르시오.

10 ① You <u>may go</u> there.
② You <u>can join</u> our club.
③ I <u>can't hear</u> your voice.
④ We <u>could see</u> the moon last night.
⑤ <u>May you visit</u> your office today?

11 ① I <u>have to take</u> a test.
② Paul <u>must work</u> hard.
③ He <u>have to eat</u> healthy food.
④ Mary <u>doesn't have to</u> cook for us.
⑤ You <u>must not bring</u> your pet here.

12 다음 우리말을 영어로 바르게 옮긴 것은?

> 나는 내일 일찍 일어날 필요가 없다.

① I don't get up early tomorrow.
② I can't get up early tomorrow.
③ I may not get up early tomorrow.
④ I must not get up early tomorrow.
⑤ I don't have to get up early tomorrow.

[13-15] 우리말과 일치하도록 밑줄 친 부분을 바르게 고치시오.

13 우리 아빠는 트럭을 운전하실 수 있다.
→ My dad <u>can drives</u> a truck.

→ _____

14 너는 영화를 보는 동안 휴대 전화를 사용해서는 안 된다.
→ You <u>don't have to</u> use your cell phone during the movie.

→ _____

15 나는 내 지갑을 찾을 수 없다.
→ I <u>may not find</u> my wallet.

→ _____

[16-18] 우리말과 일치하도록 ( ) 안의 말을 이용하여 문장을 완성하시오.

16 그는 이 숙제를 오늘 끝내야 한다. (finish)

→ He _____ this homework today.

17 그녀는 안경을 쓸 필요가 없다. (wear)

→ She _____ glasses.

18 우리는 거리에 쓰레기를 버려서는 안 된다. (throw)

→ We _____ trash on the street.

WORD LIST

- **borrow** 빌리다
- **lift** 들어올리다
- **student ID card** 학생증
- **fix** 수리하다
- **answer** 대답하다
- **chef** 요리사
- **restroom** 화장실
- **follow** 따르다
- **rule** 규칙
- **seat belt** 안전벨트
- **lie** 거짓말
- **hit** 때리다
- **cross** (가로질러) 건너다
- **advice** 충고
- **worry** 걱정하다
- **enough** 충분한
- **pay** 지불하다
- **fight** 싸우다
- **swimsuit** 수영복
- **touch** 만지다
- **wild** 야생의
- **shout** 소리지르다
- **see a doctor** 병원에 가다
- **horse** 말
- **waste** 낭비하다
- **return** 돌려주다
- **keep one's promise** 약속을 지키다
- **understand** 이해하다
- **spell** 철자를 말하다[쓰다]
- **cold** 감기
- **pet** 애완동물
- **throw trash** 쓰레기를 버리다

ESSENTIAL RULES OF
ENGLISH GRAMMAR

CHAPTER
09

일반동사 2

일반동사의 현재진행형 1

- I **am swimming** in the sea.

A

일반동사의 현재진행형

일반동사의 현재진행형은 '~하는 중이다'의 의미로, 지금 진행 중인 일을 나타낸다.

I *eat* breakfast every day.
I **am eating** breakfast now.

B

일반동사 현재진행형의 형태

1 「be동사 + 동사원형-ing」 형태로 쓰고, be동사는 주어의 인칭과 수를 따른다.

I	am	
You/We/They	are	동사원형-ing
He/She/It	is	

I **am watching** TV now.
The kids **are playing** in the yard.
The baby **is crying**.
It **is snowing** outside.

2 동사원형-ing 만드는 법

대부분의 동사	동사원형 + -ing	doing going eating playing watching reading singing crying
-e로 끝나는 동사	e를 빼고 + -ing	come → coming live → living make → making write → writing (예외: see → seeing)
-ie로 끝나는 동사	ie를 y로 고치고 + -ing	lie → lying die → dying tie → tying
〈단모음 + 단자음〉으로 끝나는 동사	자음을 한 번 더 쓰고 + -ing	sit → sitting run → running cut → cutting swim → swimming get → getting begin → beginning

I **am going** to the mall.
We **are making** sandwiches.
The cat **is lying** on the bed.
They **are sitting** on the carpet.

PRACTICE

🔍 Answer Key p-9

STEP 1

주어진 동사의 동사원형-ing형을 쓰시오.

0 go → _____going_____   **1** sit → _____

2 sing → _____   **3** cry → _____

4 live → _____   **5** die → _____

6 watch → _____   **7** stay → _____

8 buy → _____   **9** come → _____

10 get → _____   **11** read → _____

STEP 2

( ) 안의 말을 이용하여 현재진행형 긍정문을 완성하시오.

0 Lucy _____is sleeping_____ now. (sleep)

1 He _____ at me. (smile)

2 They _____ in the park. (run)

3 Nora _____ her room. (clean)

4 I _____ in my diary now. (write)

5 Mary _____ a scarf around her neck. (tie)

6 The students _____ at the bus stop. (stand)

STEP 3

그림을 보고 보기에서 알맞은 말을 골라 현재진행형을 써서 문장을 완성하시오.

0   **1**   **2**   **3**

보기	lie	cut	speak	~~ride~~

0 Jack _____is riding_____ a bike.

1 I _____ on the grass.

2 They _____ in English.

3 She _____ a chocolate cake.

일반동사의 현재진행형 2

- I **am not going** to the bank.
- **Are you going** to the bank?

A 일반동사 현재진행형의 부정문

「be동사 + not + 동사원형-ing」 형태로 쓴다.

I You/We/They He/She/It	am are is	not	동사원형-ing

I **am not working** now.
They **aren't watching** a movie.
She **is not driving** a car.
Lisa **isn't making** dinner.

B 일반동사 현재진행형의 의문문

「be동사 + 주어 + 동사원형-ing?」 형태로 쓴다.

be동사 + 주어 + 동사원형-ing?			긍정의 대답	부정의 대답
Am/Are/Is	주어	동사원형-ing?	Yes, 주어 + am/are/is.	No, 주어 + am not/aren't/isn't.

A: **Am I speaking** fast?
B: **Yes, you are. / No, you aren't.**

A: **Are you playing** computer games?
B: **Yes, I am. / No, I'm not.**

A: **Are they taking** a test?
B: **Yes, they are. / No, they aren't.**

A: **Is your dad coming** home now?
B: **Yes, he is. / No, he isn't.**

PRACTICE

🔍 Answer Key p-9

STEP 1 ( ) 안에서 알맞은 말을 고르시오.

0 (Be, Are) you crying?

1 Is she (cut, cutting) the bread?

2 They (isn't, aren't) working hard.

3 I (am, do) not thinking about him.

4 James (is not, not is) looking at you.

5 (Is, Does) Olivia taking a photo?

6 Are you (use, using) that program?

STEP 2 ( ) 안의 말을 이용하여 현재진행형 부정문을 완성하시오.

0 The dog _____isn't barking_____. (bark)

It is sleeping.

1 They _____ soccer. (play)

They are watching a soccer game.

2 She _____ her face. (wash)

She is brushing her teeth.

3 I _____ on the phone. (talk)

I am writing an email.

4 David _____ in the park. (walk)

He is running at the gym.

STEP 3 보기에서 알맞은 말을 골라 적절한 형태로 바꾸어 현재진행형 대화를 완성하시오.

보기	~~listen~~	put	stay	wear

0 A: _____Are_____ you _____listening_____ to me?
   B: Yes, I am.

1 A: _____ she _____ a sweater?
   B: No, she isn't.

2 A: _____ they _____ at the hotel?
   B: No, they aren't.

3 A: _____ Don _____ books on the desk?
   B: Yes, he is.

UNIT 03 일반동사의 미래형 1

- I **will go** there by bus.
- He **is going to take** a plane.

A 일반동사의 미래형

1 일반동사의 미래형은 '~할 것이다'의 의미로, 앞으로 일어날 일에 대한 예측이나 의지, 예정된 계획 등을 나타낸다. 주로 「will + 동사원형」이나 「be going to + 동사원형」 형태로 쓴다.

   I **will do** my best.
   I **am going to visit** my grandmother this Saturday.

2 주로 tomorrow, next week/month/year, soon 등 미래를 나타내는 표현과 함께 쓴다.

   I **will see** you *tomorrow*.
   Jack **will be** in London *next year*.
   We**'re going to move** *soon*.

B will + 동사원형

I **will help** you.
Peter **will be** twelve years old next year.
The movie **will start** at eight o'clock.

cf. 「대명사 주어 + will」은 줄임말로 쓸 수 있다.

I will → I'll	You will → You'll	He will → He'll	She will → She'll
It will → It'll	We will → We'll	They will → They'll	

C be going to + 동사원형

I You/We/They He/She/It	am are is	going to	동사원형

I **am going to order** pizza for dinner.
They**'re going to play** board games after school.
She**'s going to be** a mother soon.

PRACTICE

🔍 Answer Key p.9

STEP 1

( ) 안에서 알맞은 말을 고르시오.

0 It (be, (is)) going to rain soon.

1 We will (meet, meets) tomorrow.

2 He is going to (pass, passes) the test.

3 Alex will (be, is) busy next year.

4 The train (will leave, will leaving) the station at 5:00 p.m.

5 Tina (going, is going) to have a birthday party next week.

6 They (be going to, are going to) go on a picnic on Saturday.

STEP 2

그림을 보고 will과 ( ) 안의 말을 이용하여 문장을 완성하시오. (긍정문으로 쓸 것)

0   **1**   **2**   **3**

0 I ____will tell____ you a secret. (tell)

1 I _____ you later. (call)

2 The baseball game _____ soon. (begin)

3 He _____ to the movies this weekend. (go)

STEP 3

be going to와 ( ) 안의 말을 이용하여 문장을 완성하시오. (긍정문으로 쓸 것)

0 We ____are going to play____ tennis tomorrow. (play)

1 I _____ at home today. (stay)

2 She _____ some eggs soon. (boil)

3 They _____ chicken for dinner. (eat)

4 I _____ a tree on Sunday. (plant)

5 A new restaurant _____ tomorrow. (open)

6 We _____ Hong Kong next week. (visit)

7 My brother _____ abroad next year. (study)

일반동사의 미래형 2

- I **won't give up**.
- **Are you going to try** again?

will의 부정문과 의문문

1 will의 부정문은 주어의 인칭과 수에 관계없이 주어 뒤에 「will not + 동사원형」 형태로 쓴다.

주어	will not + 동사원형 (= won't + 동사원형)

Ted **will not change** his mind.
They **won't tell** you their secret.
I **won't be** late again.

2 will의 의문문은 주어의 인칭과 수에 관계없이 「Will + 주어 + 동사원형?」 형태로 쓴다.

A: **Will Josh keep** his promise?
B: Yes, he will. / No, he won't.

be going to의 부정문과 의문문

1 be going to의 부정문은 「be동사 + not + going to + 동사원형」 형태로 쓰고, be동사는 주어의 인칭과 수를 따른다.

I	am			
You/We/They	are	not	going to	동사원형
He/She/It	is			

I'm not going to buy this camera.
We**'re not going to sing** in the festival.
Tommy **is not going to forgive** me.

2 be going to의 의문문은 「be동사 + 주어 + going to + 동사원형?」 형태로 쓴다.

A: **Are you going to stay** at home this Sunday?
B: Yes, I am. / No, I'm not.

PRACTICE

🔍 Answer Key p.9

 STEP 1　( ) 안에서 알맞은 말을 고르시오.

0 (Is, Will) she win the game?

1 We will (not fight, fight not) again.

2 (Be, Is) Jack going to wait for us?

3 Mike (won't, not will) come with us.

4 Are you (go, going) to wash this shirt?

5 Will James (agrees, agree) with you?

6 We are (going not to, not going to) move to Seoul.

STEP 2　그림을 보고 will과 ( ) 안의 말을 이용하여 문장을 완성하시오.

0	1	2	3

0 I _____won't answer_____ your question. (not/answer)

1 He _____ fast food. (not/eat)

2 We _____ the elevator. (not/take)

3 _____ you _____ our soccer club? (join)

STEP 3　be going to와 ( ) 안의 말을 이용하여 문장을 완성하시오.

0 Amber _____is not going to wear_____ this hat. (not/wear)
She doesn't like it.

1 They _____ soon. (not/sleep)
They are watching a movie.

2 I _____ my raincoat. (not/bring)
The weather is going to be nice.

3 A: _____ James _____ a bus to the library? (take)
B: No, he will take the subway.

GRAMMAR FOR WRITING

 보기에서 알맞은 말을 골라 우리말을 영어로 옮기시오.

[0-4]

보기	make	~~drink~~	shop	read	fly

0 Tom은 사과 주스를 마시고 있다.

→ Tom _____is drinking_____ apple juice.

1 새들이 하늘을 날고 있다.

→ Birds _____ in the sky.

2 나는 그 책을 읽고 있지 않다.

→ I _____ that book.

3 우리는 눈사람을 만들고 있다.

→ We _____ a snowman.

4 Linda는 온라인으로 쇼핑하고 있니?

→ _____ online?

[5-10] (( ) 안의 말을 이용할 것)

보기	be	buy	invite	try	go	change

5 그들이 그것을 다시 시도할까? (will)

→ _____ that again?

6 우리는 새 오븐을 살 것이다. (be going to)

→ We _____ a new oven.

7 나는 내 헤어스타일을 바꾸지 않을 것이다. (will)

→ I _____ my hairstyle.

8 너는 이번 여름에 시카고에 갈 거니? (be going to)

→ _____ to Chicago this summer?

9 Bob은 내년에 6학년이 될 것이다. (will)

→ Bob _____ in the sixth grade next year.

10 그녀는 자신의 생일 파티에 Andy를 초대하지 않을 것이다. (be going to)

→ She _____ Andy to her birthday party.

108

B 그림을 보고 보기에서 알맞은 말을 골라 적절한 형태로 바꾸어 현재진행형 문장을 완성하시오.

보기	eat
---	play
	sell
	sit
	~~walk~~

0 A boy _____is walking_____ his dog.

1 A woman _____ ice cream.

2 A father and son _____ badminton.

3 Two girls _____ on the bench.

4 Some children _____ lunch on the grass.

C 그림을 보고 ( ) 안의 말을 이용하여 대화를 완성하시오.

0   1   2   3

0 A: May I take your order?
B: Yes. I _____will have_____ pizza. (will, have)

1 A: You are late again!
B: Sorry. I _____ late next time. (will, be)

2 A: Do you have any plans for this weekend?
B: Yes. I _____ a mountain with my dad.
(be going to, climb)

3 A: _____ he _____ the race? (be going to, win)
B: Yes. He is running very fast.

REVIEW TEST

[1-2] 다음 중 동사원형-ing형이 <u>잘못</u> 연결된 것을 고르시오.

1
① do – doing　　② run – running
③ lie – lieing　　④ play – playing
⑤ come – coming

2
① die – dying　　② live – living
③ make – making　　④ cut – cutting
⑤ begin – begining

3 빈칸에 들어갈 말로 알맞지 <u>않은</u> 것은?

I will leave _____.

① soon　　　　② tonight
③ yesterday　　④ tomorrow
⑤ next week

[4-5] 빈칸에 공통으로 들어갈 말을 고르시오.

4
• We _____ enjoying the party. • They _____ going to meet on Saturday.

① be　　② is　　③ are
④ do　　⑤ will

5
• _____ the shop be open tomorrow? • We _____ go to New York next month.

① Be[be]　　② Are[are]　　③ Do[do]
④ Does[does]　　⑤ Will[will]

6 빈칸에 들어갈 말이 나머지 넷과 <u>다른</u> 것은?
① Winter _____ coming.
② Joe _____ staying in Paris.
③ She _____ waiting for a bus.
④ The telephone _____ ringing.
⑤ The boys _____ playing soccer.

[7-8] 다음 중 밑줄 친 부분이 <u>잘못된</u> 것을 고르시오.

7
① <u>Is</u> she <u>drying</u> her hair?
② They <u>don't eating</u> lunch.
③ Kelly <u>is traveling</u> in China.
④ <u>Are you learning</u> Japanese?
⑤ I <u>am not using</u> your pen.

8
① Chris <u>will do</u> the dishes.
② <u>Will she bring</u> her children?
③ I'm <u>going to clean</u> the floor.
④ Mary <u>going to wash</u> her shoes.
⑤ She <u>won't give up</u> her dream.

빈출

9 밑줄 친 부분의 쓰임이 나머지 넷과 <u>다른</u> 것은?

① They <u>are going to</u> help us.
② I <u>am going to</u> finish my work today.
③ The bus <u>is going to</u> the library now.
④ My dad <u>is going to</u> buy a new car.
⑤ She <u>is going to</u> spend her vacation in Spain.

서술형

[10-11] 빈칸에 알맞은 말을 써서 대화를 완성하시오.

10
A: Is Kevin singing a song?
B: No, _____ _____. He's listening to music.

11
A: Are you going to meet Mike tonight?
B: Yes, _____ _____.

12 다음 우리말을 영어로 바르게 옮긴 것은?

> 그 요리사는 국에 소금을 추가하지 않을 것이다.

① The cook will add not salt to the soup.
② The cook will not adds salt to the soup.
③ The cook will not add salt to the soup.
④ The cook is going to add salt to the soup.
⑤ The cook is not going add salt to the soup.

서술형

[13-15] 우리말과 일치하도록 ( ) 안의 말을 이용하여 문장을 완성하시오.

13 바람이 세게 불고 있다. (blow)

→ The wind _____ _____ hard.

14 우리는 그 식당에 가지 않을 것이다. (go)

→ We _____ _____ _____ _____ _____ to the restaurant.

15 너 지금 컴퓨터 사용 중이니? (use)

→ _____ _____ _____ the computer now?

서술형

[16-17] 우리말과 일치하도록 ( ) 안에 주어진 말을 바르게 배열하시오.

16 나는 그녀에게 말을 걸 것이다.
(going to, am, talk, I)

→ _____ to her.

17 내일 날씨가 화창할까? (it, be, will, sunny)

→ _____ tomorrow?

서술형

18 다음을 현재진행형 부정문으로 바꿔 쓰시오.

Wendy wears a watch.

→ _____

WORD LIST

- **yard** 마당
- **tie** 묶다
- **cut** 깎다, 자르다
- **begin** 시작하다
- **mall** 쇼핑몰
- **carpet** 카펫
- **write in one's diary** 일기를 쓰다
- **scarf** 스카프
- **neck** 목
- **bus stop** 버스 정류장
- **take a test** 시험을 보다
- **look at** ~을 보다
- **bark** 짖다
- **sweater** 스웨터
- **plane** 비행기
- **soon** 곧
- **move** 이사하다
- **go on a picnic** 소풍을 가다
- **boil** 삶다
- **plant** 심다
- **abroad** 해외에서, 해외로
- **give up** 포기하다
- **change one's mind** 마음을 바꾸다
- **join** 가입하다, ~을 함께 하다
- **invite** 초대하다
- **sell** 팔다
- **enjoy** 즐기다
- **telephone** 전화기
- **dry** 말리다
- **spend** (시간을) 보내다
- **add** 추가하다
- **blow** (바람이) 불다

ESSENTIAL RULES OF
ENGLISH GRAMMAR

CHAPTER
10

비교

UNIT 01 비교급

• He is **older than** me.

A 비교급

1 비교급은 두 개의 대상을 비교할 때 쓰는 형용사, 부사의 형태이다.

Steve is *tall*.
Steve is **taller** than Mike.

2 「비교급 + than」 형태로 쓰여 '~보다 더 …한/하게'의 의미를 나타낸다.

My hair is **darker than** Susan's.
Peter studies **harder than** me.

cf. 비교급 앞에 much(훨씬)를 써서 비교급을 강조할 수 있다.
Asia is **much** *larger* than Europe.

B 비교급 만드는 법

비교급: 「형용사/부사 + -er」 또는 「more + 형용사/부사」

대부분의 형용사/부사	+ -er	older smaller colder faster smarter
-e로 끝나는 형용사/부사	+ -r	large → larger nice → nicer wise → wiser cute → cuter
〈단모음 + 단자음〉으로 끝나는 형용사/부사	자음을 한 번 더 쓰고 + -er	big → big**ger** thin → thin**ner** hot → hot**ter**
-y로 끝나는 형용사/부사	y를 i로 고치고 + -er	heavy → heav**ier** early → earl**ier** easy → eas**ier** funny → funn**ier**
3음절 이상의 형용사/부사와 -ous, -ful, -ive 등으로 끝나는 2음절 형용사/부사	more + 형용사/부사	difficult → **more** difficult expensive → **more** expensive interesting → **more** interesting famous → **more** famous quickly → **more** quickly
예외	good/well → **better** bad → **worse** many/much → **more** little → **less**	

My room is **smaller** than my brother's.
Your suitcase is **heavier** than mine.
This shirt is **more expensive** than that one.
Lisa sings **better** than Simon.

PRACTICE

🔍 Answer Key p.10

 STEP 1　그림을 보고 주어진 단어의 비교급을 쓰시오.

0 small – <u>smaller</u>　　**1** difficult – _____　　**2** heavy – _____

3 cheap – _____　　**4** hard – _____　　**5** big – _____

STEP 2　( ) 안에서 알맞은 말을 고르시오.

0 You are (young, younger) than me.

1 Her voice is (loud, louder) than mine.

2 Angela reads (much, more) than me.

3 China is (larger, more larger) than Japan.

4 Max walked (slowlier, more slowly) than me.

5 He talks (much faster, more faster) than you.

STEP 3　( ) 안의 말을 이용하여 비교급 문장을 완성하시오.

0 Your cat is _____fatter than_____ mine. (fat)

1 I get up _____ my sister. (early)

2 This coffee is _____ the tea. (hot)

3 He eats _____ his father. (little)

4 Your new cell phone is _____ mine. (good)

5 The book was _____ the movie. (interesting)

• The Nile River is **the longest** river in the world.

A 최상급

1 최상급은 세 개 이상의 대상을 비교할 때 쓰는 형용사, 부사의 형태이다.

Steve is *tall*.
Steve is *taller* than Mike.
Steve is **the tallest** student in the class.

2 「the + 최상급」 형태로 쓰여 '가장 ~한/하게'의 의미를 나타낸다.

He is **the richest** man in the world.
This is **the nicest** room in the hotel.

B 최상급 만드는 법

최상급: 「형용사/부사 + -est」 또는 「most + 형용사/부사」

대부분의 형용사/부사	+ -est	oldest smallest coldest fastest smartest
-e로 끝나는 형용사/부사	+ -st	large → largest nice → nicest wise → wisest cute → cutest
〈단모음 + 단자음〉으로 끝나는 형용사/부사	자음을 한 번 더 쓰고 + -est	big → biggest thin → thinnest hot → hottest
-y로 끝나는 형용사/부사	y를 i로 고치고 + -est	heavy → heaviest early → earliest easy → easiest funny → funniest
3음절 이상의 형용사/부사와 -ous, -ful, -ive 등으로 끝나는 2음절 형용사/부사	most + 형용사/부사	difficult → **most** difficult expensive → **most** expensive interesting → **most** interesting famous → **most** famous quickly → **most** quickly
예외		good/well → **best** bad → **worst** many/much → **most** little → **least**

This is the **oldest** tree in the park.
It's the **biggest** supermarket in town.
This is the **most expensive** diamond in the world.
John has the **worst** grades in his class.

PRACTICE

🔍 Answer Key p-10

STEP 1

주어진 단어의 최상급을 쓰시오.

0 loud → <u>loudest</u>

1 many → _____

2 nice → _____

3 thin → _____

4 well → _____

5 interesting → _____

6 pretty → _____

7 little → _____

8 fast → _____

STEP 2

( ) 안에서 알맞은 말을 고르시오.

0 It is the (better, ⓑest) song on this album.

1 Jeju is (largest, the largest) island of Korea.

2 He is the (wisest, most wise) man in our town.

3 Yesterday was the (colder, coldest) day of this year.

4 He is the (greatest, most greatest) writer in our country.

5 It is the (more difficult, most difficult) question on the test.

6 This cake is the (much popular, most popular) dessert in our café.

STEP 3

( ) 안의 말을 이용하여 최상급 문장을 완성하시오.

0 His bedroom is _____the cleanest_____ room in the house. (clean)

1 It was _____ movie of the year. (bad)

2 He is _____ man in this company. (busy)

3 Baseball is _____ sport for me. (exciting)

4 Health is _____ thing of all. (important)

5 Summer is _____ season of the year. (hot)

6 Mary is _____ person in her family. (young)

GRAMMAR FOR WRITING

보기에서 알맞은 말을 골라 적절한 형태로 바꾸어 우리말을 영어로 옮기시오.

[0-4]

보기	thick	quickly	good	heavy	~~warm~~

0 오늘은 어제보다 더 따뜻했다.

→ Today was _____warmer than_____ yesterday.

1 소는 토끼보다 더 무겁다.

→ Cows are _____ rabbits.

2 이 책은 그 잡지보다 더 두껍다.

→ This book is _____ the magazine.

3 네 카메라는 내 것보다 더 좋다.

→ Your camera is _____ mine.

4 나는 James보다 더 빨리 질문에 대답했다.

→ I answered the question _____ James.

[5-10]

보기	good	easy	big	smart	popular	tall

5 이것은 서울에서 가장 높은 빌딩이다.

→ This is _____ building in Seoul.

6 역사는 나에게 가장 쉬운 과목이다.

→ History is _____ subject for me.

7 Mark는 그의 반에서 가장 인기 있는 학생이다.

→ Mark is _____ student in his class.

8 그것은 세계에서 가장 똑똑한 로봇이다.

→ It is _____ robot in the world.

9 그녀는 그 식당에서 가장 훌륭한 요리사이다.

→ She is _____ cook in the restaurant.

10 시애틀은 워싱턴주에서 가장 큰 도시이다.

→ Seattle is _____ city in Washington State.

B 다음 표를 보고 ( ) 안의 말을 이용하여 문장을 완성하시오.

[0-2]

Name	Age
Nancy	8
Jenny	11
Chris	13

0 Nancy is ___younger than___ Jenny. (young)

1 Chris is _____ Jenny. (old)

2 Nancy is _____ person of the three. (young)

[3-5]

Item	Price
cap	$10
bag	$20
shirt	$40

3 The cap is _____ the bag. (cheap)

4 The shirt is _____ the bag. (expensive)

5 The shirt is _____ item of the three. (expensive)

C 그림을 보고 ( ) 안의 말을 이용하여 문장을 완성하시오.

0   **1**   **2**   **3**

0 Jack's birthday is _____sooner_____ than his dad's. (soon)

1 Jane is _____ of the three. (short)

2 This chair is _____ than that chair. (comfortable)

3 It is _____ painting in this museum. (famous)

REVIEW TEST

[1-3] 빈칸에 들어갈 알맞은 말을 고르시오.

1

Sam is _____ than his brother.

① big   ② bigger
③ more big   ④ biggest
⑤ most big

2

This is the _____ place in the city.

① beautifuler   ② beautifulest
③ much beautiful   ④ more beautiful
⑤ most beautiful

3

Her room is _____ cleaner than mine.

① many   ② much
③ more   ④ very
⑤ the

서술형

[4-5] ( ) 안의 말을 이용하여 비교급 문장을 완성하시오.

4

Amy's feet are _____ than mine. (small)

5

Tony studies _____ than Dan. (hard)

[6-8] 다음 중 밑줄 친 부분이 잘못된 것을 고르시오.

6
① My sister is wiser than me.
② The bus is slower than the train.
③ Julie sleeps littler than Lucy.
④ Women usually live longer than men.
⑤ The bed is more comfortable than the sofa.

7
① She is the best player on the team.
② This is the newest bike in the shop.
③ He is the greatest actor in Hollywood.
④ Tennis is the difficultest exercise for me.
⑤ The Sahara is the largest desert in Africa.

8
① This is the easiest question of all.
② This computer is oldest than mine.
③ Time is more important than money.
④ This week is colder than last week.
⑤ The giraffe is the tallest animal at the zoo.

빈출

9 다음 우리말을 영어로 바르게 옮긴 것은?

Mary는 Tom보다 훨씬 더 빨리 달린다.

① Mary runs much faster than Tom.
② Mary runs more faster than Tom.
③ Mary runs the fastest than Tom.
④ Tom runs much faster than Mary.
⑤ Tom runs more faster than Mary.

서술형

[10-11] ( ) 안의 말을 이용하여 최상급 문장을 완성하시오.

10 He was _____ character on the show. (funny)

11 New York is _____ city in the world. (exciting)

[12-13] 빈칸에 들어갈 말이 바르게 짝지어진 것을 고르시오.

12
- My cell phone is thinner _____(A)_____ yours.
- He is the _____(B)_____ famous king in history.

	(A)		(B)
①	of	……	much
②	of	……	most
③	than	……	much
④	than	……	more
⑤	than	……	most

13
- John is _____(A)_____ tallest of the five boys.
- Math is _____(B)_____ interesting than science for me.

	(A)		(B)
①	the	……	much
②	the	……	more
③	most	……	much
④	most	……	more
⑤	most	……	most

서술형 **빈출**

14 다음 두 문장이 같은 의미가 되도록 ( ) 안의 말을 이용하여 문장을 완성하시오.

The students came later than the teacher.

→ The teacher came _____ the students. (early)

서술형

[15-17] 우리말과 일치하도록 ( ) 안의 말을 이용하여 문장을 완성하시오.

15 나는 Judy보다 춤을 더 잘 출 수 있다. (well)

→ I can dance _____ Judy.

16 이번 여름은 지난 여름보다 더 덥다. (hot)

→ This summer is _____ last summer.

17 이것은 이 식당에서 가장 맛있는 음식이다. (delicious, dish)

→ This is _____ in the restaurant.

WORD LIST

- **Asia** 아시아 (대륙) _____
- **wise** 현명한 _____
- **thin** 얇은, 마른 _____
- **interesting** 재미있는 _____
- **famous** 유명한 _____
- **quickly** 빨리 _____
- **suitcase** 여행 가방 _____
- **cheap** (값이) 싼 _____
- **hard** 단단한, 어려운, 열심히 _____
- **fat** 살찐 _____
- **hotel** 호텔 _____
- **town** 마을 _____
- **grade** 성적 _____
- **island** 섬 _____
- **clean** 깨끗한 _____
- **company** 회사 _____
- **sport** 운동, 스포츠 _____
- **important** 중요한 _____
- **season** 계절 _____
- **history** 역사 _____
- **subject** 과목 _____
- **item** 항목, 품목 _____
- **comfortable** 편안한 _____
- **painting** 그림 _____
- **place** 장소 _____
- **player** 선수 _____
- **desert** 사막 _____
- **giraffe** 기린 _____
- **character** 등장인물 _____
- **math** 수학 _____
- **science** 과학 _____
- **dish** 요리 _____

ESSENTIAL RULES OF
ENGLISH GRAMMAR

CHAPTER
11

to부정사

명사처럼 쓰는 to부정사

• I want **to have** some pizza.

A to부정사

to부정사는 「to + 동사원형」 형태로, 문장에서 명사, 형용사, 부사처럼 쓰인다.

I like **to exercise**.
I don't have time **to exercise**.
I went to the gym **to exercise**.

B 명사처럼 쓰는 to부정사

to부정사가 명사처럼 문장에서 주어, 목적어, 보어로 쓰여, '~하는 것'이라는 의미를 나타낸다.

Paul wants a dog.
Paul wants **to have** a dog.

1 주어 역할: ~하는 것은

to부정사가 주어로 쓰일 경우 보통 주어 자리에 It을 쓰고 to부정사를 뒤로 보낸다.

It is exciting **to travel**. (= To travel is exciting.)
It is easy **to solve** this puzzle. (= To solve this puzzle is easy.)

2 목적어 역할: ~하는 것을

to부정사가 want, need, hope, plan, decide, like, agree 등의 동사 뒤에서 목적어로 쓰인다.

You *need* **to sleep**.
I *hope* **to see** you again.
Jason *decided* **to learn** Chinese.

3 보어 역할: ~하는 것(이다)

to부정사가 보어로 쓰여 주어를 보충 설명한다.

My dream is **to become** a singer.
His goal is **to win** the game.

PRACTICE

🔍 Answer Key p.11

STEP 1

( ) 안에서 알맞은 말을 고르시오.

0 You need (be, ⟨to be⟩) quiet.

1 (Play, To play) with Linda is fun.

2 We decided to (buy, bought) a chair.

3 I want (know, to know) your name.

4 Her job is to (help, helps) sick people.

5 (It, That) is boring to stay at home alone.

6 Tina and I (like, to like) to watch movies.

7 It was great (work, to work) with you.

STEP 2

보기에서 알맞은 말을 골라 적절한 형태로 바꾸어 문장을 완성하시오. (단, 한 번씩만 쓸 것)

보기	draw	go	sell	meet	~~be~~

0 I want _____to be_____ a police officer.

1 Jenny likes _____ cartoons.

2 They agreed _____ at seven o'clock.

3 We are planning _____ to France.

4 Mark decided _____ his house.

STEP 3

사진을 보고 ( ) 안의 말을 이용하여 문장을 완성하시오.

0  **1**  **2**  **3**

0 It is helpful _____to read_____ books. (read)

1 It is good _____ vegetables. (eat)

2 His hobby is _____ cookies. (bake)

3 My goal is _____ English well. (speak)

UNIT 02

형용사, 부사처럼 쓰는 to부정사

- I want something **to eat**.
- We will go out **to eat** dinner.

A 형용사처럼 쓰는 to부정사

to부정사가 형용사처럼 명사나 대명사를 꾸며주며, '~할'이라는 의미를 나타낸다.

Sam has <u>many</u> *books*.
Sam has *books* **to read**.

이때 to부정사는 명사나 대명사를 뒤에서 꾸며준다.

She has *homework* **to do**.
I have *a present* **to give** you.
We need *someone* **to help** us.

B 부사처럼 쓰는 to부정사

to부정사가 부사처럼 동사나 형용사 등을 꾸며주며, 목적, 감정의 원인 등을 나타낸다.

I ran <u>fast</u>.
I ran **to catch** the bus.

1 목적: ~하기 위해

to부정사가 동사의 목적을 나타낸다.

I *studied* hard **to pass** the exam.
Bill *went out* **to meet** his friend.
They *came* **to ask** me some questions.

2 감정의 원인: ~해서

to부정사가 happy, glad, sad, sorry 등 감정을 나타내는 형용사 뒤에 쓰여 감정의 원인을 나타낸다.

I'm *happy* **to come** back home.
I'm *glad* **to see** you.
I'm *sorry* **to hear** that.

PRACTICE

🔍 Answer Key p.11

 STEP 1

밑줄 친 to부정사가 꾸며주는 말에 동그라미 하시오.

0 We have (five boxes) to move.

1 There is a message to read.

2 It is time to leave now.

3 I have something to tell you.

4 It is a great way to spend a holiday.

5 I don't have enough time to sleep.

6 There are many places to visit in Seoul.

7 Do you have any money to buy some food?

STEP 2

자연스러운 문장이 되도록 알맞게 연결하시오.

0 We practiced hard •   • ⓐ to buy a new car.

1 She is saving money •   • ⓑ to take a walk.

2 Ryan went to the park •   • ⓒ to check my email.

3 They went to the station •   • ⓓ to win the game.

4 I turned on the computer •   • ⓔ to take the train.

STEP 3

보기에서 알맞은 말을 골라 적절한 형태로 바꾸어 대화를 완성하시오.

보기	wear	ask	hear	meet	~~study~~

0 A: Is Ben home?
   B: No. He went to the library _____to study_____.

1 A: Did you call me?
   B: Yes. I had some questions _____ you.

2 A: Cindy will move to Canada next month.
   B: Oh, I'm sad _____ that.

3 A: Are these your sunglasses?
   B: Yes. I bought them _____ on my trip.

4 A: Did you like the party yesterday?
   B: Yes, I did. I was happy _____ new people.

GRAMMAR FOR WRITING

A 보기에서 알맞은 말을 골라 적절한 형태로 바꾸어 우리말을 영어로 옮기시오.

보기	do	exercise	get	listen	~~choose~~

0 좋은 선물을 고르는 것은 어렵다.

→ It's hard _____to choose_____ a good gift.

1 나는 운동하기 위해 일찍 일어났다.

→ I got up early _____.

2 Tim은 음악을 듣는 것을 좋아한다.

→ Tim likes _____ to music.

3 내 목표는 좋은 성적을 받는 것이다.

→ My goal is _____ good grades.

4 나는 오늘 할 일이 많다.

→ I have many things _____ today.

B ( ) 안의 말을 이용하여 우리말을 영어로 옮기시오.

0 우리는 콘서트에 가는 것을 계획했다. (plan, go)

→ We _____planned to go_____ to the concert.

1 거짓말을 하는 것은 잘못된 것이다. (wrong, tell)

→ It is _____ a lie.

2 나는 주스를 만들기 위해 과일을 조금 샀다. (some fruit, make)

→ I bought _____ juice.

3 Ben은 열심히 공부하기로 결심했다. (decide, study)

→ Ben _____ hard.

4 나는 그 소식을 들어서 기쁘다. (happy, hear)

→ I'm _____ the news.

5 그는 신선한 공기를 좀 쐬러 밖으로 나갔다. (go outside, get)

→ He _____ some fresh air.

6 이것들은 도서관에 반납할 책들이다. (the books, return)

→ These are _____ to the library.

C 주어진 동사를 동사원형 또는 to부정사 중 적절한 형태로 써서 문장을 완성하시오.

0 fix   a. I will _____fix_____ my bike.

                    b. I need _____to fix_____ my computer.

1 wash   a. I _____ my hair every morning.

                    b. I don't want _____ the dishes.

2 help   a. Daniel will _____ his teacher.

                    b. They go there _____ the children.

3 take   a. Did you _____ these photos?

                    b. His dream is _____ great photos.

4 travel   a. My brother will _____ to India this year.

                    b. Andy hopes _____ around the country someday.

5 drink   a. It is important _____ enough water.

                    b. I always _____ coffee in the morning.

D 그림을 보고 ( ) 안의 말을 이용하여 문장을 완성하시오.

0    **1**    **2**    **3**

0 Emily planned _____to go_____ to a festival. (go)

1 She waited in a long line _____ a ticket. (buy)

2 There were many things _____. (enjoy)

3 She was excited _____ some famous singers. (see)

REVIEW TEST

[1-2] 빈칸에 들어갈 알맞은 말을 고르시오.

1

> I have a present _____ you.

① give   ② gives   ③ gave
④ to give   ⑤ will give

2

> It is important _____ an honest person.

① be   ② is   ③ to is
④ to be   ⑤ to being

3 빈칸에 들어갈 말로 알맞지 <u>않은</u> 것은?

> She wants to _____.

① help you
② take a bath
③ become a soldier
④ order pizza for dinner
⑤ travels around the world

빈출

[4-6] 다음 중 보기의 밑줄 친 부분과 쓰임이 같은 것을 고르시오.

4

> 보기   We agreed <u>to change</u> the plan.

① His job is <u>to fix</u> cars.
② He wants <u>to go</u> to the movies.
③ Alex studied hard <u>to be</u> a lawyer.
④ I have little time <u>to sleep</u> tonight.
⑤ It was hard <u>to answer</u> the question.

5

> 보기   Tom was glad <u>to find</u> his wallet.

① It is time <u>to go</u> to school.
② I have a shirt <u>to wash</u>.
③ I was excited <u>to buy</u> a new bike.
④ His dream is <u>to be</u> a great actor.
⑤ They decided <u>to help</u> poor people.

6

> 보기   He exercised <u>to be</u> strong.

① I need <u>to pack</u> my bag.
② Her favorite activity is <u>to play</u> chess.
③ There are rules <u>to remember</u>.
④ Jane visited Paris <u>to meet</u> Eva.
⑤ I don't have enough money <u>to eat</u> at this restaurant.

서술형

[7-8] 빈칸에 알맞은 말을 써서 문장을 완성하시오.

7

> We planned _____ spend our vacation in Singapore.

8

> _____ is exciting to ride a roller coaster.

130

[9-10] 다음 중 밑줄 친 부분이 잘못된 것을 고르시오.

9 ① We are happy to invite you.
② I want to take a picture with you.
③ Sam wants something to drank.
④ It's important to bring your passport.
⑤ Tim went to Canada to study English.

10 ① We need to leave now.
② I hope to visit New York.
③ She likes listen to the radio.
④ Daniel wants to learn French.
⑤ Tina decided to walk home.

11 다음 우리말을 영어로 바르게 옮긴 것은?

> 좋은 친구를 사귀는 것은 어렵다.

① To make good friends be difficult.
② It is good to make friends difficult.
③ It is difficult to make good friends.
④ This is difficult to make good friends.
⑤ It makes good friends to be difficult.

서술형

[12-13] to부정사를 이용하여 다음 두 문장을 연결하시오.

12 Susan raised her hand. She wanted to ask a question.

→ Susan raised her hand _____ _____.

13 I was sorry. I heard about his accident.

→ I was sorry _____.

서술형

[14-15] 우리말과 일치하도록 (   ) 안의 말을 이용하여 문장을 완성하시오.

14 그들의 계획은 그 미술관을 방문하는 것이다. (visit)

→ Their plan is _____ the art gallery.

15 Dave는 친구들과 온라인 게임을 하는 것을 좋아한다. (play)

→ Dave likes _____ online games with his friends.

서술형

[16-17] 우리말과 일치하도록 (   ) 안에 주어진 말을 바르게 배열하시오.

16 Nick은 재킷을 한 벌 사기 위해 쇼핑몰에 갔다. (to, a jacket, buy)

→ Nick went to the mall _____.

17 나는 아침을 먹을 시간이 없다. (to, time, breakfast, eat)

→ I don't have _____.

WORD LIST

- **solve** 풀다 _____
- **hope** 바라다 _____
- **decide** 결심하다, 결정하다 _____
- **agree** 동의하다 _____
- **dream** 꿈 _____
- **goal** 목표 _____
- **sell** 팔다 _____
- **cartoon** 만화 _____
- **helpful** 도움이 되는 _____
- **hobby** 취미 _____
- **catch the bus** 버스를 (잡아)타다 _____
- **holiday** 휴가, 방학 _____
- **practice** 연습하다 _____
- **save money** 돈을 저축하다 _____
- **check** 확인하다 _____
- **turn on** 켜다 _____
- **choose** 고르다 _____
- **get good grades** 좋은 성적을 받다 _____
- **wrong** 잘못된 _____
- **outside** 밖으로 _____
- **return** 돌려주다, 반납하다 _____
- **someday** 언젠가 _____
- **lawyer** 변호사 _____
- **wallet** 지갑 _____
- **pack** (짐을) 꾸리다 _____
- **roller coaster** 롤러코스터 _____
- **take a picture** 사진을 찍다 _____
- **passport** 여권 _____
- **make friends** 친구를 사귀다 _____
- **raise** 들어올리다 _____
- **accident** 사고 _____
- **art gallery** 미술관 _____

ESSENTIAL RULES OF ENGLISH GRAMMAR

CHAPTER

12

접속사

and, but, or

- I have a cat **and** a dog.

A

and: 그리고, ~와/과

1 내용상 서로 비슷한 것을 연결한다.

you **and** I, bread **and** milk, fresh **and** new …

2 단어와 단어, 문장과 문장 등을 연결한다.

It is *cold **and** dry* in winter.
John is my neighbor, **and** *he's very kind*.

cf. 세 개 이상의 단어를 연결할 때는 「A, B, and C」의 형태로 쓴다.
I like **basketball, baseball, and soccer**. (~~basketball and baseball and soccer~~)

B

but: 그러나, ~지만

1 내용상 서로 반대인 것을 연결한다.

small **but** strong, nice **but** expensive, smart **but** lazy …

2 단어와 단어, 문장과 문장 등을 연결한다.

The hotel is *old **but** clean*.
She is thin, **but** *she eats a lot*.

C

or: 또는, ~거나

1 둘 이상의 선택해야 할 것들을 연결한다.

coffee **or** tea, he **or** she, win **or** lose …

2 단어와 단어, 문장과 문장 등을 연결한다.

They will go there by *bus **or** subway*.
We can order pizza, **or** *I can cook pasta*.

PRACTICE

🔍 Answer Key p.12

STEP 1

( ) 안에서 알맞은 말을 고르시오.

0 Mark (and, or) Ben are friends.

1 I like fish, (but, or) I don't like meat.

2 I'll give the book to you on Monday (but, or) Tuesday.

3 It is an interesting (and, or) useful website.

4 You can choose chicken (but, or) pizza for dinner.

5 I know his face, (but, or) I can't remember his name.

6 The new dress is beautiful, (and, but) it is so expensive.

7 I'll go to England, Italy, (and, but) Germany this summer.

STEP 2

사진을 보고 빈칸에 and, but, or 중 알맞은 접속사를 넣어 문장을 완성하시오.

0   **1**    **2**    **3**

0 I need a pen _____and_____ paper.

1 I tried yoga, _____ it was difficult.

2 Jim can sing _____ dance well.

3 A: Is he a police officer _____ a firefighter?
    B: He is a firefighter.

STEP 3

보기에서 알맞은 말을 골라 문장을 완성하시오.

보기	and	but	or

0 The orange is fresh _____and_____ delicious.

1 The test was difficult, _____ I passed it.

2 I went to the park with Tom, Jane, _____ Peter.

3 Gina and I will meet at the theater, _____ we will meet at my house.

UNIT 02

when, before, after, because

• I wear a helmet **when** I ride a bike.

when, before, after는 시간을, because는 원인을 나타내는 접속사로 문장과 문장을 연결한다.

A when: ~할 때

He plays soccer **when** he has free time.
You have to be careful **when** you cross the street.
When I came home, my dog barked at me.

B before: ~하기 전에

I wash my hands **before** I eat.
We checked the weather **before** we went out.
Before he left, he turned off the lights.

C after: ~한 후에

Sarah got to the bus stop **after** the bus left.
He took a nap **after** he walked his dog.
After I finished my homework, I watched TV.

> *cf.* 시간을 나타내는 접속사가 이끄는 절에서는 미래를 나타내더라도 현재시제를 쓴다.
> *When* I **grow up**, I will be a designer. (~~will grow up~~)
> We will go to the movies *after* we **take** the test. (~~will take~~)

D because: ~하기 때문에

because가 이끄는 문장이 원인을, 나머지 문장이 결과를 나타낸다.

I stayed at home **because** I was tired.
Joe went to see a doctor **because** he had a cold.
Because the camera was expensive, I didn't buy it.

PRACTICE

🔍 Answer Key p.12

( ) 안에서 알맞은 말을 고르시오.

0 It was snowing (when), because) we arrived in New York.

1 I was late (before, because) I missed the school bus.

2 I'll visit your office when I (have, will have) time.

3 Can I use your computer (after, because) you use it?

4 (When, Because) he was three years old, he lived in Jeju.

5 I went to the restroom (before, because) the class began.

자연스러운 문장이 되도록 알맞게 연결하시오.

0 I met my friends   •————————• ⓐ after I had lunch.

1 I tasted the pasta   •   • ⓑ when you get home.

2 I wanted to be a nurse   •   • ⓒ because she is friendly.

3 I don't go to school today •   • ⓓ because it is a holiday.

4 We like Mary very much   •   • ⓔ before I added more sauce.

5 It will be dark   •   • ⓕ when I was young.

( ) 안의 말을 이용하여 다음 두 문장을 연결하시오.

0 She left home. I arrived. (before)

  → She left home _____ before I arrived _____ .

1 Dan was happy. He heard the news. (when)

  → Dan was happy _____ .

2 We'll go to the restaurant. The concert is over. (after)

  → We'll go to the restaurant _____ .

3 I need an umbrella. It is raining. (because)

  → I need an umbrella _____ .

GRAMMAR FOR WRITING

A 보기에서 알맞은 말을 골라 우리말을 영어로 옮기시오.

[0-3]

보기	and	but	or

0 남자들과 여자들 → men _____and_____ women

1 닭고기 또는 소고기 → chicken _____ beef

2 맵지만 맛있는 → spicy _____ delicious

3 사고 팔다 → buy _____ sell

[4-7]

보기	when	before	after	because

4 나는 많이 먹었기 때문에 배가 부르다. → I'm full _____ I ate a lot.

5 나는 운동을 하고 난 후에 기분이 좋다. → I feel great _____ I exercise.

6 내가 전화했을 때 Nora는 자고 있었다. → Nora was sleeping _____ I called.

7 나는 그들이 도착하기 전에 음식을 요리했다. → I cooked the meal _____ they arrived.

B ( ) 안의 말을 이용하여 우리말을 영어로 옮기시오.

0 나는 Bob을 좋아하지만, 그의 형은 좋아하지 않는다. (like)

→ I like Bob, _____but I don't like_____ his brother.

1 Nancy는 자전거에서 떨어졌을 때 울었다. (fall)

→ Nancy cried _____ off her bike.

2 그림에 사자들과 얼룩말들이 있다. (lions, zebras)

→ There are _____ in the picture.

3 나는 그 책을 읽은 후에 Chris에게 그것을 빌려줬다. (read)

→ _____ the book, I lent it to Chris.

4 날씨가 나빴기 때문에 우리는 집에 있었다. (the weather, bad)

→ We stayed at home _____.

5 너는 왼손으로 글씨를 쓰니, 아니면 오른손으로 글씨를 쓰니? (left hand, right hand)

→ Do you write with your _____?

C 보기에서 알맞은 말을 골라 ( ) 안의 말과 함께 써서 문장을 완성하시오. (단, 한 번씩만 쓸 것)

보기	It's too heavy.
	~~I came to Seoul.~~
	He wears glasses.
	He watched the horror movie.

0 I lived in London _____before I came to Seoul_____ . (before)

1 I can't move the box _____ . (because)

2 He couldn't sleep _____ . (after)

3 He looks great _____ . (when)

D 그림을 보고 보기에서 알맞은 말을 골라 ( ) 안의 말과 함께 써서 대화를 완성하시오. (단, 한 번씩만 쓸 것)

| 보기 | and | but | or |

0 Jamie: I want to order steak ____and french fries____ . (french fries)

1 Waiter: I'm sorry, _____ french fries today. (we don't have)

2 Jamie: Can I order salad _____ ? (soup)

3 Waiter: Yes, we have potato soup and a green salad.

Jamie: Okay. I'll have steak _____ , then. (a green salad)

[1-2] 빈칸에 들어갈 알맞은 말을 고르시오.

1

> It was cold _____ snowy today.

① and ② but ③ or
④ before ⑤ after

2

> I'll call you _____ I get back.

① and ② but ③ or
④ when ⑤ because

서술형

[3-5] 보기에서 알맞은 말을 골라 문장을 완성하시오.

보기	but	before	because

3

The dancer practices a lot _____ the show begins.

4

I can't talk to you now _____ I'm in a hurry.

5

I want to call him, _____ I don't know his phone number.

[6-7] 다음 중 밑줄 친 부분이 <u>잘못된</u> 것을 고르시오.

6
① She was sad, <u>but</u> she didn't cry.
② She can speak English <u>and</u> French.
③ Andrew had juice <u>and</u> toast for breakfast.
④ They will visit Korea, <u>and</u> Japan, and China.
⑤ You can take a bus <u>or</u> train to the mountains.

7
① We'll leave <u>when</u> the rain stops.
② I'm happy <u>because</u> I passed the test.
③ I'll finish the work <u>before</u> I go home.
④ I'll buy this T-shirt <u>after</u> I like the color.
⑤ <u>When</u> I saw her, she smiled at me.

서술형

[8-9] 빈칸에 공통으로 들어갈 말을 쓰시오.

8
• I was tired _____ happy.
• We tried hard, _____ we lost the game.

9
• Jessica will leave for London today _____ tomorrow.
• Do you want to watch TV, _____ will you listen to music?

10 다음 중 빈칸에 before가 들어갈 수 없는 것은?

① I knocked on the door _____ I opened it.

② I read the email twice _____ I sent it.

③ Peter exercised _____ he went to bed.

④ We laughed _____ the story was funny.

⑤ He looked at the mirror _____ he went out.

13 다음 우리말을 영어로 바르게 옮긴 것은?

> Jenny는 추울 때 목도리를 한다.

① Jenny wears a scarf after it's cold.

② Jenny wears a scarf when it's cold.

③ Jenny wears a scarf before it's cold.

④ It's cold because Jenny wears a scarf.

⑤ It's cold when Jenny wears a scarf.

빈출

[11-12] 빈칸에 들어갈 말이 바르게 짝지어진 것을 고르시오.

11
- Is this coat yours __(A)__ Jane's?
- I bought apples, oranges, __(B)__ bananas.

	(A)		(B)
①	and	⋯⋯	but
②	but	⋯⋯	and
③	but	⋯⋯	or
④	or	⋯⋯	and
⑤	or	⋯⋯	but

12
- We will eat dinner when he __(A)__.
- After I __(B)__ my homework, I'll go out.

	(A)		(B)
①	comes	⋯⋯	finish
②	comes	⋯⋯	will finish
③	will come	⋯⋯	finish
④	will come	⋯⋯	will finish
⑤	came	⋯⋯	finished

서술형 빈출

[14-16] 우리말과 일치하도록 ( ) 안의 말을 이용하여 문장을 완성하시오.

14 나는 수학과 과학을 좋아한다. (math, science)

→ I like _____.

15 콘서트를 다녀온 후에 우리는 매우 행복했다. (go)

→ We were very happy _____ to the concert.

16 James는 늦게 일어났기 때문에 학교에 지각했다. (get up late)

→ James was late for school _____ _____.

WORD LIST

- **dry** 건조한
- **basketball** 농구
- **lose** 잃다, 지다
- **order** 주문하다
- **meat** 고기
- **useful** 유용한
- **remember** 기억하다
- **yoga** 요가
- **firefighter** 소방관
- **helmet** 헬멧
- **free time** 여가 시간
- **careful** 조심하는, 주의 깊은
- **cross** (길을) 건너다
- **bark** 짖다
- **turn off** 끄다
- **get to** ~에 도착하다
- **take a nap** 낮잠을 자다
- **grow up** 자라다
- **have a cold** 감기에 걸리다
- **office** 사무실
- **restroom** 화장실
- **over** 끝이 난
- **beef** 소고기
- **full** 배부른
- **lend** 빌려주다
- **glasses** 안경
- **french fries** 감자튀김
- **in a hurry** 서둘러, 바쁜
- **toast** 토스트
- **knock** 두드리다, 노크하다
- **twice** 두 번
- **be late for** ~에 늦다

ESSENTIAL RULES OF
ENGLISH GRAMMAR

CHAPTER
13

의문문, 명령문, 감탄문

who, what

• **Who** is your grandfather?

A 의문사

의문사는 '누가, 언제, 어디서, 무엇을, 어떻게, 왜' 등을 물을 때 의문문의 맨 앞에 쓰는 말이다.
의문사로 시작하는 의문문에는 Yes/No로 대답하지 않는다.

A: **Who** is that woman?
B: She's my English teacher.

B who: 누가, 누구를

1 사람에 대해 물을 때 쓰는 의문사이다.

Who is in the kitchen?

2 문장 안에서 주어 또는 목적어로 쓰인다. 목적어로 쓰인 경우 who 대신 whom을 쓰기도 한다.

Who is your favorite actor?
Who closed the door?
Who(m) did Mike meet yesterday?

cf. Whose + 명사: 누구의 (~)
Whose *hat* is this?

C what: 무엇이, 무엇을

1 사물에 대해 물을 때 쓰는 의문사이다.

What is in your bag?

2 문장 안에서 주어 또는 목적어로 쓰인다.

What is her name?
What are you thinking now?
What does he do in his free time?

3 what + 명사: 무슨 (~), 어떤 (~)

What *size* are these shoes?
What *book* did you read?

PRACTICE

🔍 Answer Key p-13

STEP 1

( ) 안에서 알맞은 말을 고르시오.

0 (Who, (What)) color is his car?

1 (Who, Whom) teaches you science?

2 (Who, What) do you do after school?

3 (Who, Whose) idea was this?

4 (Whom, Whose) did you call last night?

STEP 2

그림을 보고 빈칸에 알맞은 말을 써서 대화를 완성하시오.

0    **1**    **2**    **3**

0 A: _____What_____ time is it?
B: It's 2:40 p.m.

1 A: _____ ate my cake?
B: I don't know.

2 A: _____ did you buy yesterday?
B: I bought this T-shirt.

3 A: _____ is the girl next to you?
B: She's my sister.

STEP 3

빈칸에 알맞은 말을 써서 밑줄 친 부분을 묻는 의문문을 완성하시오.

0 I ate <u>ramen</u> last night.

→ _____What_____ did you eat last night?

1 It's <u>my</u> turn.

→ _____ turn is it?

2 <u>Jake</u> was at the door.

→ _____ was at the door?

3 They invited <u>their friends</u> to the party.

→ _____ did they invite to the party?

when, where, why

- **When** is your birthday?

A when: 언제

시간, 날짜 등을 물을 때 쓰는 의문사이다.

When is the concert?
When did you start your job?
When will Emma come home?

cf. 구체적인 시간을 물을 경우 when 대신 what time을 쓸 수 있다.
<u>**What time**</u> does the movie start?
　　= When

B where: 어디에, 어디서

위치, 장소 등을 물을 때 쓰는 의문사이다.

Where is my bag?
Where are you going now?
Where did they come from?

C why: 왜

1 원인, 이유 등을 물을 때 쓰는 의문사이다.

Why are you late?
Why did Peter call you?
Why do you like cats?

2 why로 묻는 질문에 대한 대답에는 주로 because(왜냐하면)가 사용된다.

A: **Why** are you so angry?
B: I'm angry **because** someone stole my bike.

A: **Why** did Jane go to the hospital?
B: **Because** she hurt her leg.

PRACTICE

Answer Key p-13

 STEP 1

( ) 안에서 알맞은 말을 고르시오.

0 A: (When, Why) is she crying?
B: Because she watched a sad movie.

1 A: (When, Where) will you go to America?
B: Next week.

2 A: (When, Where) is the post office?
B: It is on the corner.

3 A: (What, When) time does the train arrive?
B: It arrives at two o'clock.

4 A: (Where, Why) are you tired?
B: Because I went to bed late last night.

 STEP 2

자연스러운 대화가 되도록 알맞게 연결하시오.

0 Where is the restroom? • • ⓐ He will get here at 7:00 p.m.
1 Why do you like Bill? • • ⓑ They studied in the library.
2 Where did they study? • • ⓒ Because I had a stomachache.
3 When will Mike get here? • • ⓓ It's on the second floor.
4 Why did you take some medicine? • • ⓔ I like him because he's nice.

 STEP 3

빈칸에 알맞은 말을 써서 밑줄 친 부분을 묻는 의문문을 완성하시오.

0 I eat lunch at noon.
→ _____When_____ do you eat lunch?

1 The movie theater is on Main Street.
→ _____ is the movie theater?

2 I like chocolate because it's sweet.
→ _____ do you like chocolate?

3 He went to church last Sunday.
→ _____ did he go to church?

4 They played basketball in the backyard.
→ _____ did they play basketball?

UNIT

03 how

• **How** is the weather?

A how: 어떻게, 어떤, 얼마나 ~한/하게

1 상태, 수단, 방법 등을 물을 때 쓰는 의문사이다.

How are you today?
How was the math test?
How can I get to the museum?

2 「how + 형용사/부사」의 형태로 쓰여 '얼마나 ~한/하게'의 의미를 나타낸다.

· how old: 몇 살의, 얼마나 오래된   · how tall: 얼마나 키가 큰/높은
· how long: 얼마나 긴/오랫동안   · how far: 얼마나 먼
· how often: 얼마나 자주   · how much: 얼마(의)

How old are you?
How old is this tree?

How tall is he?
How tall is the building?

How long is this river?
How long will David stay here?

How far is the airport?
How far is your house from school?

How often do you exercise?
How often does this bus come?

How much are these socks?
How much did you pay for lunch?

cf. how many + 셀 수 있는 명사: 얼마나 많은 수의 ~
　　how much + 셀 수 없는 명사: 얼마나 많은 양의 ~
How many *classes* do you have today?
How much *money* do you have?

PRACTICE

🔍 Answer Key p·13

STEP 1

( ) 안에서 알맞은 말을 고르시오.

0 A: (What, ⃝How) do you spell your name?
B: F.R.E.D.

1 A: (How many, How much) are these jeans?
B: They are $30.

2 A: (What, How) do I get to the subway station?
B: You can take bus number fifteen.

3 A: (How far, How long) is the beach from here?
B: It's 2 km away.

STEP 2

보기에서 알맞은 말을 골라 대화를 완성하시오.

보기	How old	How long	How often	How many

0 A: _____How old_____ is your dog?
B: He is four years old.

1 A: _____ is your summer vacation?
B: It's for a month.

2 A: _____ sisters do you have?
B: I have two sisters.

3 A: _____ do you practice the piano?
B: I practice it twice a week.

STEP 3

빈칸에 알맞은 말을 써서 밑줄 친 부분을 묻는 의문문을 완성하시오.

0 I call her <u>once a week</u>.
→ _____How often_____ do you call her?

1 The book was <u>boring</u>.
→ _____ was the book?

2 I go to school <u>on foot</u>.
→ _____ do you go to school?

3 My brother is <u>160 cm tall</u>.
→ _____ is your brother?

부가의문문

• This textbook is yours, **isn't it**?

A 부가의문문

사실을 확인하거나 상대방에게 동의를 구하기 위해 평서문 뒤에 붙이는 간단한 의문문으로, '그렇지?', '그
렇지 않니?'의 의미를 나타낸다.

Tom is a nurse, **isn't he**?
Jenny can play the piano, **can't she**?
You didn't come to school yesterday, **did you**?

B 부가의문문 만드는 법

1 긍정문 뒤에는 부정 의문문을 쓰고, 부정문 뒤에는 긍정 의문문을 쓴다. 부가의문문의 시제는 앞의
평서문과 같은 시제를 쓴다.

It *is* cold today, **isn't** it?
He *didn't* break the cup, **did** he?

2 부가의문문의 주어: 평서문의 주어를 주격 대명사로 바꿔 쓴다.

The play wasn't interesting, was **it**?
Bill and Mike are close friends, aren't **they**?

3 부가의문문의 동사: be동사와 조동사는 그대로, 일반동사는 주어와 시제에 따라 do/does/did로
바꿔 쓴다.

1) be동사의 부가의문문: ~, be동사 (+ not) + 대명사?

You *are* sleepy now, **aren't you**?
Emma *wasn't* at home last night, **was she**?

2) 조동사의 부가의문문: ~, 조동사 (+ not) + 대명사?

You *can* swim, **can't you**?
They *won't* keep their promise, **will they**?

3) 일반동사의 부가의문문: ~, do/does/did (+ not) + 대명사?

Mary *wears* glasses, **doesn't she**?
You *didn't tell* him the truth, **did you**?

PRACTICE

🔍 Answer Key p.13

STEP 1

( ) 안에서 알맞은 말을 고르시오.

0 This room is quiet, (is, ⓘsn't) it?

1 You can't play tennis, (can, do) you?

2 Bella speaks fast, doesn't (her, she)?

3 They dance well, (don't, aren't) they?

4 You were sick yesterday, (aren't, weren't) you?

5 Adam went to Jeonju last year, (doesn't, didn't) he?

6 Kelly and Joe are from Canada, (isn't she, aren't they)?

STEP 2

빈칸에 알맞은 말을 보기에서 골라 기호를 쓰시오.

보기	ⓐ isn't she	ⓑ are they	ⓒ does he
	ⓓ ~~did you~~	ⓔ can't he	ⓕ will they

0 You didn't eat lunch, _____ⓓ_____?

1 Lucy is fourteen years old, _____?

2 They won't find us, _____?

3 He doesn't know me, _____?

4 Jim can speak German, _____?

5 These apples aren't fresh, _____?

STEP 3

빈칸에 알맞은 말을 써서 부가의문문을 완성하시오.

0 She is a dentist, _____isn't she_____?

1 They don't get up early, _____?

2 We will meet in the library, _____?

3 Jake bought a new car, _____?

4 You were at the concert, _____?

5 He can't ride a bike, _____?

6 This plant needs more water, _____?

명령문, 감탄문

- **Take** a taxi.
- **What a great idea!**

 A 명령문

상대방에게 명령하거나 제안하는 내용의 문장으로, 주어(you) 없이 동사원형으로 시작한다.

Look at the sky.

1 동사원형 ~: ~해라

Be quiet.
Eat more vegetables.

2 Don't[Do not] + 동사원형: ~하지 마라

Don't be afraid.
Do not move.

3 Let's + 동사원형: ~하자

Let's go.
Let's start the test.

cf. Let's not + 동사원형: ~하지 말자
　　Let's not waste time.

 B 감탄문

기쁨, 슬픔, 놀라움 등의 감정을 표현하는 문장으로, '매우 ~하구나!'의 의미를 나타낸다.

What a nice day (it is)!

1 what으로 시작하는 감탄문: What + a(n) + 형용사 + 명사 (+ 주어 + 동사)!

What a brave girl (she is)!
What an amazing story (it is)!

cf. what으로 시작하는 감탄문에서 명사가 복수형이거나 셀 수 없는 명사인 경우 a(n)를 쓰지 않는다.
　　What cute *puppies* they are! (~~What a cute puppies~~)

2 how로 시작하는 감탄문: How + 형용사/부사 (+ 주어 + 동사)!

How kind (he is)!
How beautiful the picture is!
How well you sing!

PRACTICE

🔍 Answer Key p.13

STEP 1

( ) 안에서 알맞은 말을 고르시오.

0 (What, (How)) fast the train is!

1 (What, How) a lovely baby!

2 (Finish, Finishes) your homework today.

3 (Don't, Let's) forget your umbrella. It's going to rain.

STEP 2

그림을 보고 보기에서 알맞은 말을 골라 명령문을 완성하시오.

보기	~~Come~~	Wear	Be	Let's not	Let's	Don't

0 ___Come___ here. **1** _____ careful. **2** _____ have some pizza.

3 _____ your seat belt. **4** _____ fight again. **5** _____ smoke here.

STEP 3

다음 문장을 ( ) 안의 말로 시작하는 감탄문으로 바꿔 쓰시오.

0 It is a very old house. (what)
→ _____What an old house_____ it is!

1 The model is very tall. (how)
→ _____ the model is!

2 They are nice teachers. (what)
→ _____ they are!

3 These questions are very difficult. (how)
→ _____ these questions are!

GRAMMAR FOR WRITING

A 보기에서 알맞은 말을 골라 우리말을 영어로 옮기시오.

[0-3]

보기	Who	~~What~~	When	Where

0 너의 꿈은 무엇이니? → ___What___ is your dream?

1 누가 여기 가장 먼저 왔니? → _____ came here first?

2 너는 어디서 신발을 사니? → _____ do you buy your shoes?

3 너는 언제 이 사진을 찍었니? → _____ did you take this photo?

[4-7] (필요하면 형태를 바꿀 것)

보기	enter	stay	press	try

4 다시 시도해라. → _____ again.

5 여기에 머무르자. → _____ here.

6 그 버튼을 눌러라. → _____ the button.

7 그 방에 들어가지 마라. → _____ the room.

B ( ) 안의 말을 이용하여 우리말을 영어로 옮기시오.

0 너는 얼마나 자주 이발을 하니? (get)

→ ___How often do you get___ a haircut?

1 잔디 위를 걷지 마라. (walk)

→ _____ on the grass.

2 뉴욕은 서울에서 얼마나 머니? (New York)

→ _____ from Seoul?

3 이것은 정말 훌륭한 그림이구나! (great, picture)

→ _____ this is!

4 너는 커피를 마시지 않아, 그렇지? (drink, coffee)

→ You _____, _____?

5 그 수업은 지루했어, 그렇지 않니? (boring)

→ The class _____, _____?

C 빈칸에 알맞은 의문사를 써서 대화를 완성하시오.

0 A: _____Who_____ is that girl?
B: She is my girlfriend.

1 A: _____ is your birthday?
B: It's October 17.

2 A: _____ are you sad?
B: Because my best friend is sick.

3 A: _____ does Jason live?
B: He lives in San Francisco.

4 A: _____ is your favorite subject?
B: I love music the most.

5 A: _____ does your dad get to work?
B: He goes to work by bus.

D 그림을 보고 ( ) 안의 말을 이용하여 명령문 또는 감탄문을 완성하시오.

0   **1**   **2**   **3**

0 __Let's take a picture__ with the flowers. They're pretty. (take a picture)
1 _____ the box is! I can't move it. (heavy)
2 _____ it is! I want to eat some ice cream. (hot, day)
3 _____ now. We will get wet. (not, go out)

REVIEW TEST

[1-3] 빈칸에 들어갈 알맞은 말을 고르시오.

1

_____ buy that computer. It's too expensive.

① Be   ② Do   ③ Don't
④ Let   ⑤ Let's

2

_____ funny our teacher is!

① When   ② Where   ③ Why
④ What   ⑤ How

3

A: _____ water did you drink?
B: I drank two glasses of water.

① Who   ② Why
③ How   ④ How many
⑤ How much

서술형

[4-5] 빈칸에 알맞은 의문사를 써서 대화를 완성하시오.

4

A: _____ is the elevator?
B: It's near the restroom.

5

A: _____ won the contest?
B: Nick did.

[6-7] 다음 중 밑줄 친 부분이 잘못된 것을 고르시오.

6

① <u>Do</u> the dishes.
② <u>Read</u> this book.
③ <u>Let's</u> take a break.
④ <u>Stop</u> at the red lights.
⑤ <u>Not play</u> computer games.

7

① He will wash the car, <u>won't he</u>?
② His idea was great, <u>wasn't he</u>?
③ She wasn't at school, <u>was she</u>?
④ You bought a new coat, <u>didn't you</u>?
⑤ They can't come to the party, <u>can they</u>?

서술형

[8-9] 빈칸에 알맞은 말을 써서 부가의문문을 완성하시오.

8

Mike doesn't have a little brother, _____?

9

We can borrow a camera from Jenny, _____?

[10-11] 다음 중 대화가 자연스럽지 <u>않은</u> 것을 고르시오.

10 ① A: Whose cell phone is that?
　　　B: That's Leo's.
　　② A: When did he leave?
　　　B: He left two days ago.
　　③ A: What is your hobby?
　　　B: I read the book yesterday.
　　④ A: Where do you have lunch?
　　　B: I have lunch in the cafeteria.
　　⑤ A: How was your trip to Italy?
　　　B: It was great.

11 ① A: How much is this bicycle?
　　　B: It's $200.
　　② A: How often does your club meet?
　　　B: Once a week.
　　③ A: How long is the bridge?
　　　B: It's fifty years old.
　　④ A: How tall is the tower?
　　　B: It's ten meters tall.
　　⑤ A: How many tickets do you need?
　　　B: I need three tickets.

[12-13] 빈칸에 들어갈 말이 바르게 짝지어진 것을 고르시오.

12

| A: _____(A)_____ are you so happy? |
| B: _____(B)_____ my exams are over. |

	(A)		(B)
①	Who	……	When
②	When	……	Because
③	Where	……	When
④	Why	……	Because
⑤	How	……	Before

13

| • _____(A)_____ a smart boy he is! |
| • _____(B)_____ sweet these cookies are! |

	(A)		(B)
①	What	……	What
②	What	……	How
③	Who	……	What
④	How	……	How
⑤	How	……	What

[14-16] 우리말과 일치하도록 ( ) 안의 말을 이용하여 문장을 완성하시오.

14 병원이 몇 시에 문을 닫니? (time)

→ _____ does the hospital close?

15 오늘 밤에 영화를 보자. (watch)

→ _____ a movie tonight.

16 그것은 정말 재미있는 이야기구나!
(interesting, story)

→ _____ it is!

WORD LIST

- **size** 크기, 사이즈 _____
- **call** 전화하다 _____
- **turn** 차례 _____
- **steal** 훔치다 _____
- **hurt** 다치게 하다 _____
- **stomachache** 복통 _____
- **medicine** 약 _____
- **backyard** 뒤뜰 _____
- **pay** 지불하다 _____
- **spell** 철자를 말하다 _____
- **jeans** 청바지 _____
- **subway station** 지하철역 _____
- **on foot** 걸어서, 도보로 _____
- **break** 깨다, 휴식 _____
- **play** 연주하다, 연극 _____
- **close** 친한, 닫다 _____
- **sleepy** 졸린 _____
- **dentist** 치과 의사 _____
- **plant** 식물 _____
- **afraid** 두려워하는 _____
- **brave** 용감한 _____
- **lovely** 사랑스러운 _____
- **enter** 들어가다 _____
- **press** 누르다 _____
- **try** 노력하다, 시도하다 _____
- **button** 버튼 _____
- **subject** 과목 _____
- **wet** 젖은 _____
- **contest** 대회, 시합 _____
- **borrow** 빌리다 _____
- **cafeteria** 카페테리아, 구내식당 _____
- **bicycle** 자전거 _____

MEMO

지은이

NE능률 영어교육연구소

NE능률 영어교육연구소는 혁신적이며 효율적인 영어 교재를 개발하고
영어 학습의 질을 한 단계 높이고자 노력하는 NE능률의 연구조직입니다.

GRAMMAR Inside 〈Starter〉

펴 낸 이	주민홍
펴 낸 곳	서울특별시 마포구 월드컵북로 396(상암동) 누리꿈스퀘어 비즈니스타워 10층
	㈜NE능률 (우편번호 03925)
펴 낸 날	2022년 1월 5일 개정판 제1쇄 발행
	2024년 9월 15일 제16쇄
전 화	02 2014 7114
팩 스	02 3142 0356
홈페이지	www.neungyule.com
등록번호	제1-68호
I S B N	979-11-253-3706-5 53740
정 가	14,500원

NE 능률

고객센터

교재 내용 문의: contact.nebooks.co.kr (별도의 가입 절차 없이 작성 가능)
제품 구매, 교환, 불량, 반품 문의: 02-2014-7114
☎ 전화문의는 본사 업무시간 중에만 가능합니다.

GRAMMAR Inside

Answer Key

A 4-level grammar course
with abundant writing practice

Compact and concise English grammar
간결하고 정확한 문법 설명

Extensive practice in sentence writing
다양한 유형의 영어 문장 쓰기

Full preparation for middle school tests
내신 완벽 대비

+ Workbook with additional exercises
풍부한 양의 추가 문제

NE능률 교재 MAP

아래 교재 MAP을 참고하여 본인의 현재 혹은 목표 수준에 따라 교재를 선택하세요.
NE능률 교재들과 함께 영어실력을 쑥쑥~ 올려보세요!
MP3 등 교재 부가 학습 서비스 및 자세한 교재 정보는 www.nebooks.co.kr 에서 확인하세요.

문법
구문
서술형

초1-2	초3	초3-4	초4-5	초5-6
	그래머버디 1	그래머버디 2	그래머버디 3	Grammar Bean 3
	초등영어 문법이 된다 Starter 1	초등영어 문법이 된다 Starter 2	Grammar Bean 1	Grammar Bean 4
		초등 Grammar Inside 1	Grammar Bean 2	초등영어 문법이 된다 2
		초등 Grammar Inside 2	초등영어 문법이 된다 1	초등 Grammar Inside 5
			초등 Grammar Inside 3	초등 Grammar Inside 6
			초등 Grammar Inside 4	

초6-예비중	중1	중1-2	중2-3	중3
능률중학영어 예비중	능률중학영어 중1	능률중학영어 중2	Grammar Zone 기초편	능률중학영어 중3
Grammar Inside Starter	Grammar Zone 입문편	1316 Grammar 2	Grammar Zone 워크북 기초편	문제로 마스터하는 중학영문법 3
원리를 더한 영문법 STARTER	Grammar Zone 워크북 입문편	문제로 마스터하는 중학영문법 2	1316 Grammar 3	Grammar Inside 3
	1316 Grammar 1	Grammar Inside 2	원리를 더한 영문법 2	열중 16강 문법 3
	문제로 마스터하는 중학영문법 1	열중 16강 문법 2	중학영문법 총정리 모의고사 2	중학영문법 총정리 모의고사 3
	Grammar Inside 1	원리를 더한 영문법 1	쓰기로 마스터하는 중학서술형 2학년	쓰기로 마스터하는 중학서술형 3학년
	열중 16강 문법 1	중학영문법 총정리 모의고사 1	중학 천문장 3	
	쓰기로 마스터하는 중학서술형 1학년	중학 천문장 2		
	중학 천문장 1			

예비고–고1	고1	고1-2	고2-3	고3
문제로 마스터하는 고등영문법	Grammar Zone 기본편 1	필히 통하는 고등 영문법 실력편	Grammar Zone 종합편	
올클 수능 어법 start	Grammar Zone 워크북 기본편 1	필히 통하는 고등 서술형 실전편	Grammar Zone 워크북 종합편	
천문장 입문	Grammar Zone 기본편 2	TEPS BY STEP G+R Basic	올클 수능 어법 완성	
	Grammar Zone 워크북 기본편 2		천문장 완성	
	필히 통하는 고등 영문법 기본편			
	필히 통하는 고등 서술형 기본편			
	천문장 기본			

수능 이상/ 토플 80-89 · 텝스 600-699점	수능 이상/ 토플 90-99 · 텝스 700-799점	수능 이상/ 토플 100 · 텝스 800점 이상		
TEPS BY STEP G+R 1	TEPS BY STEP G+R 2	TEPS BY STEP G+R 3		

workbook

GRAMMAR Inside

STARTER

A 4-level grammar course
with abundant writing practice

NE_ Neungyule

CONTENTS

GRAMMAR BASICS

01 단어의 종류

A 다음 중 단어의 종류가 <u>다른</u> 하나에 O표 하시오.

0 we, this, he, it, (here), you

1 can, run, after, may, go, must

2 very, at, under, behind, on, in

3 like, know, walk, will, buy, often

4 book, Brazil, time, oops, window, Peter

5 and, but, or, sometimes, when, because

6 friend, Mr. Kim, Japan, make, London, library

7 happy, sadly, small, young, handsome, good

B 다음 문장을 읽고, 밑줄 친 단어의 종류가 무엇인지 보기에서 골라 쓰시오.

보기	명사 대명사 동사 형용사 부사 전치사 접속사 감탄사

0 I know <u>Eric</u>.   명사

1 Ian is <u>always</u> kind.   _____

2 <u>She</u> is my mother.   _____

3 The building is <u>tall</u>.   _____

4 He speaks <u>slowly</u>.   _____

5 Jenny is a <u>pretty</u> girl.   _____

6 <u>Wow</u>, it is amazing!   _____

7 I <u>have</u> two brothers.   _____

8 A book is <u>on</u> the table.   _____

9 <u>Health</u> is very important.   _____

10 Is she a doctor <u>or</u> a nurse?   _____

11 We <u>are</u> middle school students.   _____

02 문장의 구성

A 다음 문장을 읽고, 주어에는 O표, 동사에는 밑줄을 그으시오.

0 He walks.

1 I live in Seoul.

2 She is a teacher.

3 My room is small.

4 Michael likes movies.

5 New York is a big city.

6 You look happy today.

7 The soccer team practices on Mondays.

8 Ms. Jackson sings beautifully.

9 Alice and her husband have a son.

10 The paintings are in London now.

B 다음 문장을 읽고, 목적어에는 O표, 보어에는 △표 하시오.

0 I like baseball.

1 He feels happy.

2 My sister is a singer.

3 He studies history.

4 John loves her very much.

5 Emily drinks milk every day.

6 Robert sent me an email.

7 My friends call me Annie.

8 He became a famous actor.

9 Ms. Anderson teaches us English.

10 The restaurant became popular.

UNIT 01

셀 수 있는 명사

A 밑줄 친 부분이 명사이면 O표, 명사가 아니면 X표 하시오.

0 She eats an <u>egg</u> every day. _____O_____

1 Jim is a <u>banker</u>. _____

2 <u>There</u> is a magazine on the table. _____

3 The sun <u>rises</u> every day. _____

4 He has a <u>mirror</u>. _____

5 I <u>have</u> a dream. _____

6 He rides a <u>bicycle</u>. _____

7 Look at <u>the</u> sky. _____

8 There is a <u>dog</u> in the living room. _____

9 She plays the guitar in the <u>evening</u>. _____

10 Mary goes <u>to</u> the beach in summer. _____

B 주어진 명사의 복수형을 쓰시오.

0 a cat – two ____cats____

1 a book – two _____

2 a roof – three _____

3 a class – two _____

4 a tooth – four _____

5 a puppy – two _____

6 a foot – four _____

7 a day – three _____

8 a deer – five _____

9 a knife – three _____

10 a man – two _____

11 a house – two _____

12 a story – ten _____

4

C 주어진 명사를 ( ) 안의 말과 함께 써서 문장을 완성하시오.

0 bag
a. I have a _____ bag _____.
b. I have ____ two bags ____. (two)

1 watch
a. Ted has a _____.
b. Ted has _____. (three)

2 mouse
a. There is a _____ in the field.
b. There are _____ in the field. (four)

3 blackboard
a. My school has a _____.
b. My school has _____. (three)

4 spoon
a. I put a _____ in the basket.
b. I put _____ in the basket. (five)

5 lady
a. There is a _____ at the bus stop.
b. There are _____ at the bus stop. (two)

WRITING PRACTICE

( ) 안의 말을 이용하여 우리말을 영어로 옮기시오.

0 이 방에는 두 개의 문이 있다. (door)
→ There are ____ two doors ____ in this room.

1 그들은 아기가 두 명 있다. (baby)
→ They have _____.

2 나는 상자 열 개가 필요하다. (box)
→ I need _____.

3 엄마는 매일 당근 한 개를 드신다. (carrot)
→ Mom eats a _____ every day.

4 가게 안에 세 명의 여자들이 있다. (woman)
→ There are _____ in the store.

5 그는 정원에 나무 네 그루를 가지고 있다. (tree)
→ He has _____ in his garden.

UNIT 02

셀 수 없는 명사

A 셀 수 없는 명사를 문장에서 찾아 O표 하시오.

0 We want ⓦater.

1 Love is wonderful.

2 We want happiness.

3 My cousin's name is Andy.

4 There is sand in my shoes.

5 They need money.

6 We buy bread here.

7 They are from France.

8 Seoul is a great city.

9 There is salt on the table.

10 My dad enjoys coffee on weekends.

B ( ) 안에서 알맞은 말을 고르시오.

0 We want (ⓦater, a water).

1 My teacher gives (an advice, advice) to us.

2 (Tony, A Tony) is my brother.

3 People love (peace, peaces).

4 They are going to (Germany, a Germany).

5 There is (juice, juices) on the floor.

6 My aunt lives in (a Florida, Florida).

7 She makes (two teas, two cups of tea).

8 We want (a milk, four bottles of milk) now.

9 I put (a cheese, a piece of cheese) in my sandwich.

10 My sister eats (bread, a slice of breads) every day.

C ( ) 안의 말을 이용하여 문장을 완성하시오.

0 I want a _____glass of water_____. (glass, water)

1 The cook has ten _____. (slice, bread)

2 I eat a _____ for lunch. (bowl, soup)

3 There are two _____ in the refrigerator. (bottle, wine)

4 Kate drinks a _____ every week. (bottle, cola)

5 There are two _____ on the plate. (piece, cake)

6 I need three _____ for the report. (piece, paper)

7 Beth needs two _____ for the salad. (slice, cheese)

8 Ron has two _____ every day. (cup, cocoa)

WRITING PRACTICE

( ) 안의 말을 이용하여 우리말을 영어로 옮기시오.

0 Brian은 나의 반 친구이다. (Brian)

→ _____Brian_____ is my classmate.

1 우리 아버지는 고기를 좋아하신다. (meat)

→ My father likes _____.

2 하버드 대학교는 케임브리지에 있다. (Cambridge)

→ Harvard University is in _____.

3 그는 건강에 대해 신경 쓴다. (health)

→ He cares about his _____.

4 그는 우리를 위해 두 잔의 커피를 만든다. (coffee)

→ He makes _____ for us.

5 사물함 안에 열 장의 종이가 있다. (paper)

→ There are _____ in the locker.

UNIT

03

관사

A

빈칸에 a나 an 중 알맞은 것을 쓰시오.

0 He has _____a_____ spoon.

1 John is _____ teacher.

2 This is _____ chair.

3 I have _____ umbrella.

4 Mr. Grey is _____ pianist.

5 I put _____ onion in the soup.

6 I need _____ lamp in my room.

7 There is _____ tiger in the zoo.

8 She has _____ idea for the project.

9 There is _____ fork on the table.

10 She eats _____ apple in the morning.

B

( ) 안에서 알맞은 말을 고르시오.

0 (The, A) moon is bright tonight.

1 Julie plays (a, the) cello.

2 (A, An) MVP award is a big prize.

3 Please close (a, the) door behind you.

4 I have (a, an) question.

5 There is an island. (An, The) island is so beautiful.

6 She has (a, the) nice voice.

7 This is (a, an) elephant.

8 (A, The) sky is clear today.

9 She has information. (An, The) information is surprising.

10 Let's look at (a, the) screen.

C ( ) 안의 말과 알맞은 관사를 함께 써서 문장을 완성하시오.

0 ____The world____ changes every day. (world)

1 Olivia has a flower. _____ is a rose. (flower)

2 There are sixty minutes in _____. (hour)

3 I play _____ after school. (violin).

4 She has _____ in her pencil case. (eraser)

5 There is _____ on the table. (keyboard)

6 Tom plays _____ on Saturdays. (flute)

7 _____ is huge. (sun)

8 We live on _____. (earth)

WRITING PRACTICE

( ) 안의 말과 알맞은 관사를 함께 써서 우리말을 영어로 옮기시오.

0 기차가 1분 뒤에 출발한다. (minute)

→ The train leaves in _____a minute_____.

1 이것은 사과 파이다. (apple pie)

→ This is _____.

2 그 설탕을 저에게 건네주세요. (sugar)

→ Pass me _____, please.

3 나는 접시 하나와 컵 두 개가 필요하다. (dish)

→ I need _____ and two cups.

4 그는 많은 옷을 갖고 있다. 그 옷들은 비싸다. (clothes)

→ He has many clothes. _____ are expensive.

5 이 강은 길다. 나는 그 강을 따라 걷는다. (river)

→ This river is long. I walk along _____.

REVIEW TEST

[1-2] 다음 중 명사의 복수형이 잘못 연결된 것을 고르시오.

1
① cup – cups   ② fox – foxes
③ boy – boys   ④ thief – thieves
⑤ woman – womans

2
① mouse – mouses   ② city – cities
③ tooth – teeth   ④ watch – watches
⑤ potato – potatoes

[3-4] 빈칸에 들어갈 말로 알맞지 않은 것을 고르시오.

3
> I need a _____.

① pencil   ② laptop   ③ bike
④ eraser   ⑤ cell phone

4
> _____ is important.

① Air   ② Friend   ③ Love
④ Water   ⑤ Honesty

서술형

[5-7] ( ) 안의 말과 알맞은 관사를 함께 써서 문장을 완성하시오.

5
> There are seven days in
> _____. (week)

6
> _____ is wonderful.
> (world)

7
> We need _____ in the
> living room. (sofa)

빈출

[8-9] 빈칸에 들어갈 말이 바르게 짝지어진 것을 고르시오.
(X는 필요 없음을 뜻함)

8
> • _____(A)_____ sky is blue today.
> • There are three _____(B)_____ on the
> desk.

   (A)   (B)
① A   ······   photos
② A   ······   photoes
③ The   ······   photos
④ The   ······   photoes
⑤ X   ······   photos

9
> • We have four _____(A)_____ in the
> room.
> • My grandparents live in _____(B)_____.

   (A)   (B)
① box   ······   Chicago
② boxs   ······   a Chicago
③ boxs   ······   Chicago
④ boxes   ······   a Chicago
⑤ boxes   ······   Chicago

[10-12] 다음 중 밑줄 친 부분이 잘못된 것을 고르시오.

10 ① I have <u>a class</u>.
② She has <u>three hats</u>.
③ Jim has <u>two sisters</u>.
④ They work for <u>peace</u>.
⑤ My uncle lives in <u>an Europe</u>.

11 ① We need <u>an apple</u>.
② My mom is <u>a chef</u>.
③ He buys <u>two piece of cake</u>.
④ <u>Italy</u> is a beautiful country.
⑤ There are <u>three men</u> in the car.

12 ① <u>Bill</u> is very smart.
② I need <u>four dishes</u>.
③ We play <u>the violin</u> on Mondays.
④ She puts <u>a sugar</u> in her tea.
⑤ There are <u>roses</u> in this garden.

서술형

[13-15] ( ) 안의 말을 이용하여 문장을 완성하시오.

13 Mr. Brown has four _____.
(child)

14 He needs _____ now.
(money)

15 There are two _____
in the oven. (slice, pizza)

서술형

[16-18] 우리말과 일치하도록 ( ) 안의 말을 이용하여
문장을 완성하시오.

16 나는 항상 우산 하나를 가지고 다닌다. (umbrella)

→ I always bring _____.

17 이 책에는 이야기가 다섯 개 있다. 그 이야기들은 무섭
다. (story)

→ There are five stories in this book.
_____ are scary.

18 Paul은 매일 우유 세 잔을 마신다. (glass, milk)

→ Paul drinks _____
every day.

CHAPTER 02 대명사

인칭대명사

A

주어진 말을 가리키는 주격 대명사를 쓰시오.

0	Emily	→	she
1	the chair	→	
2	Dad and I	→	
3	Paul	→	
4	Sam and Ted	→	
5	my mother	→	
6	the trucks	→	
7	the computer	→	
8	my friends	→	
9	Susan	→	
10	you and I	→	
11	Mr. Smith	→	
12	you and your brother	→	

B

( ) 안에서 알맞은 말을 고르시오.

0 (I, My) am a good person.

1 (You, Your) dress is cute.

2 (She, Her) has a sister.

3 (My, Mine) computer is old.

4 I feel sorry for (he, him).

5 The books are (their, theirs).

6 John knows (me, my) very well.

7 (Her, Hers) house has two bathrooms.

8 (Greg, Greg's) father is a police officer.

9 This is a nice piano. I like (it, its) sound.

10 This pie is delicious. Billy loves (it, its).

C ( ) 안의 말을 적절한 형태로 써서 문장을 완성하시오.

0 This is ___our___ apartment. (we)

1 The notebook is _____. (I)

2 I see _____ every day. (she)

3 I like _____ smile. (you)

4 _____ love music. (they)

5 The ticket is _____. (he)

6 The textbooks are _____. (we)

7 I miss _____ very much. (they)

8 Eric's parents are proud of _____. (he)

9 I know _____ phone number. (she)

10 This is my school bag. _____ is heavy. (it)

WRITING PRACTICE

알맞은 대명사를 이용하여 우리말을 영어로 옮기시오.

0 그는 키가 크다.

→ _____He_____ is tall.

1 그들은 우리를 좋아한다.

→ They like _____.

2 그들의 목소리는 아름답다.

→ _____ voices are beautiful.

3 이 스웨터는 네 것이다.

→ This sweater is _____.

4 그는 나와 자주 이야기한다.

→ He often talks with _____.

5 Jack의 생일은 내일이다.

→ _____ birthday is tomorrow.

CHAPTER 02 대명사

this, that, it

( ) 안에서 알맞은 말을 고르시오.

0 (This, (It)) is three o'clock now.

1 (That, It) is cold tonight.

2 (This, These) is your bike.

3 I need (that, those) baskets.

4 (This, These) video is funny.

5 (This, It) is bright outside.

6 (That, Those) skirt is pretty.

7 (This, These) oranges are fresh.

8 (That, It) is 5 km from here to my house.

B

그림을 보고 보기에서 알맞은 말을 골라 문장을 완성하시오.

보기	this	that	these	those

0 _____These_____ are my hairpins.

1 _____ is my cousin.

2 _____ are my puppies.

3 _____ is our teacher.

4 _____ are my shoes.

5 _____ is my cake!

C 보기에서 알맞은 말을 골라 문장을 완성하시오. (단, 한 번씩만 쓸 것)

[0-2]

보기	~~this~~	these	it

0 _____This_____ is a nice car.

1 _____ is Wednesday today.

2 _____ are my friends.

[3-5]

보기	that	those	it

3 I want _____ flowers.

4 _____ hotel is great.

5 _____ is nine o'clock in the morning.

알맞은 대명사를 이용하여 우리말을 영어로 옮기시오.

0 밖에 비가 온다.

→ _____It_____ is rainy outside.

1 이것은 내 보고서이다.

→ _____ is my report.

2 저 여자아이들은 내 여동생들이다.

→ _____ girls are my sisters.

3 오늘은 8월 10일이다.

→ _____ is August 10 today.

4 저 아이는 나의 반 친구 Tom이다.

→ _____ is my classmate Tom.

5 이 잡지들은 무료이다.

→ _____ magazines are free.

REVIEW TEST

[1-2] 빈칸에 들어갈 알맞은 말을 고르시오.

1
_____ are my grandparents.

① This   ② That   ③ These
④ It   ⑤ We

2
Jeff is friendly. I like _____ very much.

① he   ② his   ③ him
④ their   ⑤ them

서술형

[3-5] ( ) 안의 말을 적절한 형태로 써서 문장을 완성하시오.

3
Helen lives with _____. (I)

4
These toys are _____. (they)

5
_____ hair is long. (she)

6
빈칸에 공통으로 들어갈 말은?

• _____ is Friday today.
• I like this doll. _____ is very cute.

① This   ② That   ③ These
④ It   ⑤ They

[7-8] 빈칸에 들어갈 말로 알맞지 않은 것을 고르시오.

7
This is _____ room.

① my   ② your   ③ his
④ hers   ⑤ our

8
He cooks dinner for _____.

① me   ② our   ③ you
④ her   ⑤ them

빈출

9 다음 중 밑줄 친 부분을 가리키는 대명사가 잘못된 것은?

① I like John's smile. → his
② Our teachers are nice. → We
③ I usually study with Jim. → him
④ This purse is Sarah's. → hers
⑤ You and Tim are good friends. → You

[10-12] 다음 중 밑줄 친 부분이 잘못된 것을 고르시오.

10 ① <u>Its</u> mouth is big.
② It is <u>her</u> camera.
③ We talk about <u>him</u>.
④ The cookies are for <u>mine</u>.
⑤ <u>Daniel's</u> sister is two years old.

11 ① <u>That</u> is my school.
② <u>Those</u> are my socks.
③ <u>This</u> seats are ours.
④ <u>These</u> are their photos.
⑤ <u>This</u> apartment is very small.

12 ① <u>This</u> is 2:30 p.m. now.
② I like <u>that</u> singer.
③ Jack loves <u>his</u> cats.
④ I need <u>Chloe's</u> address.
⑤ <u>It</u> is 300 km to the airport.

13 다음 우리말을 영어로 바르게 옮긴 것은?

이분은 나의 삼촌이다.

① It is my uncle.
② This is my uncle.
③ That is my uncle.
④ These are my uncle.
⑤ Those are my uncle.

서술형

[14-15] 빈칸에 알맞은 대명사를 써서 문장을 완성하시오.

14 This building is tall. _____ is eighty meters high.

15 Lucy likes comic books. She reads _____ every weekend.

서술형

[16-18] 우리말과 일치하도록 (   ) 안의 말을 이용하여 문장을 완성하시오.

16 오늘은 화요일이다. (Tuesday)

→ _____ today.

17 나는 그를 매일 만난다. (meet)

→ _____ every day.

18 저 병들은 비어 있다. (bottle)

→ _____ are empty.

UNIT 01

be동사의 현재형 1

A 　주어진 주어에 맞게 빈칸에 알맞은 be동사와 줄임말을 각각 쓰시오.

0　He 　　<u>　is　</u>　 → 　<u>　He's　</u>

1　They 　<u>　　　　　</u>　 → 　<u>　　　　　</u>

2　I 　<u>　　　　　</u>　 → 　<u>　　　　　</u>

3　She 　<u>　　　　　</u>　 → 　<u>　　　　　</u>

4　You 　<u>　　　　　</u>　 → 　<u>　　　　　</u>

5　It 　<u>　　　　　</u>　 → 　<u>　　　　　</u>

6　We 　<u>　　　　　</u>　 → 　<u>　　　　　</u>

7　Sarah 　<u>　　　　　</u>　 → 　<u>　　　　　</u>

8　Jake 　<u>　　　　　</u>　 → 　<u>　　　　　</u>

B 　( ) 안에서 알맞은 말을 고르시오.

0　Dad (is, are) in the garden.

1　They (is, are) writers.

2　(Its, It's) beautiful.

3　I (am, is) 150 cm tall.

4　(She's, We're) neighbors.

5　This song (am, is) popular.

6　Sophia (is, are) from Russia.

7　You (is, are) a great pianist.

8　(You, He) is in the bathroom.

9　Sam and his brother (is, are) smart.

10　You and Jina (is, are) my good friends.

C ( ) 안의 말과 be동사의 현재형을 이용하여 문장을 완성하시오.

0 _____It is_____ my smartphone. (it)

1 _____ designers. (we)

2 _____ proud of you. (I)

3 _____ hungry. (the children)

4 _____ Peter's notebook. (it)

5 _____ in the restaurant. (he)

6 _____ far from here. (the airport)

7 _____ a nice person. (you)

8 _____ our English teacher. (she)

9 _____ handsome. (they)

10 _____ classmates. (Lucy and I)

WRITING PRACTICE

( ) 안의 말을 이용하여 우리말을 영어로 옮기시오.

0 우리는 부엌에 있다. (we)

→ _____We are_____ in the kitchen.

1 나는 그녀에게 화가 난다. (I)

→ _____ angry at her.

2 너는 친절하다. (you)

→ _____ kind.

3 이 기차는 매우 빠르다. (this train)

→ _____ very fast.

4 Victoria는 대학생이다. (Victoria)

→ _____ a college student.

5 우리 부모님은 의사이다. (my parents)

→ _____ doctors.

UNIT 02

be동사의 현재형 2

A

( ) 안에서 알맞은 말을 고르시오.

0 Fred (is not, are not) a pilot.

1 (Is, Are) they friendly?

2 (Is, Are) you Korean?

3 You (isn't, aren't) short.

4 (Is, Are) your brother lazy?

5 (Is, Are) it your textbook?

6 (I'm not, I amn't) fourteen years old.

7 These (not are, are not) my cats.

8 Jeff (is not, are not) in his room.

9 He and I (am not, are not) cousins.

10 (Is, Are) you and Mike in the same class?

B

빈칸에 be동사 현재형의 부정형과 그 줄임말을 각각 쓰시오.

0 His bike _____is not_____ old.   →   His bike _____isn't_____ old.

1 You _____ rude.   →   You _____ rude.

2 He _____ shy.   →   He _____ shy.

3 I _____ good at math.   →   _____ good at math.

4 It _____ Sunday today.   →   It _____ Sunday today.

5 We _____ twins.   →   We _____ twins.

6 She _____ my best friend.   →   She _____ my best friend.

7 That _____ a good idea.   →   That _____ a good idea.

8 This pool _____ deep.   →   This pool _____ deep.

9 These shoes _____ new.   →   These shoes _____ new.

10 Her name _____ Serena.   →   Her name _____ Serena.

C ( ) 안의 말과 be동사를 이용하여 현재형 의문문과 대답을 완성하시오.

0 A: _____Is he_____ a champion? (he)
   B: Yes, _____he is_____.

1 A: _____ ready now? (you)
   B: No, _____.

2 A: _____ cloudy outside? (it)
   B: Yes, _____.

3 A: _____ in the classroom? (Bill)
   B: No, _____.

4 A: _____ a scientist? (your mother)
   B: Yes, _____.

5 A: _____ famous in Asia? (they)
   B: No, _____.

WRITING PRACTICE

( ) 안의 말을 이용하여 우리말을 영어로 옮기시오.

0 그는 배우가 아니다. (he)
   → _____He is not_____ an actor.

1 나는 슬프지 않다. (I)
   → _____ sad.

2 너 배고프니? (you)
   → _____ hungry?

3 지금 8시이니? (it)
   → _____ eight o'clock now?

4 Jane은 프랑스 사람이 아니다. (Jane)
   → _____ French.

5 그들은 소풍 때문에 들떠 있니? (they)
   → _____ excited about the picnic?

UNIT 03

be동사의 과거형

A

( ) 안에서 알맞은 말을 고르시오.

0 She (was̄, were) late for school.

1 We (was, were) very thirsty.

2 It (wasn't, weren't) my mistake.

3 Your answer (was, were) right.

4 They (were not, not were) musicians.

5 (Was, Were) the math test difficult?

6 He (is, was) a baker two years ago.

7 Mike and I (was, were) not close.

8 They (are, were) at the theater last night.

9 I (am, was) in New York last winter.

10 A: Was the game exciting?
B: No, it (isn't, wasn't).

B

보기에서 알맞은 말을 골라 문장을 완성하시오.

보기	was	were	wasn't	weren't

0 I _____was_____ sleepy last night. I was too tired.

1 It _____ cold yesterday. It was warm.

2 The trip _____ fun. It was terrible.

3 The cake was great. It _____ delicious.

4 The children _____ quiet. They were noisy.

5 The pictures _____ nice. They were beautiful.

6 Alice was sick. She _____ in the hospital yesterday.

7 Those shoes _____ on sale yesterday. They were cheap.

8 Harry and Ron _____ in the book club. They were in the chess club.

C ( ) 안의 말과 be동사를 이용하여 과거형 의문문과 대답을 완성하시오.

0 A: _____Was he_____ a good dancer? (he)

B: Yes, _____he was_____.

1 A: _____ afraid? (you)

B: No, _____.

2 A: _____ expensive? (the watch)

B: Yes, _____.

3 A: _____ kind to you? (they)

B: Yes, _____.

4 A: _____ in the cafeteria? (Jake and Kevin)

B: No, _____.

5 A: _____ happy about the news? (Chris)

B: Yes, _____.

WRITING PRACTICE

( ) 안의 말을 이용하여 우리말을 영어로 옮기시오.

0 그 영화는 지루했다. (the movie)

→ _____The movie was_____ boring.

1 물은 차갑지 않았다. (the water)

→ _____ cold.

2 그 방들은 크지 않았다. (the rooms)

→ _____ large.

3 나는 지난주에 바빴다. (I)

→ _____ busy last week.

4 우리는 어제 동물원에 있었다. (we)

→ _____ at the zoo yesterday.

5 너의 남동생들은 어젯밤에 너와 함께 있었니? (your brothers)

→ _____ with you last night?

U N I T
04

There is/are

A ( ) 안에서 알맞은 말을 고르시오.

0 There (is, are) a calendar on the wall.

1 There (is, are) five people on the bus.

2 (Is, Are) there an onion in the refrigerator?

3 There (is, are) two pens on the desk.

4 There (is, are) orange juice in the glass.

5 There (is, are) ten books on the bookshelf.

6 There (was, were) a package in the mailbox.

7 There (is, are) not many people at the mall.

8 There (was, were) two pianos in the music room.

9 There (was, were) a big TV in the living room.

10 (Is, Are) there puppies in her house?

B 그림을 보고 There is 또는 There are를 넣어 문장을 완성하시오.

0   **1**   **2**   **3**

0 _____There is_____ a cup on the table.

1 _____ two beds in the hotel room.

2 _____ bread on the plate.

3 _____ many cars on the road.

C 보기에서 알맞은 말을 골라 주어진 조건에 맞게 써서 문장을 완성하시오. (단, 한 번씩만 쓸 것)

보기	There is	There are	There was	There were

[0-3] (긍정문으로)

0 _____There is_____ a coin in my pocket.

1 _____ beautiful parks in Vancouver.

2 _____ six monkeys at the zoo last year.

3 _____ a festival at our school two weeks ago.

[4-7] (부정문으로)

4 _____ a cloud in the sky yesterday.

5 _____ a bookstore on this street.

6 _____ many guests at the party last night.

7 _____ many museums in this city.

WRITING PRACTICE

다음 우리말을 영어로 옮기시오.

0 길모퉁이에 카페가 하나 있다.
→ _____There is_____ a café on the corner.

1 책상 위에 프린터가 한 대 있니?
→ _____ a printer on the desk?

2 여기에 꽃집이 하나 있었다.
→ _____ a flower shop here.

3 이 가게에는 모자가 많이 있다.
→ _____ many hats in this store.

4 바구니 안에 사과가 다섯 개 있었다.
→ _____ five apples in the basket.

5 이 웹 사이트에는 많은 오류가 있지 않다.
→ _____ many errors on this website.

REVIEW TEST

[1-3] 빈칸에 들어갈 알맞은 말을 고르시오.

1

David _____ a painter now.

① am　　② are　　③ is
④ was　　⑤ were

2

We _____ at the beach yesterday.

① am　　② are　　③ is
④ was　　⑤ were

3

_____ those stores open now?

① Am　　② Are　　③ Is
④ Was　　⑤ Were

서술형

[4-6] 보기에서 알맞은 말을 골라 문장을 완성하시오.

| 보기 | are | isn't | was |

4

Amy and Steve _____ dentists.

5

I _____ tired last night.

6

Robert _____ my father.
He is my uncle.

7 다음 중 보기의 밑줄 친 부분과 의미가 같은 것은?

| 보기 | Sarah is in France. |

① My dog is cute.
② Her name is Dorothy.
③ He is at the bus stop.
④ This is my new bike.
⑤ Today is Andrew's birthday.

8 다음 중 밑줄 친 부분의 줄임말이 잘못된 것은?

① She is sad. → She's
② I am not okay. → I'm not
③ It is nine o'clock now. → Its'
④ They are nurses. → They're
⑤ We are late for the movie. → We're

9 빈칸에 들어갈 말이 바르게 짝지어진 것은?

A: __(A)__ Mr. Jones a history
　　teacher?
B: No, he __(B)__ .

	(A)		(B)
①	Is	……	is
②	Is	……	isn't
③	Was	……	isn't
④	Was	……	was
⑤	Are	……	wasn't

[10-12] 보기에서 알맞은 말을 골라 문장을 완성하시오.

| 보기 | There is | There are | There was |

10 _____ many leaves on the playground.

11 _____ a river in Paris.

12 _____ a big fire last night.

[13-14] 다음 중 밑줄 친 부분이 잘못된 것을 고르시오.

13 ① It is noisy here.
② Rick is not a child.
③ The cups weren't clean.
④ Yesterday's test wasn't difficult.
⑤ We are in Rome two days ago.

14 ① I'm in the bank.
② They aren't sisters.
③ He is always honest.
④ There are a subway station near here.
⑤ Paul and I were on the same team last year.

15 다음 우리말을 영어로 바르게 옮긴 것은?

| 너는 택시 안에 있었니? |

① Is you in the taxi?
② Am you in the taxi?
③ Are you in the taxi?
④ Was you in the taxi?
⑤ Were you in the taxi?

[16-17] 우리말과 일치하도록 ( ) 안의 말을 이용하여 문장을 완성하시오.

16 그 길에는 많은 나무가 있었다. (many trees)

→ _____
on the street.

17 어제는 날씨가 화창했니? (sunny)

→ _____
yesterday?

[18-19] 우리말과 일치하도록 ( ) 안에 주어진 말을 바르게 배열하시오.

18 저 만화들은 재미있니?
(funny, are, cartoons, those)

→ _____ ?

19 이것은 내 책가방이 아니다.
(is, schoolbag, not, this, my)

→ _____ .

CHAPTER 04 일반동사 1

일반동사의 현재형 1

A 주어진 동사의 3인칭 단수 현재형을 쓰시오.

0 come → _____comes_____

1 talk → _____

2 mix → _____

3 jump → _____

4 try → _____

5 pass → _____

6 fly → _____

7 miss → _____

8 write → _____

9 ask → _____

10 buy → _____

11 see → _____

12 brush → _____

B ( ) 안에 주어진 동사의 현재형을 써서 문장을 완성하시오.

0 My uncle _____drives_____ a truck. (drive)

1 She _____ at home. (study)

2 Dad _____ dinner for us. (make)

3 Lisa and Kelly _____ glasses. (wear)

4 Jake _____ to the radio. (listen)

5 We _____ our classroom every day. (clean)

6 I _____ in the park on Sundays. (walk)

7 Nick _____ online classes every day. (take)

8 Victor _____ his homework after 6:00 p.m. (do)

9 My grandmother always _____ in this chair. (sit)

10 Jane and I often _____ fashion magazines. (read)

C 주어진 동사의 현재형을 써서 문장을 완성하시오.

0 love   a. Lucy ____ loves ____ hot chocolate.

                    b. We ____ love ____ hot chocolate.

1 go   a. I _____ to bed late.

                    b. Clara _____ to bed late.

2 know   a. We _____ Peter very well.

                    b. Mary _____ Peter very well.

3 teach   a. Mr. Peterson _____ science.

                    b. They _____ science.

4 cry   a. My little brother _____ all the time.

                    b. The babies _____ all the time.

5 have   a. I _____ a headache.

                    b. She _____ a headache.

WRITING PRACTICE

( ) 안의 말을 이용하여 우리말을 영어로 옮기시오.

0 Julie는 매우 빠르게 수영한다. (swim)

→ Julie ____ swims ____ very fast.

1 7월에는 비가 많이 내린다. (rain)

→ It _____ a lot in July.

2 Betty는 아침에 머리를 빗는다. (brush)

→ Betty _____ her hair in the morning.

3 형과 나는 컴퓨터를 함께 쓴다. (use)

→ My brother and I _____ the computer together.

4 그녀는 물건을 잘 고친다. (fix)

→ She _____ things well.

5 나는 아침으로 시리얼을 먹는다. (eat)

→ I _____ cereal for breakfast.

UNIT 02

일반동사의 현재형 2

A

( ) 안에서 알맞은 말을 고르시오.

0　I (~~don't~~, doesn't) like bananas.

1　He doesn't (have, has) classes today.

2　Ellen (don't, doesn't) call me.

3　(Do, Does) you like orange juice?

4　Alice (don't, doesn't) work at a bank.

5　You (don't, doesn't) have enough time.

6　(Do, Does) your parents travel a lot?

7　Does he (live, lives) in this apartment?

8　They (don't, doesn't) watch basketball games.

9　Tim and Jake (don't, doesn't) exercise hard.

10　Brian (don't, doesn't) spend much money on clothes.

B

( ) 안의 말을 이용하여 현재형 부정문을 완성하시오. (줄임말로 쓸 것)

0　I _____don't play_____ the violin. (play)

1　He _____ English. (speak)

2　I _____ cheese. (eat)

3　She _____ a gift. (want)

4　Chris _____ 3D movies. (like)

5　We _____ a car. (have)

6　My brother _____ bad words. (use)

7　They _____ emails to us. (write)

8　Sumi _____ her notebook to her friends. (lend)

9　My grandparents _____ with us. (live)

10　The children _____ in restaurants. (run)

C   ( ) 안의 말을 이용하여 현재형 의문문을 완성하시오.

0   A: _____Does_____ Sarah _____sing_____ well? (sing)

B: Yes, she does.

1   A: _____ he _____ here? (stay)

B: No, he doesn't.

2   A: _____ you _____ his last name? (know)

B: Yes, I do.

3   A: _____ she _____ a boyfriend? (have)

B: No, she doesn't.

4   A: _____ your friends _____ tablet PCs? (use)

B: Yes, they do.

5   A: _____ they _____ tea every morning? (drink)

B: No, they don't.

WRITING PRACTICE

( ) 안의 말을 이용하여 우리말을 영어로 옮기시오.

0   Sam에게 계획이 있니? (have)

→ _____Does_____ Sam _____have_____ a plan?

1   Eric은 도서관에서 공부하지 않는다. (study)

→ Eric _____ in the library.

2   너는 내 도움이 필요하니? (need)

→ _____ you _____ my help?

3   우리는 학교에 버스를 타고 가지 않는다. (take)

→ We _____ a bus to school.

4   그녀는 식물을 키우지 않는다. (grow)

→ She _____ plants.

5   우리의 미술 수업은 오전 10시에 시작하니? (start)

→ _____ our art class _____ at 10:00 a.m.?

UNIT 03

일반동사의 과거형 1

A 주어진 동사의 과거형을 쓰시오.

0 open → _opened_

1 love → _____

2 take → _____

3 cry → _____

4 want → _____

5 drop → _____

6 cut → _____

7 give → _____

8 teach → _____

9 swim → _____

10 come → _____

11 lose → _____

12 drink → _____

B ( ) 안에서 알맞은 말을 고르시오.

0 Fred (sit, sat) on the sofa.

1 I (watch, watched) a movie last weekend.

2 Dad (read, reads) the letter last night.

3 The festival ended (last week, next week).

4 The rain (stop, stopped) suddenly.

5 We (hears, heard) a strange noise outside.

6 Susan (do, did) the dishes after dinner.

7 We (run, ran) to school this morning.

8 Emily (has, had) an exam last Thursday.

9 Josh (finds, found) his wallet yesterday.

10 I (meet, met) him at the station thirty minutes ago.

C ( ) 안에 주어진 동사의 과거형을 써서 문장을 완성하시오.

0 I _____ate_____ pizza for lunch. (eat)

1 We _____ a new tent. (buy)

2 It _____ a lot last week. (snow)

3 Colin _____ a big kite. (make)

4 The baseball player _____ the ball. (hit)

5 Janet _____ in Paris for two months. (stay)

6 Brenda _____ the school bus this morning. (miss)

7 Yumi and Lisa _____ to the park yesterday. (go)

8 Greg _____ computer games last night. (play)

9 They _____ a vacation to the mountains. (plan)

10 He _____ a new activity. (try)

WRITING PRACTICE

( ) 안의 말을 이용하여 우리말을 영어로 옮기시오.

0 Chuck은 우리에게 거짓말을 했다. (tell)

→ Chuck _____told_____ a lie to us.

1 그들은 새 집으로 이사했다. (move)

→ They _____ to a new house.

2 우리는 어젯밤에 전화로 이야기를 나누었다. (chat)

→ We _____ on the phone last night.

3 나는 벽에 걸린 그림을 봤다. (see)

→ I _____ a picture on the wall.

4 나는 어제 Amy의 집에서 잤다. (sleep)

→ I _____ at Amy's house yesterday.

5 겨울 방학이 지난주에 시작했다. (start)

→ Winter vacation _____ last week.

UNIT 04

일반동사의 과거형 2

A

( ) 안에서 알맞은 말을 고르시오.

0 I (don't, (didn't)) exercise yesterday.

1 Did he (see, sees) these photos?

2 We (don't, didn't) play soccer last Friday.

3 He didn't (pass, passed) the exam.

4 She didn't (buy, buys) the scarf.

5 (Do, Did) you cook dinner yesterday?

6 I (don't, didn't) finish the book last week.

7 Victor didn't (do, did) his math homework.

8 Did they (go, went) to the shopping mall?

9 He (doesn't, didn't) have an umbrella last night.

10 Sam and I (don't, didn't) meet last weekend.

B

( ) 안의 말을 이용하여 과거형 부정문을 완성하시오. (줄임말로 쓸 것)

0 He _____didn't wear_____ a hat. (wear)

1 Tom _____ our gift. (like)

2 It _____ yesterday. (rain)

3 You _____ the door. (lock)

4 We _____ a key. (have)

5 Mark _____ a taxi last night. (take)

6 The computer _____ well. (work)

7 We _____ the concert. (enjoy)

8 Jim _____ to school yesterday. (go)

9 I _____ my cousin last summer. (visit)

10 She _____ to the interview this morning. (come)

C　( ) 안의 말을 이용하여 과거형 의문문을 완성하시오.

0　A: _____Did_____ you _____talk_____ with Chris yesterday? (talk)

　　B: No, I didn't.

1　A: _____ they _____ to the city hall? (walk)

　　B: Yes, they did.

2　A: _____ your father _____ the door? (fix)

　　B: Yes, he did.

3　A: _____ she _____ the picture to you? (give)

　　B: No, she didn't.

4　A: _____ he _____ the tickets? (buy)

　　B: Yes, he did.

5　A: _____ you _____ a good grade on the test? (get)

　　B: No, I didn't.

WRITING PRACTICE

( ) 안의 말을 이용하여 우리말을 영어로 옮기시오.

0　그들은 제시간에 도착하지 않았다. (arrive)

　→ They _____didn't arrive_____ on time.

1　나는 열심히 노력하지 않았다. (try)

　→ I _____ hard.

2　너는 얼음 위에서 넘어졌니? (fall)

　→ _____ you _____ on the ice?

3　그는 차를 빨리 운전하지 않았다. (drive)

　→ He _____ the car fast.

4　그들은 지난 일요일에 테니스를 쳤니? (play)

　→ _____ they _____ tennis last Sunday?

5　그 개는 사람들을 향해 짖지 않았다. (bark)

　→ The dog _____ at people.

REVIEW TEST

1 다음 중 동사의 3인칭 단수 현재형이 <u>잘못</u> 연결된 것은?

① eat – eats   ② go – goes

③ swim – swims   ④ play – plaies

⑤ catch – catches

2 다음 중 동사의 과거형이 <u>잘못</u> 연결된 것은?

① sit – sat   ② come – came

③ put – put   ④ plan – planed

⑤ hear – heard

[3-4] 빈칸에 들어갈 알맞은 말을 고르시오.

3

> My father _____ his car every Saturday.

① wash   ② washes

③ don't wash   ④ doesn't washes

⑤ didn't washed

4

> We _____ to this town last year.

① move   ② moves

③ moved   ④ don't move

⑤ didn't moved

서술형

[5-6] ( ) 안의 말을 이용하여 문장을 완성하시오.

5

> He _____ in the festival last night. (sing)

6

> Jessica _____ here now. (not / live)

서술형

[7-8] 빈칸에 알맞은 말을 써서 대화를 완성하시오.

7

> A: Does your sister ride a bike?
> B: No, _____ _____ .

8

> A: Did you and Bill break this window?
> B: Yes, _____ _____ .

9 빈칸에 들어갈 말이 바르게 짝지어진 것은?

> • Ted _____(A)_____ us the truth.
> • _____(B)_____ Misun and Sumi eat lunch together every day?

      (A)   (B)

① tell ...... Do

② tell ...... Did

③ tells ...... Does

④ told ...... Do

⑤ told ...... Does

[10-12] 다음 중 밑줄 친 부분이 <u>잘못된</u> 것을 고르시오.

10 ① I <u>don't drink</u> cola.
② Peter <u>doesn't like</u> that subject.
③ She <u>doesn't speak</u> Chinese.
④ Mr. Lee <u>doesn't teach</u> science.
⑤ This shop <u>don't sell</u> sweaters.

11 ① It <u>snowed</u> last Christmas.
② He <u>cutted</u> the meat with a knife.
③ We <u>enjoyed</u> the festival last night.
④ I <u>dropped</u> a spoon in the restaurant.
⑤ Lucy and I <u>studied</u> for an exam.

12 ① <u>Do you have</u> a pen now?
② <u>Did she help</u> you yesterday?
③ <u>Does he work</u> in this office?
④ <u>Did Tom bought</u> this app yesterday?
⑤ <u>Did they post</u> photos online?

빈출

13 다음 중 대화가 자연스럽지 <u>않은</u> 것은?

① A: Do they know you?
B: Yes, they do.
② A: Does Betty put honey in her tea?
B: No, she doesn't.
③ A: Does Sam exercise every day?
B: No, he didn't.
④ A: Did you clean the house?
B: Yes, I did.
⑤ A: Do Chris and Tom have the tickets?
B: Yes, they do.

서술형 빈출

[14-16] 우리말과 일치하도록 ( ) 안의 말을 이용하여 문장을 완성하시오.

14 우리는 2년 전에 고양이가 한 마리 있었다. (have)

→ We _____ a cat two years ago.

15 Jeff는 패스트푸드를 먹지 않는다. (eat)

→ Jeff _____ fast food.

16 그가 너에게 이메일을 보냈니? (send)

→ _____ he _____ an email to you?

서술형

[17-18] 우리말과 일치하도록 ( ) 안에 주어진 말을 바르게 배열하시오.

17 그녀는 너의 생일을 기억하니?
(she, remember, does, your birthday)

→ _____ ?

18 Jane은 그녀의 지갑을 가져오지 않았다.
(not, her wallet, Jane, bring, did)

→ _____ .

UNIT 01 형용사

A

( ) 안에서 알맞은 말을 고르시오.

0 The music (loud is, (is loud)).

1 Your cat is (love, lovely)!

2 I need (some, any) sleep.

3 We had (some, any) snacks.

4 Do you have (some, any) ideas?

5 They didn't want (some, any) help.

6 The cake (smells good, good smells).

7 Paul tried (something new, new something).

8 Sam is always (friend, friendly) to his neighbors.

9 The card games (interesting are, are interesting).

10 Did he make (delicious anything, anything delicious)?

B

보기에서 알맞은 말을 골라 문장을 완성하시오. (단, 한 번씩만 쓸 것)

[0-3]

보기	dirty	wrong	~~windy~~	heavy

0 It is a _____windy_____ day. It is cold too.

1 This suitcase is _____. It is over 20 kg.

2 We took the _____ bus. We were late.

3 We cleaned our house. It isn't _____ now.

[4-7]

보기	big	expensive	healthy	tired

4 This coat is _____. It is $300.

5 It is a _____ company. Many people work for it.

6 I feel _____ now. I didn't sleep well last night.

7 My mom is _____. She exercises every morning.

C 빈칸에 some 또는 any를 넣어 문장을 완성하시오.

0 Do you want _____ some _____ donuts?

1 Robert put _____ salt in the soup.

2 We don't have _____ time now.

3 I have _____ friends in Italy.

4 Will you have _____ dessert?

5 She bought _____ apples at the store.

6 He didn't make _____ mistakes.

7 Do you want _____ milk?

8 There is _____ food in the kitchen.

9 Do we have _____ guests today?

10 I didn't meet _____ interesting people at the party.

WRITING PRACTICE

( ) 안의 말을 이용하여 우리말을 영어로 옮기시오.

0 그는 새 셔츠가 필요하다. (new, shirt)

→ He needs a _____ new shirt _____.

1 그 영화는 지루했다. (boring)

→ The movie _____.

2 그것은 멋진 콘서트였다. (wonderful, concert)

→ It was a _____.

3 Amy는 갈색 눈을 가지고 있다. (brown, eyes)

→ Amy has _____.

4 우리는 그를 위해 특별한 것을 샀다. (special, something)

→ We bought _____ for him.

5 Tony는 그 사건 이후로 유명해졌다. (become, famous)

→ Tony _____ after the event.

UNIT 02 부사

A

주어진 형용사의 부사형을 쓰시오.

0	nice	→	_nicely_
1	wise	→	_____
2	good	→	_____
3	heavy	→	_____
4	hard	→	_____
5	lucky	→	_____
6	new	→	_____
7	clear	→	_____
8	warm	→	_____
9	quiet	→	_____
10	beautiful	→	_____
11	happy	→	_____
12	strange	→	_____

B

( ) 안에서 알맞은 말을 고르시오.

0   The man drove (fast, fastly).

1   We (real, really) love you.

2   I am (very sorry, sorry very).

3   Daniel (kind, kindly) helped us.

4   We (final, finally) finished the work.

5   He opened the door (easy, easily).

6   Susan speaks Korean (perfect, perfectly).

7   The train arrived at the station (late, lately).

8   She smiled (bright, brightly).

9   (Sad, Sadly), they didn't come to my party.

10   He (often go, often goes) to the ice cream shop.

C   ( ) 안의 말을 알맞은 곳에 넣어 문장을 완성하시오.

0   We talk about Jessica. (often)

   → We _____ often talk about _____ Jessica.

1   She looks tired. (always)

   → She _____ .

2   He reads fashion magazines. (never)

   → He _____ .

3   My best friend borrows my books. (often)

   → _____ my books.

4   I am angry at my brother. (sometimes)

   → I _____ my brother.

5   Philip leaves his office at 6:00 p.m. (usually)

   → Philip _____ 6:00 p.m.

WRITING PRACTICE

( ) 안의 말을 이용하여 우리말을 영어로 옮기시오.

0   그는 자신의 이름을 천천히 말했다. (slow)

   → He said his name _____ slowly _____ .

1   안은 무척 어두웠다. (very, dark)

   → It was _____ inside.

2   나는 질문에 빨리 대답했다. (quick)

   → I answered the question _____ .

3   그들은 역에 일찍 도착했다. (early)

   → They arrived at the station _____ .

4   우리 교실은 대개 깨끗하다. (usually, clean)

   → Our classroom _____ .

5   Sarah는 절대 계단을 이용하지 않는다. (never, use)

   → Sarah _____ the stairs.

REVIEW TEST

[1-3] 빈칸에 들어갈 알맞은 말을 고르시오.

1

She has a _____ voice.

① well ② quite ③ sweet
④ nicely ⑤ wonderfully

2

The old man is _____.

① friendly ② poorly ③ sadly
④ luckily ⑤ happily

3

I crossed the road _____.

① easy ② quick ③ slow
④ safe ⑤ carefully

4 밑줄 친 부분의 성격이 나머지 넷과 <u>다른</u> 것은?

① The baby cried <u>loudly</u>.
② She is a <u>hard</u> worker.
③ We came home <u>quickly</u>.
④ Henry speaks Spanish <u>well</u>.
⑤ He got up <u>early</u> this morning.

빈출

[5-6] ( ) 안의 말이 들어갈 위치를 고르시오.

5

(usually)
He ① goes ② to ③ school ④ early ⑤.

6

(always)
They ① are ② proud ③ of ④ their ⑤ son.

서술형

[7-8] 빈칸에 some 또는 any를 넣어 문장을 완성하시오.

7

We didn't catch _____ fish in the river.

8

I have _____ news for you.

[9-10] 다음 중 밑줄 친 부분이 <u>잘못된</u> 것을 고르시오.

9 ① He is <u>very kind</u>.
② I was <u>really busy</u>.
③ Karen has <u>long hair</u>.
④ This lotion <u>smells good</u>.
⑤ It <u>snowed heavy</u> last night.

10 ① I baked <u>some cookies</u>.
② Did he buy <u>any books</u>?
③ We didn't have <u>any money</u>.
④ Do you want <u>some water</u>?
⑤ I don't have <u>some friends</u> here.

빈출

[11-12] 빈칸에 들어갈 말이 바르게 짝지어진 것을 고르시오.

11

| • ___(A)___ apples are green. |
| • There isn't ___(B)___ paper in the printer. |

	(A)		(B)
①	Some	······	some
②	Some	······	any
③	Any	······	some
④	Any	······	any
⑤	답 없음		

12

| • It is ___(A)___ outside. |
| • James talked ___(B)___ . |

	(A)		(B)
①	bright	······	quiet
②	bright	······	quietly
③	brightly	······	quiet
④	brightly	······	quietly
⑤	답 없음		

서술형

[13-14] 밑줄 친 부분을 바르게 고치시오.

13 Josh is a good runner. He runs <u>very fastly</u>.

→ _____

14 She is brave. She <u>never is afraid</u> of anything.

→ _____

서술형

[15-17] 우리말과 일치하도록 ( ) 안의 말을 이용하여 문장을 완성하시오.

15 나는 그 문제를 쉽게 풀었다. (easy)

→ I solved the problem _____.

16 나는 하늘에서 이상한 것을 보았다.
(strange, something)

→ I saw _____ in the sky.

17 Mary는 자주 친구들에게 전화를 한다.
(call, often)

→ Mary _____ her friends.

서술형

[18-19] 우리말과 일치하도록 ( ) 안에 주어진 말을 바르게 배열하시오.

18 흥미롭게도, 우리는 비밀의 방을 발견했다.
(found, interestingly, secret room, we, a)

→ _____.

19 로마는 오래된 도시이다.
(city, an, Rome, old, is)

→ _____.

CHAPTER 06 전치사

장소를 나타내는 전치사

A

( ) 안에서 알맞은 말을 고르시오.

0 There are roses (in, at) the garden.

1 Jim stood next to (I, me).

2 Jay put his bag (in, on) the desk.

3 Paula was behind (we, us).

4 I had coffee (at, on) the café.

5 There are dishes (in, on) the shelf.

6 He had some money (in, at) his pocket.

7 We enjoyed our vacation (in, at) Sydney.

8 I put my cell phone (at, under) my pillow.

9 There was a nice painting (at, on) the wall.

10 They took a photo (front of, in front of) the tower.

B

그림을 보고 보기에서 알맞은 말을 골라 문장을 완성하시오. (단, 한 번씩만 쓸 것)

| 0 | 1 | 2 | 3 |

| 보기 | | in | at | ~~on~~ | behind |

0 The dog was _____on_____ the sofa.

1 I was _____ Jerry in line.

2 I put my clothes _____ the box.

3 A girl played with sand _____ the beach.

C ( ) 안에서 알맞은 말을 골라 문장을 완성하시오.

0 (at, next to)

    a. A bakery is _____at_____ the corner.

    b. There is a supermarket ____next to____ my house.

1 (in, behind)

    a. I sat _____ Jeremy in the classroom.

    b. We took a walk _____ the park.

2 (at, in front of)

    a. Robert spent the day _____ the TV.

    b. They had dinner _____ the Chinese restaurant.

3 (under, on)

    a. The glass fell _____ the floor.

    b. They had a picnic _____ a big tree.

WRITING PRACTICE

( ) 안의 말을 이용하여 우리말을 영어로 옮기시오.

0 우리는 벤치 위에 앉았다. (the bench)

    → We sat _____on the bench_____.

1 Jim은 지금 학교에 있다. (school)

    → Jim is _____ now.

2 나는 감자들을 그릇 안에 넣었다. (the bowl)

    → I put potatoes _____.

3 나는 문 앞에서 이 상자를 찾았다. (the door)

    → I found this box _____.

4 그의 사무실은 서점 옆에 있다. (the bookstore)

    → His office is _____.

5 나의 고양이는 커튼 뒤에서 잔다. (the curtain)

    → My cat sleeps _____.

UNIT 02

시간을 나타내는 전치사

A

( ) 안에서 알맞은 말을 고르시오.

0 The bus left (in, (at)) 3:15 p.m.

1 I get up late (in, on) Sundays.

2 Steve starts work (in, at) nine o'clock.

3 Jay gave me chocolate (at, on) Valentine's Day.

4 Jake plays baseball (in, on) the afternoon.

5 Thursday comes (before, after) Wednesday.

6 It rained a lot (for, during) the summer.

7 We enjoy beautiful flowers (in, on) spring.

8 He lived in this town (for, during) thirty years.

9 My sister doesn't eat snacks (in, at) night.

10 We have three morning classes (before, after) lunch.

B

빈칸에 in, at, on 중 알맞은 전치사를 넣어 문장을 완성하시오.

0 The contest is _____on_____ April 5.

1 Children's Day is _____ May.

2 Daniel went to the dentist _____ Friday.

3 It wasn't very cold _____ the evening.

4 School is over _____ five o'clock.

5 The man died _____ November 2.

6 The last train leaves _____ midnight.

7 Mom gave me a gift _____ my birthday.

8 She won the gold medal _____ 2020.

9 The students have lunch _____ noon.

10 Americans eat turkey _____ Thanksgiving Day.

C 보기에서 알맞은 말을 골라 대화를 완성하시오. (단, 한 번씩만 쓸 것)

보기	~~in~~	at	on	after	during

0 A: Do you exercise after dinner?

B: No, I exercise _____in_____ the morning.

1 A: Did you finally find your notebook?

B: Yes, I did. I found it _____ five days.

2 A: Did you have a party _____ Christmas Eve?

B: Yes, we did. It was great.

3 A: Was the movie boring?

B: Yes, I fell asleep _____ the movie.

4 A: Are you at home in the afternoon?

B: No, I usually come home _____ 7:00 p.m.

WRITING PRACTICE

( ) 안의 말을 이용하여 우리말을 영어로 옮기시오.

0 Andy는 2015년에 초등학교에 입학했다. (2015)

→ Andy entered elementary school _____in 2015_____.

1 나는 한 시간 동안 수학을 공부했다. (an hour)

→ I studied math _____.

2 콘서트는 밤 10시 전에 끝난다. (10:00 p.m.)

→ The concert finishes _____.

3 우리는 방과 후에 Chris를 만났다. (school)

→ We met Chris _____.

4 나는 화요일마다 피아노 레슨을 받는다. (Tuesdays)

→ I take piano lessons _____.

5 그들은 시험 보는 동안 부정행위를 했다. (the test)

→ They cheated _____.

REVIEW TEST

[1-3] 빈칸에 들어갈 알맞은 말을 고르시오.

1

My neighbor plays loud music _____ night.

① in   ② at   ③ on
④ for   ⑤ during

2

There are four people _____ this car.

① in   ② at   ③ after
④ for   ⑤ during

3

Mina rode her bike _____ thirty minutes.

① in   ② at   ③ on
④ for   ⑤ during

4 빈칸에 들어갈 말로 알맞지 <u>않은</u> 것은?

Juliet stood behind _____.

① me   ② us   ③ Mike
④ they   ⑤ the tree

서술형

[5-7] 우리말과 일치하도록 빈칸에 알맞은 전치사를 쓰시오.

5 그는 회의하는 동안 어떤 말도 하지 않았다.

→ He didn't say anything _____ the meeting.

6 그녀는 목욕 후에 낮잠을 잔다.

→ She takes a nap _____ a bath.

7 나는 빵 위에 치즈 한 장을 얹었다.

→ I put a slice of cheese _____ the bread.

서술형

[8-10] 빈칸에 공통으로 들어갈 전치사를 쓰시오.

8
- It is very hot _____ summer.
- Ann works _____ this office.

9
- We have five classes _____ Wednesdays.
- There are some cookies _____ the plate.

10
- My father is _____ work now.
- This supermarket closes _____ 10:00 p.m.

빈출

[11-12] 빈칸에 들어갈 말이 나머지 넷과 다른 것을 고르시오.

11 ① Some dogs are _____ the grass.
② Peter visited me _____ Saturday.
③ I saw him _____ the train station.
④ There is a clock _____ the wall.
⑤ He came back to Korea _____ July 4.

12 ① I met my husband _____ school.
② Mike called me _____ noon.
③ We were _____ home last night.
④ He had lunch _____ eleven o'clock.
⑤ They went to Germany _____ winter.

[13-14] 다음 중 밑줄 친 부분이 잘못된 것을 고르시오.

13 ① We had a great time in London.
② Your bag is on the chair.
③ The cat is next to the desk.
④ She parked in front the building.
⑤ I bought some milk at the store.

14 ① The meeting finished at 5:00 p.m.
② My birthday is in November.
③ We take a walk behind dinner.
④ They go to church on Sundays.
⑤ I play basketball after school.

서술형 빈출

[15-16] 대화가 성립하도록 ( ) 안에서 알맞은 말을 고르시오.

15
A: Did you go to Busan ⓐ (in, during) the vacation?
B: Yes. I stayed there ⓑ (for, during) a week.

ⓐ _____ ⓑ _____

16
A: Did you meet Julie ⓐ (at, on) the airport?
B: Yes, I did. I met her ⓑ (in, at) 11:30 a.m.

ⓐ _____ ⓑ _____

서술형

[17-18] 우리말과 일치하도록 ( ) 안에 주어진 말을 바르게 배열하시오.

17 나는 경기 전에 물을 마셨다.
(before, water, drank, the game)

→ I _____.

18 비행기에서 한 영화배우가 내 옆에 앉았다.
(to, sat, me, next, a movie star)

→ _____
on the plane.

UNIT 01

동사의 종류 1

A

주어진 문장의 형태를 보기에서 고르시오.

보기	ⓐ 주어 + 동사
	ⓑ 주어 + 동사 + 목적어
	ⓒ 주어 + 동사 + 간접목적어 + 직접목적어

0 We want some ice cream.   ⓑ

1 I like comic books. _____

2 Ellen cried during the movie. _____

3 We bought the kids toys. _____

4 Jack used my cell phone. _____

5 He bought me a hamburger. _____

6 I slept for twelve hours last night. _____

7 Grace read the notice carefully. _____

8 A famous singer lived in this house. _____

B

보기에서 알맞은 말을 골라 문장을 완성하시오. (과거형으로 쓸 것)

[0-3]

보기	come	~~sleep~~	happen	jump

0 I _____slept_____ all day long.

1 The cat _____ very high.

2 Nate _____ from Spain.

3 The accident _____ suddenly.

[4-7]

보기	drink	kick	know	meet

4 He _____ a cup of cocoa.

5 I _____ Fred last Sunday.

6 David _____ the soccer ball.

7 They _____ my email address.

C ( ) 안에 주어진 말을 바르게 배열하여 문장을 완성하시오.

0 My neighbor _____gave me this table_____. (this table, me, gave)

1 My tutor _____. (me, Chinese, teaches)

2 Justin _____. (us, gave, these tickets)

3 She didn't _____. (us, the truth, tell)

4 He _____ yesterday. (me, an umbrella, lent)

5 Mom _____. (made, a chocolate cake, us)

6 Tom often _____. (buys, lunch, me)

7 Jessica _____. (her room, me, showed)

8 I _____. (my friends, sent, photos)

WRITING PRACTICE

( ) 안의 말을 이용하여 우리말을 영어로 옮기시오.

0 그녀는 매일 밤 일기를 쓴다. (keep, a diary)

→ She _____keeps a diary_____ every night.

1 그 군인은 안전하게 도착했다. (arrive, safely)

→ The soldier _____.

2 Janet은 팝송을 좋아한다. (like, pop songs)

→ Janet _____.

3 그들은 네 명의 아이가 있다. (have, children)

→ They _____.

4 엄마는 내게 닭고기 수프를 만들어주셨다. (make, chicken soup)

→ Mom _____.

5 여행 가이드는 우리에게 지도를 보여주었다. (show, the map)

→ The tour guide _____.

UNIT 02

동사의 종류 2

A

( ) 안에서 알맞은 말을 고르시오.

0 You look (sad, sadly).

1 We (feel, smell) hungry.

2 This bread smells (good, well).

3 Your idea (tastes, sounds) great.

4 Your shirt (looks, sounds) tight on you.

5 His gift made me (happy, happily).

6 Nick looked (sickness, sick) this morning.

7 We found the exam (hard, hardly).

8 Her sandwiches tasted (strange, strangely).

9 His name is William. We (make, call) him Bill.

10 The air conditioner (keeps, finds) the rooms cool.

B

보기에서 알맞은 말을 골라 문장을 완성하시오. (단, 한 번씩만 쓸 것)

[0-3]

보기	are	became	look	sounded

0 Brenda _____became_____ a lawyer.

1 His voice _____ beautiful.

2 These puzzles _____ easy.

3 Those boys _____ basketball players.

[4-7]

보기	feels	looked	smells	tasted

4 The soup _____ salty.

5 The perfume _____ sweet.

6 This teddy bear _____ soft.

7 Chris _____ angry yesterday.

C ( ) 안에 주어진 말을 바르게 배열하여 문장을 완성하시오.

0 The game _____made us rivals_____. (rivals, made, us)

1 People _____. (called, a hero, her)

2 His letter _____. (me, made, angry)

3 Coffee _____. (me, keeps, awake)

4 The ice _____. (kept, fresh, the fish)

5 We always _____. (him, Captain Park, call)

6 I _____. (the internet, found, slow)

7 The war _____. (the countries, made, poor)

8 My sister never _____. (clean, her room, keeps)

WRITING PRACTICE

( ) 안의 말을 이용하여 우리말을 영어로 옮기시오.

0 밤에 날씨가 추워졌다. (cold)
→ It _____became cold_____ at night.

1 Mary는 긴장감을 느꼈다. (nervous)
→ Mary _____.

2 그 아기는 건강해 보인다. (healthy)
→ The baby _____.

3 Jack의 이야기는 지루하게 들렸다. (boring)
→ Jack's story _____.

4 그의 사업은 그를 부유하게 만들었다. (make, rich)
→ His business _____.

5 나는 그 침대가 편안하다는 것을 알게 되었다. (find, the bed, comfortable)
→ I _____.

REVIEW TEST

[1-3] 빈칸에 들어갈 말로 알맞지 <u>않은</u> 것을 고르시오.

1
> This pizza _____ wonderful.

① is   ② looks   ③ smells
④ watches   ⑤ tastes

2
> He is _____.

① young   ② smart
③ quietly   ④ a scientist
⑤ a good student

3
> Amy sends _____ Christmas cards every year.

① me   ② he   ③ them
④ Susan   ⑤ her mom

서술형

[4-6] 보기에서 알맞은 말을 골라 문장을 완성하시오.
(과거형으로 쓸 것)

보기	hear look show

4
John _____ serious this morning.

5
I _____ the news from Sue.

6
My dad _____ me some pictures yesterday.

빈출

[7-8] 다음 중 보기와 문장의 형태가 같은 것을 고르시오.

7

보기	Sam ran fast.

① That sounds perfect.
② I found the idea creative.
③ The sun rises in the east.
④ They have a nice house.
⑤ Danny told me his secret.

8

보기	Karen bought me ice cream.

① We laughed a lot.
② I have two brothers.
③ The milk tasted sour.
④ Minsu taught James taekwondo.
⑤ Mom always keeps this door open.

빈출

[9-10] 밑줄 친 부분의 쓰임이 나머지 넷과 <u>다른</u> 것을 고르시오.

9
① She <u>told</u> us a joke.
② Tom <u>told</u> a lie again.
③ He <u>told</u> me his dream.
④ We <u>told</u> Jane our address.
⑤ Our teacher <u>told</u> us her love story.

10 ① Sujin <u>made</u> us tea.

② Dad <u>made</u> me this chair.

③ She <u>made</u> her daughter gloves.

④ The movie <u>made</u> me sad.

⑤ Andrew <u>made</u> us breakfast.

14 내 유니폼은 경기 중에 더러워졌다.
(become, dirty)

→ My uniform _____
during the game.

[11-12] 다음 중 밑줄 친 부분이 <u>잘못된</u> 것을 고르시오.

11 ① I <u>opened the box</u>.

② David <u>studies alone</u>.

③ He <u>felt thirsty</u> last night.

④ The boy <u>likes dogs</u> very much.

⑤ Steve <u>gave we this present</u>.

15 Tony는 어제 그의 집을 페인트칠했다.
(paint, his house)

→ Tony _____
yesterday.

12 ① We <u>are classmates</u>.

② His new hair <u>looks nicely</u>.

③ That man <u>wrote this novel</u>.

④ She <u>made her father cookies</u>.

⑤ They <u>bought the child a new bike</u>.

서술형

[16-17] 우리말과 일치하도록 ( ) 안에 주어진 말을 바르게 배열하시오.

16 은행은 사람들에게 돈을 빌려준다.
(money, people, lend)

→ Banks _____.

서술형

[13-15] 우리말과 일치하도록 ( ) 안의 말을 이용하여 문장을 완성하시오.

13 Mike는 항상 미소를 짓는다. (smile)

→ Mike always _____.

17 이 핸드크림은 내 손을 부드럽게 유지해준다.
(keeps, soft, my hands)

→ This hand cream _____

_____.

UNIT 01

can, may

A

( ) 안에서 알맞은 말을 고르시오.

0　Rick can (play, plays) tennis well.

1　She (can, cans) dance very well.

2　Can (order I, I order) chicken?

3　Betty can (cook, cooked) pasta.

4　(May, Can) you solve this math problem?

5　Jennifer (can read, read can) Korean.

6　May (I ask, ask I) you a question?

7　You (leave may, may leave) the office now.

8　Penguins (can fly not, cannot fly) in the sky.

9　I can't (find, found) my car.

10　My brother (can't, not can) watch horror movies.

B

can 또는 can't와 ( ) 안의 말을 이용하여 문장을 완성하시오.

0　I have a lot of homework.

　　I _____can't go_____ to bed early tonight. (go)

1　This movie is for all ages.

　　Kids _____ the movie. (watch)

2　I bought new glasses.

　　I _____ things clearly now. (see)

3　We missed the train.

　　We _____ to your house on time. (get)

4　Ellen's mother is a baker.

　　She _____ delicious muffins. (bake)

5　My father is busy today.

　　He _____ dinner at home tonight. (have)

C 보기에서 알맞은 말을 골라 (   ) 안의 말과 함께 써서 대화를 완성하시오. (단, 한 번씩만 쓸 것)

보기	~~borrow~~	answer	see	speak	sit

0 A: _____ Can I borrow _____ some money? (can)

B: Sorry, I don't have any.

1 A: _____ to John? (may)

B: Sorry, he's not at home right now.

2 A: _____ next to you? (can)

B: Sure.

3 A: _____ your passport? (may)

B: Sure. Here you are.

4 A: _____ the phone? (may)

B: Of course.

WRITING PRACTICE

(   ) 안의 말을 이용하여 우리말을 영어로 옮기시오.

0 너는 네 친구들을 데리고 와도 좋다. (bring)

→ You _____ can bring _____ your friends.

1 당신의 사진들을 제 블로그에 올려도 될까요? (post)

→ _____ your pictures on my blog?

2 나는 지난밤에 그녀의 목소리를 들을 수 있었다. (hear)

→ I _____ her voice last night.

3 Emily는 매운 음식을 먹을 수 있니? (eat)

→ _____ spicy food?

4 제가 당신에게 커피 한 잔을 사드려도 될까요? (buy)

→ _____ you a cup of coffee?

5 여러분은 이제 건물에 들어오셔도 좋습니다. (enter)

→ You _____ the building now.

**UNIT
02**

must, have to

A

( ) 안에서 알맞은 말을 고르시오.

0 You must (are, be) polite to people.

1 Sam (have, has) to go home now.

2 I (have, must) to get a new shirt.

3 You must (did, do) your best.

4 We (must not, doesn't have to) waste water.

5 She (don't, doesn't) have to lose weight.

6 I'm fine. You (must not, don't have to) help me.

7 Nick (has, have) to study for the test tonight.

8 We (follow must, must follow) the traffic rules.

9 You must (write not, not write) on the library books.

10 Anna and her sister (has to, have to) do the dishes.

B

must 또는 must not과 ( ) 안의 말을 이용하여 문장을 완성하시오.

In the classroom ...

0 You _____ must come _____ to class on time. (come)

1 You _____. (run)

2 You _____ your teacher. (listen to)

3 You _____ your homework before class. (finish)

4 You _____ during class. (sleep)

5 You _____ your classroom clean. (keep)

6 You _____ bad words to your classmates. (say)

7 You _____ your cell phone during class. (use)

C 보기에서 알맞은 말을 골라 have/has to 또는 don't/doesn't have to와 함께 써서 문장을 완성하시오.

[0-2]

보기	~~clean~~	fix	tell

0 Your room is dirty. You _____ have to clean _____ it.

1 I already heard the news. You _____ me about it.

2 Rick broke his brother's bike. He _____ it.

[3-5]

보기	get up	work	take

3 He is on vacation now. He _____.

4 You _____ a taxi to the museum. You can walk there.

5 Susan's train leaves at 5:30 a.m. She _____ early.

WRITING PRACTICE

( ) 안의 말을 이용하여 우리말을 영어로 옮기시오.

0 너희들은 이 책을 읽어야 한다. (read)

→ You _____ must read _____ this book.

1 우리는 Amy를 기다릴 필요가 없다. (wait)

→ We _____ for Amy.

2 그는 그의 남동생을 돌봐야 한다. (take care of)

→ He _____ his little brother.

3 Sarah는 그에게 전화할 필요가 없다. (call)

→ Sarah _____ him.

4 나는 방과 후에 의사에게 진찰을 받아야 한다. (see)

→ I _____ a doctor after school.

5 너는 이 동물들에게 먹이를 줘서는 안 된다. (give)

→ You _____ food to these animals.

REVIEW TEST

[1-3] 빈칸에 들어갈 알맞은 말을 고르시오.

1

> _____ I have some water?

① Be   ② Am   ③ Is
④ Does   ⑤ Can

2

> The baby is one month old. He _____ walk.

① can   ② may   ③ must
④ cannot   ⑤ has to

3

> You _____ play with that knife. It's dangerous.

① can   ② must   ③ have to
④ must not   ⑤ don't have to

[4-5] 빈칸에 들어갈 말이 바르게 짝지어진 것을 고르시오.

4

> • Mike lost his key. He ___(A)___ find it.
> • You didn't finish your meal! You ___(B)___ have dessert now.

	(A)		(B)
①	have to	······	may
②	have to	······	can
③	have to	······	can't
④	has to	······	may
⑤	has to	······	can't

5

> • Brian ___(A)___ take the plane. He has a ticket for it.
> • You ___(B)___ bring your lunch. I'll bring one for you.

	(A)		(B)
①	can	······	have to
②	can	······	don't have to
③	can't	······	may
④	can't	······	have to
⑤	can't	······	don't have to

서술형

[6-8] 보기에서 알맞은 말을 골라 대화를 완성하시오. (필요하면 형태를 바꿀 것)

보기	can	have to	must not

6

> A: _____ you carry these books for me?
> B: Sure.

7

> A: You _____ play the piano at night. It's too loud.
> B: Oh, I'm sorry.

8

> A: Does Paul have any plans for the weekend?
> B: Yes, he _____ visit his grandparents.

[9-10] 다음 중 밑줄 친 부분이 잘못된 것을 고르시오.

9
① We <u>can help</u> you.
② My sister <u>can counts</u> to ten.
③ <u>May I ask</u> your phone number?
④ We <u>don't have to buy</u> the tickets.
⑤ You <u>must wear</u> a suit to the wedding.

10
① <u>Can I eat</u> the snacks?
② We <u>could meet</u> last night.
③ They <u>must not go</u> outside.
④ You <u>may search</u> on the internet.
⑤ Nate <u>has to not follow</u> the rules.

빈출

[11-12] 다음 우리말을 영어로 바르게 옮긴 것을 고르시오.

11 우리는 비싼 선물들을 살 필요가 없다.

① We cannot buy expensive gifts.
② We may not buy expensive gifts.
③ We must not buy expensive gifts.
④ We have to buy expensive gifts.
⑤ We don't have to buy expensive gifts.

12 너는 여기에 일주일간 머물러도 좋다.

① You may stay here for a week.
② You can't stay here for a week.
③ You must stay here for a week.
④ You have to stay here for a week.
⑤ You don't have to stay here for a week.

서술형

13 대화가 성립하도록 ( ) 안에서 알맞은 말을 고르시오.

A: The exam is over! We ⓐ (have to, don't have to) study today.
B: Yes, we ⓑ (can, can't) go out and play.

ⓐ _____ ⓑ _____

서술형

[14-17] 우리말과 일치하도록 ( ) 안의 말을 이용하여 문장을 완성하시오.

14 제가 화장실을 사용해도 될까요? (use)

→ _____ your bathroom?

15 Jake는 팝송을 잘 부를 수 있다. (sing)

→ Jake _____ pop songs well.

16 그녀는 오늘 숙제를 할 필요가 없다. (do)

→ She _____ her homework today.

17 그는 그의 자전거 헬멧을 써야 한다. (wear)

→ He _____ his bike helmet.

UNIT 01

일반동사의 현재진행형 1

A 주어진 동사의 동사원형-ing형을 쓰시오.

0 do → doing

1 eat → _____

2 cut → _____

3 play → _____

4 draw → _____

5 ride → _____

6 sell → _____

7 change → _____

8 look → _____

9 make → _____

10 get → _____

11 swim → _____

12 move → _____

B ( ) 안의 말을 이용하여 현재진행형 긍정문을 완성하시오.

0 The old man _____is carrying_____ a box. (carry)

1 It _____ outside. (rain)

2 I _____ to the bank. (go)

3 Dad _____ on the sofa. (lie)

4 Brian _____ in India. (travel)

5 He _____ at the mall. (shop)

6 The children _____ a song. (sing)

7 Fred and Julie _____ behind me. (sit)

8 We _____ a big event. (plan)

9 Sumi _____ her teacher a question. (ask)

10 They _____ their bags on the table. (put)

C 보기에서 알맞은 말을 골라 적절한 형태로 바꾸어 현재진행형 긍정문을 완성하시오.

[0-3]

보기	help	run	tie	~~write~~

0 Mr. Brown _____is writing_____ a new novel.

1 I _____ a ribbon.

2 Ryan _____ in the park.

3 They _____ the little children.

[4-7]

보기	cross	listen	shout	choose

4 I _____ a present.

5 Someone _____ loudly outside.

6 A boy _____ the street.

7 People _____ to music at a concert.

WRITING PRACTICE

( ) 안의 말을 이용하여 우리말을 영어로 옮기시오.

0 아빠는 식탁을 고치고 계신다. (fix)

→ Dad _____is fixing_____ the table.

1 나는 숲속에서 걷고 있다. (walk)

→ I _____ in the forest.

2 Sally는 거울을 들여다보고 있다. (look)

→ Sally _____ in the mirror.

3 내 남동생들은 옷장 안에 숨어 있다. (hide)

→ My brothers _____ in the closet.

4 그 소녀들은 카메라를 향해 미소 짓고 있다. (smile)

→ The girls _____ at the camera.

5 Ken은 카페에서 커피를 주문하고 있다. (order)

→ Ken _____ coffee at the café.

UNIT 02

일반동사의 현재진행형 2

A ( ) 안에서 알맞은 말을 고르시오.

0 I'm (studying not, ~~not studying~~).

1 Is she (play, playing) the flute?

2 Tom (isn't, aren't) laughing.

3 We are not (visit, visiting) Rome.

4 Am (walking I, I walking) too fast?

5 Is Mom (baking, bakes) cookies?

6 Are they (write, writing) a report?

7 (Is, Does) he buying fruit in the store?

8 (Is, Are) your cousins staying at your house?

9 Steve (is not, not is) brushing his teeth.

10 My brother (is, does) not wearing a coat.

B ( ) 안의 말을 이용하여 현재진행형 부정문을 완성하시오.

0 He _____isn't playing_____ tennis now. (play)
He is cleaning the court.

1 It _____ outside. (snow)
It is sunny.

2 They _____ for you. (wait)
They left an hour ago.

3 Bob _____ at the door. (stand)
He is sitting on the floor.

4 She _____ in the bed. (sleep)
She is just lying on it.

5 Jake _____ his emails now. (check)
He is playing computer games.

6 I _____ a text message. (send)
I am calling my friend.

C 보기에서 알맞은 말을 골라 적절한 형태로 바꾸어 현재진행형 대화를 완성하시오. (단, 한 번씩만 쓸 것)

보기	shake	~~print~~	jog	wash	write

0 A: _____Are_____ you _____printing_____ the report?

B: Yes, I am.

1 A: _____ you _____ on your blog?

B: No, I'm reading the news.

2 A: _____ she _____ in the park?

B: No, she's taking a rest.

3 A: _____ your dad _____ his car?

B: No, he washed it this morning.

4 A: _____ the men _____ hands?

B: Yes, they are.

WRITING PRACTICE

( ) 안의 말을 이용하여 우리말을 영어로 옮기시오.

0 그녀는 울고 있지 않다. (cry)

→ She _____isn't crying_____ .

1 나는 Fred와 이야기하고 있지 않다. (talk)

→ I _____ with Fred.

2 그 비행기는 아주 높이 날고 있지 않다. (fly)

→ The plane _____ very high.

3 우리는 지금 가방을 싸고 있지 않다. (pack)

→ We _____ our bags now.

4 그들은 산을 오르고 있니? (climb)

→ _____ the mountain?

5 너는 그림을 그리고 있니? (draw)

→ _____ a picture?

UNIT 03

일반동사의 미래형 1

A ( ) 안에서 알맞은 말을 고르시오.

0 He will ((like), likes) the idea.

1 They will (be, are) quiet in class.

2 (I, I'm) going to give him this book.

3 Ken will (meet, be meet) Mary tomorrow.

4 The store is going (open, to open) next week.

5 We will (take, to take) a bus to the airport.

6 The boy is going to (be, is) a great artist.

7 We are going (turn on, to turn on) the lights.

8 Mary (is, be) going to have fruit salad for lunch.

9 She (going, is going) to travel to Germany next year.

10 Robin and I (am, are) going to eat at the Indian restaurant.

B 보기에서 알맞은 말을 골라 will과 함께 써서 문장을 완성하시오. (긍정문으로 쓸 것)

[0-3]

보기	be	help	lend	~~visit~~

0 We _____ will visit _____ our aunt tomorrow.

1 He _____ you his textbook.

2 I _____ you with your homework.

3 Lisa _____ a good doctor in the future.

[4-7]

보기	buy	pass	plant	start

4 I _____ you a nice gift.

5 She _____ a new job.

6 You _____ the final exam easily.

7 Harry _____ a cherry tree in his garden.

C   be going to와 ( ) 안의 말을 이용하여 문장을 완성하시오. (긍정문으로 쓸 것)

0   I _____am going to keep_____ a diary. (keep)

1   I _____ her tomorrow. (call)

2   He _____ for dinner. (pay)

3   Amy _____ there by subway. (go)

4   We _____ pasta for lunch. (eat)

5   The party _____ at 6:00 p.m. (begin)

6   They _____ a new house. (build)

7   Ron _____ an action movie. (watch)

8   Jiho and I _____ every day. (exercise)

9   She _____ you a birthday cake. (make)

10   My parents _____ soon. (arrive)

WRITING PRACTICE

( ) 안의 말을 이용하여 우리말을 영어로 옮기시오.

0   그가 너에게 그것을 설명해 줄 것이다. (will, explain)

→ He _____will explain_____ it to you.

1   나는 인터넷을 검색해 볼 것이다. (be going to, search)

→ I _____ the internet.

2   그들은 곧 한국을 떠날 것이다. (be going to, leave)

→ They _____ Korea soon.

3   나는 그의 이름을 영원히 기억할 것이다. (will, remember)

→ I _____ his name forever.

4   Sarah는 새 스마트폰을 위해 돈을 모을 것이다. (be going to, save)

→ Sarah _____ money for a new smartphone.

5   우리 형은 내년에 고등학생이 될 것이다. (will, be)

→ My brother _____ a high school student next year.

UNIT
04

일반동사의 미래형 2

A

( ) 안에서 알맞은 말을 고르시오.

0 Rick (isn't, ⓦon't) forgive her.

1 (Are, Will) you dance with him?

2 Is Nora (go, going) to learn Chinese?

3 Will Emily (be, is) late for the meeting?

4 They (will not, not will) be angry at you.

5 Will she (study, studies) with you today?

6 Ted (isn't, aren't) going to buy a new bike.

7 Will (come they, they come) here by taxi?

8 (Be, Are) we going to have dinner at home?

9 I'm (not going, going not) to make the same mistake again.

10 My friends (is not, are not) going to visit me tomorrow.

B

( ) 안의 말을 이용하여 미래형 부정문을 완성하시오.

0 It _____won't be_____ cold this afternoon. (will, be)

1 She _____ the truth. (will, tell)

2 I _____ sorry to Ben. (will, say)

3 I _____ for him. (be going to, wait)

4 You _____ this time. (will, fail)

5 Brian _____ dessert. (be going to, have)

6 She _____ the train. (be going to, take)

7 They _____ their dog tonight. (will, wash)

8 We _____ sunglasses. (be going to, wear)

9 Mia and Sam _____ to the gym. (be going to, go)

10 My little sister _____ her pictures to us.
(be going to, show)

C 보기에서 알맞은 말을 골라 미래형 의문문을 완성하시오. (단, 한 번씩만 쓸 것)

[0-3] (will을 이용할 것)

보기	come	like	~~open~~	score

0 _____Will_____ you _____open_____ the box later?

1 _____ he _____ this present?

2 _____ she _____ a goal?

3 _____ Ted and Jane _____ to Korea this Saturday?

[4-7] (be going to를 이용할 것)

보기	read	watch	have	leave

4 _____ they _____ this novel?

5 _____ she _____ for Paris tonight?

6 _____ you _____ a hamburger for lunch?

7 _____ we _____ a movie this Friday?

WRITING PRACTICE

(   ) 안의 말을 이용하여 우리말을 영어로 옮기시오.

0 너는 라디오를 들을 거니? (will, listen)

→ _____Will you listen_____ to the radio?

1 Suzy는 오늘 너에게 전화하지 않을 것이다. (will, call)

→ Suzy _____ you today.

2 너는 낮잠을 잘 거니? (be going to, take)

→ _____ a nap?

3 그는 대회에서 이길까? (will, win)

→ _____ the contest?

4 나는 Nancy와 함께 여행하지 않을 것이다. (be going to, travel)

→ I _____ with Nancy.

5 진호는 오늘 밤에 태권도를 연습하지 않을 것이다. (will, practice)

→ Jinho _____ taekwondo tonight.

[1-2] 다음 중 동사원형-ing형이 잘못 연결된 것을 고르시오.

1 ① sit – sitting ② try – trying
③ tie – tying ④ call – calling
⑤ take – takeing

2 ① say – saying ② wait – waiting
③ sleep – sleeping ④ swim – swiming
⑤ wash – washing

3 빈칸에 들어갈 말로 알맞지 <u>않은</u> 것은?

Helena _____ invite Tommy tomorrow.

① will ② won't
③ is going to ④ isn't going to
⑤ are going to

[4-5] 빈칸에 들어갈 말이 바르게 짝지어진 것을 고르시오.

4
• ___(A)___ you going to take the yoga classes?
• ___(B)___ you have some tea?

	(A)		(B)
①	Are	……	Are
②	Are	……	Will
③	Be	……	Will
④	Will	……	Are
⑤	Will	……	Do

5
• I am ___(A)___ school.
• Sam ___(B)___ sleeping now. He is talking on the phone.

	(A)		(B)
①	go to	……	is
②	going to	……	is
③	going to	……	is not
④	going to go to	……	does
⑤	going to go to	……	does not

[6-7] 빈칸에 알맞은 말을 써서 대화를 완성하시오.

6
A: _____ _____ meet him on Saturday?
B: No, I won't. I'll meet him on Sunday.

7
A: Are Jim and Ron playing computer games?
B: Yes, _____ _____.

8 문장이 성립하도록 ( ) 안에서 알맞은 말을 고르시오.

The children ⓐ (aren't, don't) playing in the kitchen. They ⓑ (will, are) making a pie!

ⓐ _____ ⓑ _____

[9-10] 다음 중 밑줄 친 부분이 **잘못된** 것을 고르시오.

9 ① I <u>am thinking</u> about Jerry.
② They <u>are speak</u> English.
③ Mom <u>is not driving</u> now.
④ Is Jane <u>locking</u> the door?
⑤ He <u>is buying</u> some clothes.

10 ① <u>Is she going to call</u> you?
② The TV show <u>will start</u> soon.
③ I <u>am going to wash</u> my shirt.
④ <u>Will Susan like</u> these flowers?
⑤ <u>Do they are going to say</u> sorry to her?

11 다음 우리말을 영어로 바르게 옮긴 것은?

> 그는 내년에 LA에 없을 것이다.

① He is going to be in LA next year.
② He not going to be in LA next year.
③ He is going not to be in LA next year.
④ He is not going to be in LA next year.
⑤ He is not going to is in LA next year.

서술형

[12-14] 우리말과 일치하도록 ( ) 안의 말을 이용하여 문장을 완성하시오.

12 그녀는 패션 잡지를 읽고 있지 않다. (read)

→ She _____ _____ a fashion magazine.

13 오늘 오후에 눈이 올 것이다. (snow)

→ It _____ _____
_____ _____ this
afternoon.

14 너는 John을 위해 수프를 만들어 줄 거니? (make)

→ _____ _____
_____ soup for John?

서술형

[15-17] 우리말과 일치하도록 ( ) 안에 주어진 말을 바르게 배열하시오.

15 그들은 휴일을 기다리고 있니?
(are, waiting, they)

→ _____
for the holidays?

16 그녀는 영화관에 가지 않을 거야.
(will, go, she, not)

→ _____
to the theater.

17 너는 네 자전거를 팔 거니?
(going to, are, you, sell)

→ _____
your bike?

UNIT 01 비교급

A 주어진 단어의 비교급을 쓰시오.

0	old	→	_____older_____
1	wise	→	_____
2	long	→	_____
3	happy	→	_____
4	fat	→	_____
5	heavy	→	_____
6	warm	→	_____
7	thin	→	_____
8	famous	→	_____
9	clean	→	_____
10	little	→	_____
11	nice	→	_____
12	beautiful	→	_____

B ( ) 안에서 알맞은 말을 고르시오.

0 Peter runs (fast, (faster)) than me.

1 He eats (much, more) than his father.

2 The living room is (large, larger) than the bedroom.

3 My grades are (worse, badder) than yours.

4 Today is (hotter, more hot) than yesterday.

5 This street is (noisy, noisier) than Main Street.

6 My cat is (very, much) cuter than Steve's.

7 Sally's cell phone is (smaller, more small) than mine.

8 Gold is (expensive, more expensive) than silver.

9 The math exam was (easier, more easier) than the history exam.

10 These pants are (comfortabler, more comfortable) than the skirt.

C ( ) 안의 말을 이용하여 비교급 문장을 완성하시오.

0 Her new book is _____shorter than_____ the last one. (short)

1 My sister is _____ my brother. (smart)

2 Scissors are _____ knives. (safe)

3 I got up _____ my parents. (early)

4 You look _____ yesterday. (healthy)

5 They sang _____ us. (well)

6 This pool is _____ the kids' pool. (deep)

7 The Tokyo Tower is _____ the Seoul N Tower. (tall)

8 This novel is _____ that comic book. (funny)

9 Health is _____ money. (important)

10 This cake is _____ those cookies. (delicious)

WRITING PRACTICE

( ) 안의 말을 이용하여 우리말을 영어로 옮기시오.

0 이 셔츠는 저 티셔츠보다 더 꽉 낀다. (tight)

→ This shirt is _____tighter than_____ that T-shirt.

1 Mary는 그녀의 언니보다 더 게으르다. (lazy)

→ Mary is _____ her sister.

2 Tom은 나보다 더 높이 점프했다. (high)

→ Tom jumped _____ me.

3 그녀는 프랑스어를 나보다 더 빨리 배웠다. (quickly)

→ She learned French _____ me.

4 우리 팀이 너희 팀보다 더 강하다. (strong)

→ My team is _____ your team.

5 우리는 그들보다 공항에 더 늦게 도착했다. (late)

→ We arrived at the airport _____ them.

CHAPTER 10 비교

최상급

주어진 단어의 최상급을 쓰시오.

0	bright	→	brightest
1	funny	→	_____
2	fast	→	_____
3	large	→	_____
4	big	→	_____
5	much	→	_____
6	wise	→	_____
7	little	→	_____
8	slow	→	_____
9	difficult	→	_____
10	wonderful	→	_____
11	hot	→	_____
12	heavy	→	_____

( ) 안에서 알맞은 말을 고르시오.

0 She is the (older, ⨀oldest) woman in England.

1 He is the (taller, tallest) man in the world.

2 This is (smallest, the smallest) bird at the zoo.

3 That was the (badest, worst) accident in history.

4 His score was the (higher, highest) in his class.

5 She is the (more, most) famous violinist in the world.

6 Tim is the (busiest, most busiest) doctor in the hospital.

7 He was the (greatest, most great) writer in the world.

8 It was (most, the most) amazing moment in my life.

9 Andrew is the (laziest, most lazy) person in his family.

10 This is the (more exciting, most exciting) story in the magazine.

C 보기에서 알맞은 말을 골라 적절한 형태로 바꾸어 최상급 문장을 완성하시오. (단, 한 번씩만 쓸 것)

보기	boring	~~cold~~	good	short	young

0 It was _____the coldest_____ day this month.
It was minus eighteen degrees.

1 I have two older sisters.
I'm _____ girl in my family.

2 She won a gold medal in the Olympics.
She is _____ player in the world.

3 It was _____ movie of the year.
I fell asleep during it.

4 There are twelve months in a year.
February is _____ month of the year.

WRITING PRACTICE

( ) 안의 말을 이용하여 우리말을 영어로 옮기시오.

0 이것은 한국에서 가장 긴 다리이다. (long, bridge)
→ This is ____the longest bridge____ in Korea.

1 그는 세계에서 가장 운이 좋은 사람이다. (lucky, man)
→ He is _____ in the world.

2 그녀는 우리 반에서 가장 똑똑한 학생이다. (smart, student)
→ She is _____ in our class.

3 이것은 그 가게에서 가장 싼 넥타이이다. (cheap, tie)
→ This is _____ in the shop.

4 Peter는 우리 학교에서 가장 친절한 소년이다. (kind, boy)
→ Peter is _____ in our school.

5 그것은 이 책에서 가장 중요한 장이다. (important, chapter)
→ It is _____ in this book.

REVIEW TEST

1 다음 중 형용사/부사의 비교급이 <u>잘못</u> 연결된 것은?

① nice – nicer ② little – less
③ hard – harder ④ heavy – heavier
⑤ expensive – expensiver

2 다음 중 형용사/부사의 최상급이 <u>잘못</u> 연결된 것은?

① old – oldest ② big – biggest
③ well – best ④ easy – easyest
⑤ large – largest

[3-5] 빈칸에 들어갈 알맞은 말을 고르시오.

3
> She drives more slowly _____ me.

① in ② of ③ to
④ than ⑤ much

4
> It was the _____ news in the newspaper.

① sader ② sadder ③ sadest
④ saddest ⑤ most sad

5
> Mike exercises _____ than Jake.

① many ② much ③ more
④ good ⑤ well

[6-8] ( ) 안의 말을 이용하여 비교급 문장을 완성하시오.

6
> This dictionary is _____ than that book. (thin)

7
> Chocolate ice cream is _____ than strawberry ice cream in this store. (popular)

8
> This restaurant is _____ than that one. (bad)

[9-10] 다음 중 밑줄 친 부분이 <u>잘못된</u> 것을 고르시오.

9 ① Busan is <u>warmer than</u> Seoul.
② My desk is <u>dirtier than</u> Lina's.
③ This pie is <u>sweeter than</u> that cake.
④ Taxis are <u>more faster than</u> buses.
⑤ Basketball is <u>more interesting than</u> soccer for me.

10 ① I'm <u>the smallest</u> person in my family.
② New York is <u>the largest</u> city in the US.
③ He is <u>the most young</u> boy on the team.
④ This is <u>the most exciting</u> game on the internet.
⑤ Today is <u>the busiest</u> day of the week.

[11-12] ( ) 안의 말을 이용하여 최상급 문장을 완성하시오.

11 This is _____ scene in this movie. (good)

12 August is _____ month of the year. (hot)

[13-14] 빈칸에 들어갈 말이 바르게 짝지어진 것을 고르시오.

13
- It is the ____(A)____ beautiful painting in the museum.
- This monitor is ____(B)____ wider than that one.

	(A)		(B)
①	more	......	very
②	more	......	much
③	most	......	very
④	most	......	most
⑤	most	......	much

14
- You must speak ____(A)____ than me.
- It was the ____(B)____ storm of the summer.

	(A)		(B)
①	loud	......	worse
②	loud	......	worst
③	louder	......	worse
④	louder	......	worst
⑤	louder	......	most bad

15 다음 우리말을 영어로 바르게 옮긴 것은?

> 우유는 탄산음료보다 더 건강에 좋다.

① Milk is healthy than soda.
② Milk is healthier than soda.
③ Milk is the healthier than soda.
④ Milk is healthiest than soda.
⑤ Milk is the healthiest than soda.

[16-18] 우리말과 일치하도록 ( ) 안의 말을 이용하여 문장을 완성하시오.

16 그는 나보다 중국어를 더 잘 말한다. (well)

→ He speaks Chinese _____ me.

17 엄마는 이모보다 더 젊어 보인다. (young)

→ My mom looks _____ my aunt.

18 킬리만자로산은 아프리카에서 가장 높은 산이다. (high, mountain)

→ Mt. Kilimanjaro is _____ in Africa.

UNIT 01

명사처럼 쓰는 to부정사

A 밑줄 친 부분이 문장에서 하는 역할을 보기에서 고르시오.

| 보기 | ⓐ 주어 | ⓑ 목적어 | ⓒ 보어 |

0 Daniel wants <u>to take</u> a walk.　　　　　　　　　　ⓑ

1 Her hobby is <u>to do</u> yoga.　　　　　　　　　　_____

2 It is important <u>to be</u> kind to people.　　　　_____

3 Amy needs <u>to eat</u> something.　　　　　　　_____

4 It is wrong <u>to hit</u> your friends.　　　　　　　_____

5 His job is <u>to clean</u> this building.　　　　　　_____

6 He hopes <u>to go</u> to this university.　　　　　_____

7 I like <u>to have</u> coffee after meals.　　　　　_____

8 My goal is <u>to save</u> $1,000 this year.　　　　_____

B 주어진 동사를 동사원형 또는 to부정사 중 적절한 형태로 써서 문장을 완성하시오.

0 stay　　a. We want ____to stay____ here tonight.

　　　　　b. Will you ____stay____ here tonight?

1 play　　a. It is exciting _____ basketball.

　　　　　b. Can you _____ basketball after school?

2 paint　a. Tom will _____ the walls at home tomorrow.

　　　　　b. My plan is _____ the walls at home tomorrow.

3 buy　　a. I need _____ a new cell phone.

　　　　　b. Will Amy _____ a new cell phone?

4 join　　a. Did you _____ the movie club?

　　　　　b. It will be interesting _____ the movie club.

5 finish　a. I always _____ my homework before dinner.

　　　　　b. He hopes _____ his homework before dinner.

C 보기에서 알맞은 말을 골라 적절한 형태로 바꾸어 문장을 완성하시오. (단, 한 번씩만 쓸 것)

[0-3]

보기	design	~~hear~~	leave	lose

0 We hope _____ to hear _____ from you soon.

1 Her job is _____ clothes.

2 It is difficult _____ weight.

3 They planned _____ home before 10:00 a.m.

[4-7]

보기	touch	become	build	see

4 I decided _____ a baker.

5 It is dangerous _____ fire.

6 Grace wants _____ that musical.

7 His dream is _____ a beautiful house.

WRITING PRACTICE

( ) 안의 말을 이용하여 우리말을 영어로 옮기시오.

0 그녀의 아파트를 찾는 것은 쉬웠다. (easy, find)

→ It was _____ easy to find _____ her apartment.

1 Lisa는 한국어를 배우기로 결심했다. (decide, learn)

→ Lisa _____ Korean.

2 약속을 지키는 것은 중요하다. (important, keep)

→ It is _____ your promises.

3 우리의 계획은 마이애미로 이사하는 것이다. (move)

→ Our plan is _____ to Miami.

4 우리는 휴식을 취하는 것에 동의했다. (agree, take)

→ We _____ a break.

5 Matt는 오후에 낮잠 자는 것을 좋아한다. (like, take)

→ Matt _____ a nap in the afternoon.

UNIT 02

형용사, 부사처럼 쓰는 to부정사

A 밑줄 친 to부정사가 꾸며주는 말에 동그라미 하시오.

0 It's time to say goodbye.

1 Martin has four bags to carry.

2 Kelly has a lot of emails to send.

3 We need some friends to help us.

4 He didn't have money to buy a new car.

5 Can you give me some water to drink?

6 I don't have a dress to wear to the party.

7 Brenda has some photos to show you.

8 Is there anything to watch on TV?

B 보기에서 알맞은 말을 골라 적절한 형태로 바꾸어 대화를 완성하시오. (단, 한 번씩만 쓸 것)

보기	~~buy~~	finish	hear	get	see	ride

0 A: Did you go to the store?

　　B: Yes. I went there _____to buy_____ some milk.

1 A: Did Susan like our gift?

　　B: Yes. She was happy _____ it.

2 A: Is your dad still at the office?

　　B: Yes. He has some work _____.

3 A: Does Fred know about the accident?

　　B: Yes. He was sad _____ about it.

4 A: Do you have plans for the weekend?

　　B: I will go to the park _____ my bike.

5 A: Can you meet me tomorrow?

　　B: Sorry, I don't have time _____ you tomorrow.

C to부정사를 이용하여 다음 두 문장을 연결하시오.

0 We were happy. We saw the film.

→ We were happy _____to see the film_____ .

1 He was sad. He left his hometown.

→ He was sad _____ .

2 Janet exercises hard. She wants to be healthy.

→ Janet exercises hard _____ .

3 I picked up the phone. I wanted to call Mary.

→ I picked up the phone _____ .

4 Ted was excited. He went to the party.

→ Ted was excited _____ .

5 Dave washed his hands. He wanted to cook dinner.

→ Dave washed his hands _____ .

WRITING PRACTICE

( ) 안의 말을 이용하여 우리말을 영어로 옮기시오.

0 너에게 해 줄 조언이 몇 개 있다. (some advice, give)

→ I have _____some advice to give_____ you.

1 너를 만나서 반갑다. (glad, meet)

→ I'm _____ you.

2 너는 읽을 책이 있니? (a book, read)

→ Do you have _____ ?

3 Edward는 외출하기 위해 신발을 신었다. (put on his shoes, go)

→ Edward _____ out.

4 그는 해외로 여행가기 위해 여권을 만들었다. (a passport, travel)

→ He got _____ abroad.

5 그녀는 시험에 대해 물어보기 위해 나에게 전화했다. (call me, ask)

→ She _____ about the test.

REVIEW TEST

[1–3] 빈칸에 들어갈 알맞은 말을 고르시오.

1

> It is difficult _____ a star.

① be ② is ③ to
④ to is ⑤ to be

2

> My plan is _____ a walk in the evening.

① to ② take ③ took
④ to take ⑤ to taking

3

> He needed _____ the car.

① to ② fix ③ fixed
④ to fix ⑤ to fixed

서술형

[4–5] 빈칸에 알맞은 말을 써서 문장을 완성하시오.

4

> My goal is _____ speak English like an American.

5

> _____ was amazing to see wild animals.

빈출

[6–8] 다음 중 보기의 밑줄 친 부분과 쓰임이 같은 것을 고르시오.

6

> 보기 Kevin was happy to win a prize.

① I was sad to see your tears.
② He decided to follow the rules.
③ We want to borrow the books.
④ It was fun to play board games.
⑤ I went to the kitchen to do the dishes.

7

> 보기 I hope to visit you soon.

① It is good to help others.
② I don't have homework to do today.
③ Mom was glad to get the flowers.
④ They planned to take the KTX.
⑤ Sam came to my house to play with me.

8

> 보기 I went to a bakery to buy a cake.

① Her job is to teach children.
② It is wrong to use bad words.
③ He wanted to say sorry to me.
④ Mom boiled water to make tea.
⑤ Do you have time to talk with me?

9 빈칸에 들어갈 말로 알맞지 않은 것은?

> We _____ to watch action movies.

① like ② planned ③ want
④ make ⑤ decided

10 다음 중 밑줄 친 부분이 잘못된 것은?

① It's time <u>to go</u> to bed.
② Sujin writes notes <u>to remember</u> things.
③ I have things <u>to do</u> at the bank.
④ We promised <u>to clean</u> our room.
⑤ She was glad <u>to saw</u> her parents.

11 다음 우리말을 영어로 바르게 옮긴 것은?

> 나는 너에게 보여줄 몇 개의 동영상이 있다.

① I have some videos show you.
② I have some videos to show you.
③ I have to show some videos you.
④ I have to show you some videos.
⑤ I have show some videos to you.

[12-14] to부정사를 이용하여 다음 두 문장을 연결하시오.

12 Amy became a doctor. She wanted to help sick people.

→ Amy became a doctor _____
_____ .

13 I called Jane. I wanted to invite her to my house.

→ I called Jane _____
_____ .

14 We were happy. We met Chris.

→ We were happy _____ .

[15-18] 우리말과 일치하도록 ( ) 안에 주어진 말을 바르게 배열하시오.

15 나는 TV를 보기 위해 소파에 앉았다.
(to, TV, watch)

→ I sat on the sofa _____ .

16 나는 너에게 들려줄 이야기가 있다.
(tell, a story, to, you)

→ I have _____ .

17 무언가를 배우는 것은 멋진 일이다.
(wonderful, to, things, learn)

→ It is _____ .

18 Nancy는 제시간에 올 필요가 있다.
(on time, to, needs, be)

→ Nancy _____ .

CHAPTER 12 접속사

and, but, or

A

( ) 안에서 알맞은 말을 고르시오.

0 Jessica is tall (and, or) thin.

1 I ate lunch, (but, or) I'm still hungry.

2 This sweater is nice (and, or) cheap.

3 You can ask me questions by email (but, or) phone.

4 There are roses (and, but) tulips in the vase.

5 Is your birthday on June 26 (and, or) July 26?

6 We ran fast, (and, but) we missed the train.

7 I like to drink cola, (but, or) it isn't good for my health.

8 You can go home now, (and, or) we can watch TV together.

B

( ) 안에서 알맞은 말을 골라 문장을 완성하시오.

0 (and, or)

a. Is this seat yours _____or_____ Mike's?

b. Sam _____and_____ I are in the same class.

1 (but, or)

a. I'll have chocolate _____ ice cream.

b. I don't know Harry, _____ Lily knows him.

2 (and, but)

a. Erica is my cousin, _____ she is sixteen years old.

b. I can swim in a pool, _____ I can't swim in the sea.

3 (but, or)

a. The movie was good, _____ it was too long.

b. We can go to the concert on Saturday _____ Sunday.

4 (and, or)

a. I have tests in English, math, _____ science tomorrow.

b. Do you want to take a walk, _____ will you stay at home?

C 보기에서 알맞은 말을 골라 문장을 완성하시오. (단, 한 번씩만 쓸 것)

보기	and	but	or

[0-2]

0 Is she Korean _____or_____ Japanese?

1 Jake lived in Chicago _____ LA.

2 I'm sorry, _____ I can't help you.

[3-5]

3 This suitcase is pretty _____ too heavy.

4 Julie sang a song, _____ Kate danced.

5 I can go to your house, _____ we can meet at school.

WRITING PRACTICE

( ) 안의 말을 이용하여 우리말을 영어로 옮기시오.

0 우리는 길에서 Lisa와 Ted를 봤다. (Lisa, Ted)

→ We saw _____Lisa and Ted_____ on the street.

1 우리 할아버지는 연세가 많으시지만 건강하시다. (old, healthy)

→ My grandfather is _____.

2 너는 차를 운전할 거니, 아니면 버스를 탈 거니? (take a bus)

→ Will you drive a car _____?

3 나는 낮잠을 잤고 엄마는 책을 읽으셨다. (my mom, read)

→ I took a nap, _____ a book.

4 나는 요리하는 것은 좋아하지만, 설거지하는 것은 좋아하지 않는다. (like)

→ I like to cook, _____ to wash the dishes.

5 너는 그의 전화번호나 이메일 주소를 아니? (phone number, email address)

→ Do you know his _____?

CHAPTER 12 접속사

when, before, after, because

A

( ) 안에서 알맞은 말을 고르시오.

0 You have to knock (before, after) you enter my room.

1 (Before, Because) I was busy, I couldn't meet him.

2 He will call you after he (comes, will come) back home.

3 Brian can't drive (after, because) he is only twelve years old.

4 You must wear a seat belt (when, after) you drive.

5 Laura brushed her teeth (when, after) she had breakfast.

6 We will visit this mall when it (opens, will open) next month.

7 (When, Before) the train suddenly stopped, we were surprised.

8 You need to set the time (after, because) you turn on the oven.

B

( ) 안에서 알맞은 말을 골라 문장을 완성하시오.

0 (when, because)

a. You have to be careful _____when_____ you use a knife.

b. I don't wear this shirt _____because_____ it's too small.

1 (when, after)

a. I took a shower _____ I did yoga.

b. Peter and I became friends _____ we were young.

2 (before, because)

a. Grace took a taxi _____ she was late.

b. _____ she went to France, she was in England.

3 (when, before)

a. _____ he has free time, he goes to the gym.

b. I bought a gift for Mary _____ I went to her birthday party.

4 (after, because)

a. Tourists like Jeju Island _____ it's very beautiful.

b. _____ we visit the museum, we have to write a report.

C ( ) 안의 말을 이용하여 다음 두 문장을 연결하시오.

0 She was hungry. She didn't eat lunch. (because)

→ She was hungry _____because she didn't eat lunch_____ .

1 I have to go home. It gets too dark. (before)

→ I have to go home _____ .

2 We turned on the TV. We were bored. (because)

→ We turned on the TV _____ .

3 There was no one at home. We came back. (when)

→ There was no one at home _____ .

4 Ted turned off the computer. He played the game. (after)

→ Ted turned off the computer _____ .

5 Mr. Brown was my teacher. I was in elementary school. (when)

→ Mr. Brown was my teacher _____ .

WRITING PRACTICE

( ) 안의 말을 이용하여 우리말을 영어로 옮기시오.

0 그녀는 버스에 있었을 때 지갑을 잃어버렸다. (be)

→ She lost her wallet _____when she was_____ on the bus.

1 나는 그의 뮤직비디오를 본 후에 팬이 되었다. (watch)

→ I became a fan _____ his music videos.

2 영화가 웃겼기 때문에 나는 많이 웃었다. (the movie, funny)

→ I laughed a lot _____ .

3 나는 알람이 울렸을 때 잠에서 깼다. (my alarm, ring)

→ I woke up _____ .

4 어제는 토요일이었기 때문에 아빠는 일하러 가지 않으셨다. (it, Saturday)

→ Dad didn't go to work _____ yesterday.

5 너는 집에 들어오기 전에 신발을 벗어야 한다. (come into)

→ You have to take off your shoes _____ the house.

REVIEW TEST

[1-2] 빈칸에 들어갈 알맞은 말을 고르시오.

1

| My brother _____ I go to the same school. |

① and   ② but   ③ or
④ when   ⑤ after

2

| I will go to the pool when school _____ over. |

① be   ② is   ③ was
④ were   ⑤ will be

서술형

[3-5] 보기에서 알맞은 말을 골라 문장을 완성하시오.

| 보기 | because   or   after |

3 Do you want chocolate cake _____ cheesecake?

4 _____ it rained, I saw a rainbow.

5 I can't see anything _____ it's too dark.

[6-7] 다음 중 밑줄 친 부분이 잘못된 것을 고르시오.

6 ① Do you have a pen or a pencil?
② This soup is delicious but salty.
③ He has a daughter but two sons.
④ I usually eat breakfast, but I didn't eat it today.
⑤ The weather was great, and we had a good time.

7 ① We missed him a lot after he left.
② I like these socks before they're warm.
③ He became thirsty after he ran for an hour.
④ She took these photos when she was in Europe.
⑤ I'm learning Spanish because I want to travel to Spain.

서술형

[8-9] 빈칸에 공통으로 들어갈 말을 쓰시오.

8
• I have some bread _____ fruit in my basket.
• I met Kevin, _____ we did our homework together.

9
• Amy got up late, _____ she arrived on time.
• I want to buy the cell phone, _____ it's too expensive.

빈출

[10-11] 빈칸에 들어갈 말이 바르게 짝지어진 것을 고르시오.

10
• Will you wear a skirt ____(A)____ jeans tomorrow?
• I didn't go to the library ____(B)____ I was sick.

	(A)		(B)
①	and	······	when
②	but	······	before
③	but	······	because
④	or	······	before
⑤	or	······	because

11
• You have to close the window ____(A)____ you leave.
• I want to be a doctor ____(B)____ I grow up.

	(A)		(B)
①	or	······	but
②	or	······	when
③	before	······	but
④	before	······	when
⑤	after	······	because

12 다음 우리말을 영어로 바르게 옮긴 것은?

나는 컴퓨터를 끄기 전에 파일을 저장했다.

① I turned off the computer before I saved the file.
② I turned off the computer because I saved the file.
③ I saved the file when I turned off the computer.
④ I saved the file after I turned off the computer.
⑤ I saved the file before I turned off the computer.

서술형   빈출

[13-16] 우리말과 일치하도록 (   ) 안의 말을 이용하여 문장을 완성하시오.

13 그는 부엌과 화장실을 청소했다.
(the kitchen, the bathroom)

→ He cleaned _____
_____.

14 네가 나에게 전화했을 때 나는 저녁을 먹고 있었다.
(call)

→ I was having dinner _____
me.

15 그는 극장에 들어가기 전에 좌석 번호를 확인했다.
(enter)

→ He checked his seat number _____
_____ the theater.

16 버스가 오지 않아서 나는 집에 걸어갔다.
(the bus, come)

→ I walked home _____
_____.

UNIT 01

who, what

A

( ) 안에서 알맞은 말을 고르시오.

0 (Who, ⟨What⟩) time is it?

1 (Who, Whom) made you dinner?

2 (Who, What) is this book?

3 (Who, What) are those boys?

4 (Who, Whose) bag is it?

5 (Whom, Whose) did you see?

6 (Who, Whose) solved the problem?

7 (Who, What) size is this sweater?

8 (Who, What) color is your cell phone?

9 (Who, Whom) is your older sister?

10 (What, Whose) did you write on the paper?

B

보기에서 알맞은 말을 골라 대화를 완성하시오.

보기	Who	Whose	What

0 A: _____Whose_____ wallet is this?

   B: It's mine.

1 A: _____ language do you speak?

   B: I speak Korean.

2 A: _____ helped you with your homework?

   B: John helped me.

3 A: _____ is the Wi-Fi password?

   B: It's 2204513.

4 A: _____ house is this?

   B: It's my uncle's house.

5 A: _____ does Joe like?

   B: He likes Susan.

C 빈칸에 알맞은 말을 써서 밑줄 친 부분을 묻는 의문문을 완성하시오.

0 Emily is in the classroom.

→ _____Who_____ is in the classroom?

1 I want a bike for my birthday.

→ _____ do you want for your birthday?

2 I called Jake yesterday.

→ _____ did you call yesterday?

3 My little brother broke the window.

→ _____ broke the window?

4 It is Mary's phone number.

→ _____ phone number is it?

5 She studies history at the university.

→ _____ does she study at the university?

WRITING PRACTICE

( ) 안의 말을 이용하여 우리말을 영어로 옮기시오.

0 이 상자 안에 무엇이 있니? (be)

→ _____What is_____ in this box?

1 누가 이 노래를 불렀니? (sing)

→ _____ this song?

2 이것은 무슨 꽃이니? (flower)

→ _____ is this?

3 너의 영어 선생님은 누구셨니? (be)

→ _____ your English teacher?

4 이것들은 누구의 신발이니? (shoes)

→ _____ are these?

5 너는 방학 동안에 무엇을 했니? (do)

→ _____ during the vacation?

A

when, where, why

( ) 안에서 알맞은 말을 고르시오.

0 A: (When, Where) is the supermarket?
    B: It's on Fifth Street.

1 A: (When, Where) did you meet him?
    B: Last Tuesday.

2 A: (Where, Why) do you like Erica?
    B: Because she is very kind.

3 A: (When, Where) is he from?
    B: He is from Brazil.

4 A: (When, Why) will you bring back my book?
    B: Tomorrow.

5 A: (When, Why) did you send me an email?
    B: Because I had some files to give you.

6 A: (Why, What time) does he go to the gym?
    B: He goes there at 7:30 p.m.

B

보기에서 알맞은 말을 골라 대화를 완성하시오.

보기	When	Where	Why

0 A: _____Where_____ is Colin?
    B: He is at the shopping mall.

1 A: _____ did you buy this coat?
    B: Last winter.

2 A: _____ are you so excited?
    B: Because I will go on a trip tomorrow.

3 A: _____ is her wedding?
    B: It's this Sunday.

4 A: _____ did the teacher call them?
    B: Because they had a fight.

5 A: _____ do you want to put this table?
    B: Next to the sofa.

C 빈칸에 알맞은 말을 써서 밑줄 친 부분을 묻는 의문문을 완성하시오.

0 Amy will go to Hawaii <u>next Monday</u>.

→ _____When_____ will Amy go to Hawaii?

1 The bus stop is <u>in front of the coffee shop</u>.

→ _____ is the bus stop?

2 The accident happened <u>last night</u>.

→ _____ did the accident happen?

3 Breakfast is important <u>because it gives you energy</u>.

→ _____ is breakfast important?

4 I lived <u>in Chicago</u> when I was young.

→ _____ did you live when you were young?

5 She cried this morning <u>because she hurt her foot</u>.

→ _____ did she cry this morning?

WRITING PRACTICE

( ) 안의 말을 이용하여 우리말을 영어로 옮기시오.

0 그녀는 왜 달걀을 싫어하니? (hate)

→ _____Why does she hate_____ eggs?

1 Peter는 언제 컴퓨터를 샀니? (buy)

→ _____ his computer?

2 너는 오늘 아침에 어디에 있었니? (be)

→ _____ this morning?

3 너는 몇 시에 잠자리에 드니? (time, go)

→ _____ to bed?

4 그들은 어제 어디서 점심을 먹었니? (have)

→ _____ lunch yesterday?

5 너는 왜 문을 열어 놓았니? (keep)

→ _____ the door open?

CHAPTER 13 의문문, 명령문, 감탄문

how

( ) 안에서 알맞은 말을 고르시오.

0 A: (What, (How)) was the new restaurant?
B: It was great.

1 A: (How long, How tall) is that tower?
B: It's two hundred meters tall.

2 A: (How long, How much) is that rope?
B: It's three meters long.

3 A: (How, How often) do you know Jennifer?
B: We were in the same class.

4 A: (How many, How much) money did you pay for that jacket?
B: Only $35.

5 A: (How many, How much) people came to the magic show?
B: There were three hundred people.

보기에서 알맞은 말을 골라 대화를 완성하시오.

보기	How old How often	How tall How many	How far How much

0 A: _____How old_____ is your grandmother?
B: She is eighty-five years old.

1 A: _____ is one ticket?
B: It's $10.

2 A: _____ is your father?
B: He is 178 cm tall.

3 A: _____ do you eat out?
B: We eat out every weekend.

4 A: _____ is the train station?
B: It's about five hundred meters from here.

5 A: _____ hours does Tom work every day?
B: He works eight hours a day.

C 빈칸에 알맞은 말을 써서 밑줄 친 부분을 묻는 의문문을 완성하시오.

0 They came home <u>by taxi</u>.

→ _____ How _____ did they come home?

1 My jeans were <u>$50</u>.

→ _____ were your jeans?

2 My parents are <u>fine</u>.

→ _____ are your parents?

3 I lived in Busan <u>for ten years</u>.

→ _____ did you live in Busan?

4 She opened the door <u>with this key</u>.

→ _____ did she open the door?

5 I meet my boyfriend <u>once a week</u>.

→ _____ do you meet your boyfriend?

WRITING PRACTICE

의문사를 이용하여 우리말을 영어로 옮기시오.

0 음식은 어땠니?

→ _____ How _____ was the food?

1 네 여행은 얼마나 길었니?

→ _____ was your trip?

2 저 배우는 몇 살이니?

→ _____ is that actor?

3 너는 얼마나 많은 펜을 가지고 있니?

→ _____ pens do you have?

4 너는 얼마나 자주 영화를 보러 가니?

→ _____ do you go to the movies?

5 너는 어떻게 Andrew와 친한 친구가 되었니?

→ _____ did you become close friends with Andrew?

UNIT 04

부가의문문

A

( ) 안에서 알맞은 말을 고르시오.

0 This soup is salty, (is, ⟨isn't⟩) it?

1 I did well in the race, (did, didn't) I?

2 Dad doesn't work on Saturdays, does (Dad, he)?

3 You can't eat spicy food, (can, can't) you?

4 They were wrong, (weren't, didn't) they?

5 Julie can drive well, (can't, couldn't) she?

6 They aren't at home now, (are, aren't) they?

7 He won't forgive me, (will, won't) he?

8 Fred wasn't happy about the news, (is, was) he?

9 We have an apple pie for dessert, (haven't, don't) we?

10 It was Susan's birthday last Sunday, wasn't (she, it)?

B

빈칸에 알맞은 말을 보기에서 골라 기호를 쓰시오.

보기	ⓐ is she	ⓑ aren't you	ⓒ wasn't it	ⓓ can he
	ⓔ will you	ⓕ do they	ⓖ didn't we	ⓗ won't they

0 She isn't a farmer, _____ⓐ_____?

1 They don't like cats, _____?

2 It was too cold yesterday, _____?

3 John can't come to class today, _____?

4 We had a great time in Rome, _____?

5 You won't fight with your brother, _____?

6 You are busy this week, _____?

7 Tom and Dave will join the band, _____?

C 빈칸에 알맞은 말을 써서 부가의문문을 완성하시오.

0 The babies are lovely, ____aren't they____?

1 You won't be late, _____?

2 He isn't a student, _____?

3 Brian talked too much, _____?

4 Susan speaks Japanese, _____?

5 The fish was not fresh, _____?

6 You were on TV last night, _____?

7 We can take the first train, _____?

8 They don't know you well, _____?

9 Alan and Mary can't eat meat, _____?

10 The library wasn't open yesterday, _____?

( ) 안의 말을 이용하여 우리말을 영어로 옮기시오.

0 Nancy는 부지런해, 그렇지 않니? (diligent)

→ Nancy ____is diligent____, ____isn't she____?

1 그 영화는 재미있었어, 그렇지 않니? (interesting)

→ The movie _____, _____?

2 그들은 함께 오지 않았어, 그렇지? (come)

→ They _____ together, _____?

3 James가 이 경기를 이길 거야, 그렇지 않니? (will, win)

→ James _____ this game, _____?

4 Mary는 옷 사는 데에 돈을 많이 써, 그렇지 않니? (spend)

→ Mary _____ a lot of money on clothes, _____?

5 우리는 계획을 변경할 수 없어, 그렇지? (can, change)

→ We _____ our plan, _____?

UNIT 05

명령문, 감탄문

A

( ) 안에서 알맞은 말을 고르시오.

0 (Turn, Turns) off the TV.

1 (Let's, Lets) open the door.

2 (Do, Be) nice to your friends.

3 How smart (is she, she is)!

4 (What, How) sad that story is!

5 (Let's don't, Let's not) talk about it.

6 (What, How) cute dolls these are!

7 (Don't, Doesn't) drive too fast.

8 (What, How) a wonderful song this is!

9 (Not, Do not) cross the street here. It's dangerous.

10 I want to eat something sweet. (Don't, Let's) buy some chocolate.

B

보기에서 알맞은 말을 골라 문장을 완성하시오.

[0-3]

보기	Stay	~~Close~~	Don't speak	Don't swim

0 ____Close____ the door. It's noisy.

1 _____ loudly in the library. It's rude.

2 _____ in the lake. The water is deep.

3 _____ in bed. You need to get some rest.

[4-7] (Let's를 이용할 것)

보기	go	order	take	not / sit

4 _____ a taxi. We're late.

5 _____ pizza for lunch.

6 _____ outside. The weather is lovely.

7 _____ on that bench. It looks dirty.

C 다음 문장을 (   ) 안의 말로 시작하는 감탄문으로 바꿔 쓰시오.

0 This mountain is very high. (how)

→ _____How high_____ this mountain is!

1 He is a very brave boy. (what)

→ _____ he is!

2 The subway moves so slowly. (how)

→ _____ the subway moves!

3 This museum is great. (how)

→ _____ this museum is!

4 You have very pretty eyes. (what)

→ _____ you have!

5 Your parents are so kind. (how)

→ _____ your parents are!

(   ) 안의 말을 이용하여 우리말을 영어로 옮기시오.

0 빨리 걷자. (walk)

→ _____Let's walk_____ fast.

1 좋은 학생이 되어라. (be)

→ _____ a good student.

2 이 시험은 정말 어렵구나! (difficult)

→ _____ this test is!

3 불을 켜자. (turn on)

→ _____ the lights.

4 이것은 정말 맛있는 샌드위치구나! (delicious, sandwich)

→ _____ this is!

5 밤 10시 이후에는 내게 전화하지 마. (call)

→ _____ after 10:00 p.m.

REVIEW TEST

[1-3] 빈칸에 들어갈 알맞은 말을 고르시오.

1

> A: _____ is the funniest boy in your class?
> B: It's Jason. He always tells us funny stories.

① Who ② What ③ When
④ Where ⑤ How

2

> This musical looks interesting. _____ watch it tonight.

① Be ② Don't ③ Let
④ Let's ⑤ Let's not

3

> _____ bright the moon is!

① When ② Where ③ Why
④ What ⑤ How

[6-7] 다음 중 밑줄 친 부분이 잘못된 것을 고르시오.

6
① <u>Listen</u> carefully.
② <u>Don't be</u> afraid.
③ <u>Let's buy</u> these cups.
④ <u>Let's think not</u> about it.
⑤ <u>Don't run</u> in the classroom.

7
① Amy is not friendly, <u>is she</u>?
② The room was not clean, <u>wasn't it</u>?
③ They are your cousins, <u>aren't they</u>?
④ We parked our cars here, <u>didn't we</u>?
⑤ He doesn't like fish, <u>does he</u>?

서술형

[8-9] 빈칸에 알맞은 말을 써서 부가의문문을 완성하시오.

8

> You are tired, _____?

9

> People didn't believe the story, _____?

서술형

[4-5] 빈칸에 알맞은 의문사를 써서 대화를 완성하시오.

4

> A: _____ does she do?
> B: She is a pilot.

5

> A: _____ did you go to bed late last night?
> B: Because I had a book to read.

100

10 다음 중 대화가 자연스럽지 <u>않은</u> 것은?

① A: How many apples do we have?
  B: We only have three.
② A: What time do you get up?
  B: At 7:00 a.m.
③ A: What did you do yesterday?
  B: I slept all day.
④ A: Where is the department store?
  B: It's on Main Street.
⑤ A: Who is that man?
  B: It is Mark's watch.

[11-12] 빈칸에 들어갈 말이 바르게 짝지어진 것을 고르시오.

11
> • _____(A)_____ an easy question it is!
> • _____(B)_____ sad. Everything will be fine.

	(A)		(B)
①	What	......	Be
②	What	......	Let's
③	What	......	Don't be
④	How	......	Be
⑤	How	......	Don't be

12
> • _____(A)_____ do you check your text messages?
> • _____(B)_____ will you invite to dinner?

	(A)		(B)
①	How old	......	Who
②	How tall	......	Who
③	How far	......	What
④	How often	......	Whom
⑤	How many	......	Whom

[13-15] 우리말과 일치하도록 ( ) 안의 말을 이용하여 문장을 완성하시오.

13 이 재킷은 얼마죠? (much)

→ _____ is this jacket?

14 버스 정류장을 찾아보자. (find)

→ _____ a bus stop.

15 이것은 누구의 모자니? (cap)

→ _____ is this?

[16-17] 우리말과 일치하도록 ( ) 안에 주어진 말을 바르게 배열하시오.

16 그것은 정말 똑똑한 로봇이구나!
(smart, it, a, is, what, robot)

→ _____!

17 경기는 몇 시에 시작하니?
(start, the game, what, does, time)

→ _____?

MEMO

MEMO

MEMO

GRAMMAR Inside

workbook

A 4-level grammar course
with abundant writing practice

Compact and concise English grammar
간결하고 정확한 문법 설명

Extensive practice in sentence writing
다양한 유형의 영어 문장 쓰기

Full preparation for middle school tests
내신 완벽 대비

+ Workbook with additional exercises
풍부한 양의 추가 문제

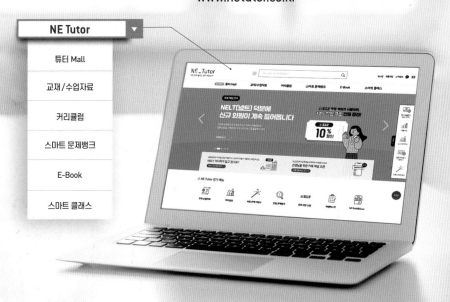

GRAMMAR Inside

STARTER

01 명사와 관사

UNIT 01 셀 수 있는 명사

PRACTICE p.11

STEP 1	1. O 2. X 3. O 4. X 5. O
STEP 2	1. roses 2. dishes 3. feet
	4. boys 5. leaves 6. cities
	7. women 8. sheep
STEP 3	1. a. potato b. potatoes
	2. a. child b. children
	3. a. knife b. knives
	4. a. fish b. fish

UNIT 02 셀 수 없는 명사

PRACTICE p.13

STEP 1	1. Friendship 2. London 3. cheese
	4. air 5. money
STEP 2	1. peace 2. health 3. New York
	4. bread 5. two glasses of juice
STEP 3	1. slices[pieces] of bread 2. bottles
	of water 3. slices[pieces] of cake
	4. bowl of soup 5. pieces of paper

UNIT 03 관사

PRACTICE p.15

STEP 1	1. an 2. a 3. an 4. a 5. an
STEP 2	1. the 2. The 3. a 4. The 5. a
STEP 3	1. an 2. The 3. the 4. the

GRAMMAR FOR WRITING pp.16-17

A   1. an email   2. three photos   3. five classes
4. a bowl of rice   5. two pieces of paper
6. three cups of tea   7. a slice[piece] of cake

B   1. the door   2. The moon   3. the violin
4. boxes   5. leaves
C   1. a cup   2. milk   3. an egg   4. sugar
5. cheese   6. a knife   7. an orange
D   1. three slices[pieces] of bread, The bread
2. two tomatoes, The tomatoes

REVIEW TEST pp.18-19

1. ④   2. ②   3. ⑤   4. ②   5. ④   6. ②   7. ③
8. an actor   9. wine   10. ⑤   11. ②   12. ①
13. the picture   14. ④   15. piece   16. sheep
17. glasses of water   18. cities   19. luck
20. the piano

1   ④ knife의 복수형은 knives이다.
2   ② deer의 복수형은 deer이다.
3   ⑤는 셀 수 있는 명사, 나머지는 셀 수 없는 물질을 나타내는 명사이다.
4   ②는 셀 수 있는 명사, 나머지는 추상적인 개념을 나타내는 셀 수 없는 명사이다.
5   ④ three bowls of soup: 수프 세 그릇
6   ② answer는 발음이 모음으로 시작하므로 앞에 an을 쓴다. (a → an)
7   ③ world는 유일한 것이므로 앞에 정관사 the를 쓴다. (A world → The world)
8   actor는 셀 수 있는 명사이고 발음이 모음으로 시작하므로 앞에 an을 쓴다.
9   wine은 셀 수 없는 명사이므로 앞에 a나 an을 쓰지 않는다.
10   ⑤ tooth의 복수형은 teeth이다. (toothes → teeth)
11   ② juice는 셀 수 없는 명사이므로 항상 단수형으로 쓴다. (juices → juice)
12   ① salt는 셀 수 없는 명사이므로 앞에 a나 an을 쓰지 않는다. (a salt → salt)
13   서로 알고 있는 것을 가리킬 때는 정관사 the를 쓴다.
14   a cup of coffee: 커피 한 잔
15   종이나 빵을 세는 단위 명사는 piece이다.
16   sheep의 복수형은 sheep이다.
17   two glasses of water: 물 두 잔
18   city의 복수형은 cities이다.
19   luck은 추상적인 개념을 나타내는 셀 수 없는 명사이므로 앞에 a나 an을 쓰지 않는다.
20   연주의 대상으로 악기를 표현할 때는 악기 이름 앞에 the를 쓴다.

UNIT 01 인칭대명사

PRACTICE   p.23

STEP 1	**1.** it **2.** she **3.** we **4.** he **5.** they
	6. you **7.** they
STEP 2	**1.** his **2.** me **3.** her **4.** us
	5. Mary's **6.** theirs
STEP 3	**1.** him **2.** our **3.** mine **4.** my
	5. hers **6.** They **7.** her **8.** Its

UNIT 02 this, that, it

PRACTICE   p.25

STEP 1	**1.** It **2.** Those **3.** This **4.** these
STEP 2	**1.** This **2.** that **3.** This **4.** These
	5. Those
STEP 3	**1.** It's[It is] rainy **2.** It's[It is] 10:30
	a.m. **3.** It's[It is] October 17
	4. It's[It is] 1 km

GRAMMAR FOR WRITING   pp.26-27

A	**1.** him **2.** Her **3.** ours **4.** That **5.** This
	6. Those **7.** These
B	**1.** your **2.** his **3.** her **4.** It **5.** These
C	**1.** his **2.** her **3.** it **4.** Their **5.** our
	6. him **7.** We **8.** mine
D	**1.** These, them **2.** That, He **3.** We

REVIEW TEST   pp.28-29

1. ③ **2.** ④ **3.** ③ **4.** her **5.** them **6.** ours
7. ① **8.** ③ **9.** ② **10.** ⑤ **11.** ⑤ **12.** ② **13.** ⑤
14. ④ **15.** They **16.** hers **17.** His eyes
18. It's[It is] 5:30 p.m.

1 these + 복수명사: 이 (~)

2 a candle을 대신하는 소유격 대명사는 its이다.

3 날씨를 나타낼 때 비인칭 주어 it을 쓴다.

4 she의 소유격 대명사 her를 써야 한다.

5 they의 목적격 대명사 them을 써야 한다.

6 we의 소유대명사 ours를 써야 한다.

7 camera의 소유 관계를 나타내는 소유격 표현이 와야 한다.

8 ③ 전치사 for의 목적어 역할을 하는 목적격 대명사를 써야 한다. (they → them)

9 ② color의 소유 관계를 나타내는 소유격 대명사가 와야 한다. (It's → Its)

10 ⑤ Tom and I는 '나'를 포함한 복수이므로 We를 써야 한다.

11 (A) '너의 것'이라는 의미의 소유대명사 yours를 쓴다.
    (B) 뒤에 shoes가 복수형이므로 these를 쓴다.

12 (A) 가까이 있는 사람을 가리킬 때 this를 쓴다.
    (B) '너를' 만나서 반갑다는 의미이므로 목적격 대명사 you를 쓴다.

13 ⑤의 her는 목적격 대명사, 나머지는 소유격 대명사이다.

14 ④의 It은 인칭대명사, 나머지는 비인칭 주어 It이다.

15 Ben과 Joe는 3인칭 복수이므로 주격 대명사로 they를 써야 한다.

16 her earphones를 가리키는 소유대명사 hers를 써야 한다.

17 he의 소유격 대명사: his

18 시간을 나타낼 때 비인칭 주어 it을 쓴다.

UNIT 01 be동사의 현재형 1

PRACTICE   p.33

STEP 1	**1.** am, I'm **2.** are, They're
	3. are, We're **4.** are, You're
	5. is, It's **6.** is, He's
STEP 2	**1.** am **2.** is **3.** are **4.** are
STEP 3	**1.** am **2.** is **3.** is **4.** are **5.** is

UNIT 02   be동사의 현재형 2

PRACTICE   p.35

STEP 1	1. Are 2. is not 3. Are 4. aren't
	5. is not 6. isn't
STEP 2	1. am not, I'm not 2. is not, isn't
	3. are not, aren't 4. is not, isn't
	5. are not, aren't 6. are not, aren't
STEP 3	1. Am I, you aren't 2. Are you, I'm
	not 3. Are you and Kate, we are
	4. Is it, it isn't

UNIT 03   be동사의 과거형

PRACTICE   p.37

STEP 1	1. was not 2. wasn't 3. Were
	4. were 5. was 6. was
STEP 2	1. wasn't 2. was 3. wasn't
	4. weren't 5. were
STEP 3	1. Was he, he was 2. Were you,
	I was / we were 3. Was the shop,
	it wasn't 4. Were they, they were

UNIT 04   There is/are

PRACTICE   p.39

STEP 1	1. were 2. is 3. aren't 4. was
	5. Are 6. Is
STEP 2	1. There is 2. There are 3. There is
STEP 3	1. There is 2. There was 3. There
	were

GRAMMAR FOR WRITING   pp.40-41

A   1. is   2. isn't[is not]   3. aren't[are not]
4. are   5. is   6. are   7. was   8. wasn't[was not]   9. was   10. Were   11. were
12. weren't[were not]
B   1. Is, it is   2. Was, he wasn't
3. Were, they weren't   4. Are, I'm not

C   1. there aren't   2. there are   3. Is there

REVIEW TEST   pp.42-43

1. ③   2. ②   3. There is   4. There are   5. ③
6. ②   7. ④   8. is   9. was   10. were   11. ④
12. ①   13. ⑤   14. ④   15. weren't[were not] easy
16. Were Liam and Jamie   17. There was rice

1 주어가 3인칭 단수이고 now로 보아 현재시제이므로 is를 쓴다.
2 주어가 2인칭이고 now로 보아 현재시제이므로 Are를 쓴다.
3 주어가 단수명사(a big tree)이므로 There is를 쓴다.
4 주어가 복수명사(four people)이므로 There are를 쓴다.
5 ③ He and I는 1인칭 복수이므로 are를 쓴다. (am → are)
6 ② yesterday로 보아 과거시제이므로 was를 쓴다. (is → was)
7 ④ Sam and Jason은 3인칭 복수이므로 aren't를 쓴다. (isn't → aren't)
8 주어가 3인칭 단수이므로 is를 쓴다.
9 주어가 1인칭 단수이고 two years ago로 보아 과거시제이므로 was를 쓴다.
10 주어가 3인칭 복수이고 last night으로 보아 과거시제이므로 were를 쓴다.
11 ④ 「Are + 2인칭 복수주어 ~?」에 대한 긍정의 대답: Yes, we are.
12 ① am not은 줄여 쓰지 않는다. (I amn't → I'm not)
13 (A) 주어가 3인칭 복수이므로 Are를 쓴다.
(B) 「Are + 3인칭 복수주어 ~?」에 대한 부정의 대답: No, they aren't.
14 (A) 주어가 복수명사(buses)이고 now로 보아 현재시제이브로 There are를 쓴다.
(B) 주어가 단수명사(a math test)이고 last Thursday로 보아 과거시제이므로 There was를 쓴다.
15 주어가 복수일 때 be동사 과거형의 부정문: weren't[were not]
16 주어가 복수일 때 be동사 과거형의 의문문: Were + 주어 ~?
17 rice는 셀 수 없는 명사이고 과거시제이므로 There was를 쓴다.

04 일반동사 1

UNIT 01 일반동사의 현재형 1

PRACTICE p.47

STEP 1	1. gets 2. flies 3. watches
	4. likes 5. says 6. teaches
	7. cries 8. fixes 9. passes
	10. carries 11. runs
STEP 2	1. studies 2. plays 3. washes
STEP 3	1. a. have b. has 2. a. brushes
	b. brush 3. a. do b. does

UNIT 02 일반동사의 현재형 2

PRACTICE p.49

STEP 1	1. don't 2. have 3. Do 4. Does
	5. don't 6. play
STEP 2	1. don't drink 2. doesn't do
	3. don't know 4. doesn't forget
	5. doesn't clean 6. doesn't have
STEP 3	1. Do, like 2. Does, go
	3. Do, speak 4. Does, use

UNIT 03 일반동사의 과거형 1

PRACTICE p.51

STEP 1	1. ate 2. did 3. had 4. ran
	5. tried 6. bought 7. chatted
	8. made 9. liked 10. played
	11. carried
STEP 2	1. lived 2. drank 3. listened
	4. came 5. cut
STEP 3	1. dropped 2. met 3. put

UNIT 04 일반동사의 과거형 2

PRACTICE p.53

STEP 1	1. break 2. Did 3. know 4. leave
	5. don't 6. didn't
STEP 2	1. didn't eat 2. didn't talk
	3. didn't play 4. didn't take
	5. didn't come 6. didn't watch
STEP 3	1. Did, paint 2. Did, ride
	3. Did, get up 4. Did, run

GRAMMAR FOR WRITING pp.54-55

A 1. doesn't[does not] play 2. Do you read
3. goes 4. watches 5. Does she drive
6. joined 7. heard 8. didn't[did not] have
9. Did you see 10. bought

B 1. don't[do not] eat 2. doesn't[does not]
like 3. lives 4. traveled 5. Did, score

C 1. swam 2. made a sandcastle 3. took a
picture 4. had a good time

REVIEW TEST pp.56-57

1. ⑤ 2. ④ 3. ② 4. ⑤ 5. ⑤ 6. doesn't[does
not] have 7. didn't[did not] rain 8. he does
9. I didn't 10. ⑤ 11. ① 12. ③ 13. ①
14. knows 15. didn't[did not] tell 16. Did, wash
17. Does Sally practice taekwondo 18. We don't
use cell phones

1 ⑤ teach의 3인칭 단수 현재형: teaches
2 ④ meet의 과거형: met
3 주어가 3인칭 단수이므로 studies를 쓰며, 부정문은
   doesn't study이다.
4 동사가 과거형이므로 과거를 나타내는 two months ago가
   알맞다.
5 주어가 3인칭 단수이므로 does[Does]를 쓴다.
6 주어가 3인칭 단수일 때 일반동사 현재형의 부정문:
   doesn't[does not] + 동사원형
7 일반동사 과거형의 부정문: didn't[did not] + 동사원형
8 「Does + 주어 + 동사원형?」에 대한 긍정의 대답: Yes, 주어 +
   does.
9 「Did + 주어 + 동사원형?」에 대한 부정의 대답: No, 주어 +
   didn't.

10 ⑤ last weekend는 과거를 나타내는 표현이므로 동사의 과거형을 쓴다. (play → played)

11 ① 주어가 3인칭 단수일 때 일반동사 현재형의 부정문: doesn't[does not] + 동사원형 (don't → doesn't [does not])

12 ③ 일반동사 과거형의 의문문: Did + 주어 + 동사원형? (found → find)

13 「Do + 주어 + 동사원형?」에 대한 대답: Yes, 주어 + do. / No, 주어 + don't.

14 know의 3인칭 단수 현재형: knows

15 일반동사 과거형의 부정문: didn't[did not] + 동사원형

16 일반동사 과거형의 의문문: Did + 주어 + 동사원형?

17 주어가 3인칭 단수일 때 일반동사 현재형의 의문문: Does + 주어 + 동사원형?

18 주어가 1인칭 복수일 때 일반동사 현재형의 부정문: don't + 동사원형

UNIT 01 형용사

PRACTICE   p.61

STEP 1   1. large house   2. any   3. interesting
         4. something strange
STEP 2   1. black   2. young   3. angry
         4. fast   5. tall
STEP 3   1. some   2. any   3. some   4. any

UNIT 02 부사

PRACTICE   p.63

STEP 1   1. newly   2. kindly   3. easily
         4. fast   5. softly   6. quickly
         7. carefully
STEP 2   1. well   2. Luckily   3. very quiet
         4. early   5. high   6. late
STEP 3   1. is always kind to everyone
         2. It often rains   3. am never bored
         with action movies   4. usually goes
         to bed

GRAMMAR FOR WRITING   pp.64-65

A   1. expensive   2. fresh   3. new   4. quietly
    5. any   6. some   7. very
B   1. suddenly   2. is always hungry
    3. carefully   4. sometimes rides
    5. something sweet
C   1. a. hard   b. hard   2. a. good   b. well
    3. a. easy   b. easily   4. a. Surprisingly
    b. Surprising
D   1. ran fast   2. came late   3. climbed high

REVIEW TEST   pp.66-67

1. ③   2. ①   3. ④   4. ④   5. ②   6. ②   7. ④
8. ③   9. ②   10. some   11. any   12. ④   13. ②
14. ⑤   15. smells good   16. Sadly   17. usually
listens to   18. We need big scissors   19. This
summer is quite hot

1   명사(girl)를 꾸며주는 형용사가 와야 한다.
2   동사(explains)를 꾸며주는 부사가 와야 한다.
3   주어(The story)를 보충 설명해 주는 형용사가 와야 한다.
4   ④는 부사, 나머지는 형용사이다.
5   ②는 형용사, 나머지는 부사이다.
6   ② 긍정문에서 '몇 개의'의 의미를 나타낼 때는 some을 쓴다.
    (any → some)
7   -thing으로 끝나는 말은 형용사가 뒤에서 꾸며준다.
8   빈도부사는 be동사의 뒤에 쓴다.
9   빈도부사는 일반동사의 앞에 쓴다.
10 긍정문에서 '조금의'의 의미를 나타낼 때는 some을 쓴다.
11 부정문에서 '조금의 (~도 없다)'의 의미를 나타낼 때는 any를
    쓴다.
12 (A) 명사(day)를 꾸며주는 형용사 lucky를 쓴다.
    (B) 문장 전체를 꾸며주는 부사 Luckily를 쓴다.
13 (A) 권유를 나타내는 의문문에서는 some을 쓴다.
    (B) 의문문에서는 any를 쓴다.
14 빈도부사의 위치: 일반동사의 앞
    동사(finishes)를 꾸며주는 부사 quickly를 쓴다.
15 형용사가 동사 뒤에 쓰여 주어(This soup)를 보충 설명해
    준다.
16 부사가 문장 전체를 꾸며준다.
17 빈도부사는 일반동사의 앞에 쓴다.
18 형용사가 명사 앞에 쓰여 명사(scissors)를 꾸며준다.
19 부사가 앞에서 형용사(hot)를 꾸며준다.

CHAPTER 06 전치사

UNIT 01 장소를 나타내는 전치사

PRACTICE
p.71

STEP 1	1. him 2. at 3. on 4. under
	5. next to 6. in 7. in front of
STEP 2	1. in 2. at 3. at 4. in 5. at
	6. in 7. in
STEP 3	1. behind 2. on 3. under
	4. next to

UNIT 02 시간을 나타내는 전치사

PRACTICE
p.73

STEP 1	1. at 2. after 3. during 4. in
	5. on 6. for 7. before
STEP 2	1. at 2. on 3. at 4. in 5. on
	6. on 7. in
STEP 3	1. before 2. for 3. during

GRAMMAR FOR WRITING
pp.74-75

A 1. next to the window 2. in New York
3. at the airport 4. behind the hill
5. before midnight 6. after school 7. for
three weeks 8. on Saturday 9. during the
vacation 10. in December
B 1. on Mondays 2. at noon 3. for two years
4. in the evening
C 1. under 2. in 3. on 4. behind

REVIEW TEST
pp.76-77

1. ① 2. ③ 3. ② 4. ① 5. ② 6. ⑤ 7. ③
8. for 9. during 10. in front of 11. at 12. after
13. before 14. ② 15. ④ 16. behind the
building 17. on Saturdays 18. in the afternoon

1 국가 앞에는 in을 쓴다.
2 날짜 앞에는 on을 쓴다.
3 ② 전치사 뒤에 대명사가 올 때는 목적격을 쓴다. (she → her)
4 in + 공간의 내부 / 계절
5 at + 장소의 한 지점 / 구체적인 시각
6 ⑤는 on, 나머지는 at
7 ③은 at, 나머지는 in
8 for + 숫자를 포함한 구체적인 기간: ~ 동안
9 during + 특정한 때를 나타내는 명사: ~ 동안
10 in front of: ~ 앞에
11 at + 구체적인 시각
12 after: ~ 후에
13 before: ~ 전에
14 ② next to: ~ 옆에 (next → next to)
15 ④ for + 숫자를 포함한 구체적인 기간: ~ 동안 (during → for)
16 behind: ~ 뒤에
17 on + 요일
18 in + 오전, 오후

CHAPTER 07 동사의 종류

UNIT 01 동사의 종류 1

PRACTICE
p.81

STEP 1	1. ⓐ 2. ⓑ 3. ⓒ 4. ⓑ 5. ⓒ
	6. ⓒ
STEP 2	1. speaks 2. helps 3. wants
	4. play
STEP 3	1. told them an amazing story
	2. made me some coffee 3. taught
	us science 4. bought Jessica some
	books 5. showed us her new shoes
	6. gave the waiter a tip

UNIT 02 동사의 종류 2

PRACTICE
p.83

STEP 1	1. angry 2. call 3. bad 4. fresh
	5. found 6. look 7. clean

| STEP 2 | **1.** tastes **2.** sounded **3.** feels |
| STEP 3 | **1.** made **2.** keeps **3.** found |

수이고 현재형이므로 smiles를 쓴다.

16 love는 목적어가 필요한 동사로, 「주어 + 동사 + 목적어」형태로 쓴다.

17 주어 + 동사 + 간접목적어 + 직접목적어

18 주어 + 동사 + 목적어 + 목적격 보어

GRAMMAR FOR WRITING

pp.84-85

A **1.** slept well **2.** lent Tom my bike
3. gave her father a letter **4.** met a classmate **5.** showed him my picture
6. became tired **7.** sounded interesting
8. made her a star **9.** tastes sour
10. found the boy rude

B **1.** kept **2.** heard **3.** watched **4.** called
5. became **6.** looked **7.** bought

C **1.** made him sick **2.** taught us English
3. found the hotel old

REVIEW TEST

pp.86-87

1. ① **2.** ③ **3.** ② **4.** ③ **5.** was **6.** gave
7. invited **8.** ② **9.** ⑤ **10.** ⑤ **11.** ④ **12.** ④
13. ⑤ **14.** looks easy **15.** smiles **16.** loves animals **17.** lent Andy my running shoes
18. found the room dirty

1 look과 같이 감각을 나타내는 동사는 보어로 형용사를 쓴다.

2 walk는 동사만으로 완전한 의미를 나타내어 ③ a park와 같은 목적어가 필요 없다.

3 ② make는 목적어가 필요한 동사이다.

4 빈칸에는 간접목적어가 와야 한다. 간접목적어가 대명사일 경우에는 목적격을 쓴다. (③ she → her)

5 주격 보어(kind)가 필요한 동사가 와야 한다.

6 간접목적어(me)와 직접목적어(a birthday gift)가 모두 필요한 동사가 와야 한다.

7 목적어(my neighbors)가 필요한 동사가 와야 한다.

8 보기와 ②는 「주어 + 동사 + 주격 보어」형태의 문장

9 보기와 ⑤는 「주어 + 동사 + 목적어 + 목적격 보어」형태의 문장

10 ⑤는 목적어가 필요한 동사, 나머지는 간접목적어와 직접목적어가 모두 필요한 동사

11 ④는 목적어와 목적격 보어가 필요한 동사, 나머지는 간접목적어와 직접목적어가 모두 필요한 동사

12 ④ taste와 같이 감각을 나타내는 동사는 보어로 형용사를 쓴다.

13 ⑤「주어 + 동사 + 간접목적어 + 직접목적어」형태로 써야 한다. (teaches music us → teaches us music)

14 look + 형용사: ~해 보이다

15 smile은 목적어나 보어가 필요 없는 동사로, 주어가 3인칭 단

CHAPTER 08 조동사

UNIT 01 can, may

PRACTICE

p.91

STEP 1	**1.** can **2.** Can **3.** I have **4.** cannot fix **5.** answer
STEP 2	**1.** can't **2.** can't **3.** can
STEP 3	**1.** May I ask **2.** Can I open **3.** May I go

UNIT 02 must, have to

PRACTICE

p.93

STEP 1	**1.** have **2.** not eat **3.** bring **4.** has to **5.** come **6.** doesn't have to **7.** must not
STEP 2	**1.** must not **2.** must **3.** must not **4.** must **5.** must
STEP 3	**1.** don't have to shout **2.** has to see **3.** don't have to wear **4.** has to work **5.** doesn't have to buy **6.** have to take

GRAMMAR FOR WRITING

pp.94-95

A **1.** Can[May] I close **2.** can't[cannot] remember **3.** can win **4.** can[may] have
5. don't have to take **6.** must not waste
7. must[have to] speak **8.** must[has to] wait
9. must not play **10.** doesn't have to go

B **1.** Can **2.** must **3.** May

C **1.** don't have to hurry **2.** must not park
3. can't[cannot] answer

REVIEW TEST

pp.96-97

1. ④ **2.** ⑤ **3.** ③ **4.** ③ **5.** ① **6.** ① **7.** can't
8. May **9.** don't have to **10.** ⑤ **11.** ③ **12.** ⑤
13. can drive **14.** must not use **15.** can't
[cannot] find **16.** must[has to] finish **17.** doesn't
have to wear **18.** must not throw

1 may와 can은 '~해도 좋다(허가)'의 의미를 나타낸다.
2 must와 have/has to는 '~해야 한다(의무)'의 의미를 나타낸다.
3 can't[cannot]: ~할 수 없다
4 must not: ~해서는 안 된다(강한 금지)
5 조동사 뒤에는 항상 동사원형을 쓴다.
6 ①은 '~해도 좋다(허가)', 나머지는 '~할 수 있다(능력, 가능)'
7 can't[cannot]: ~할 수 없다
8 may: ~해도 좋다(허가)
9 don't/doesn't have to: ~할 필요가 없다
10 ⑤ may는 '~해도 좋다(허가)'의 의미를 나타내므로, 의미상 May I visit ~?가 와야 한다.
11 ③ 주어가 3인칭 단수일 때는 has to를 쓴다. (have to eat → has to eat)
12 don't/doesn't have to: ~할 필요가 없다
13 조동사 뒤에는 항상 동사원형을 쓴다.
14 must not: ~해서는 안 된다(강한 금지)
15 can't[cannot]: ~할 수 없다
16 must와 have/has to는 '~해야 한다(의무)'의 의미를 나타낸다.
17 don't/doesn't have to: ~할 필요가 없다
18 must not: ~해서는 안 된다(강한 금지)

CHAPTER 09 일반동사 2

UNIT 01 일반동사의 현재진행형 1

PRACTICE p.101

STEP 1 **1.** sitting **2.** singing **3.** crying
4. living **5.** dying **6.** watching

7. staying **8.** buying **9.** coming
10. getting **11.** reading
STEP 2 **1.** is smiling **2.** are running **3.** is
cleaning **4.** am writing **5.** is tying
6. are standing
STEP 3 **1.** am lying **2.** are speaking
3. is cutting

UNIT 02 일반동사의 현재진행형 2

PRACTICE p.103

STEP 1 **1.** cutting **2.** aren't **3.** am **4.** is
not **5.** Is **6.** using
STEP 2 **1.** aren't[are not] playing **2.** isn't
[is not] washing **3.** am not talking
4. isn't[is not] walking
STEP 3 **1.** Is, wearing **2.** Are, staying
3. Is, putting

UNIT 03 일반동사의 미래형 1

PRACTICE p.105

STEP 1 **1.** meet **2.** pass **3.** be **4.** will
leave **5.** is going **6.** are going to
STEP 2 **1.** will call **2.** will begin **3.** will go
STEP 3 **1.** am going to stay **2.** is going to
boil **3.** are going to eat **4.** am
going to plant **5.** is going to open
6. are going to visit **7.** is going to
study

UNIT 04 일반동사의 미래형 2

PRACTICE p.107

STEP 1 **1.** not fight **2.** Is **3.** won't
4. going **5.** agree **6.** not going to
STEP 2 **1.** won't[will not] eat
2. won't[will not] take **3.** Will, join
STEP 3 **1.** aren't[are not] going to sleep
2. am not going to bring
3. Is, going to take

A　**1.** are flying　**2.** am not reading　**3.** are making　**4.** Is Linda shopping　**5.** Will they try　**6.** are going to buy　**7.** won't[will not] change　**8.** Are you going to go　**9.** will be　**10.** isn't[is not] going to invite

B　**1.** is selling　**2.** are playing　**3.** are sitting　**4.** are eating

C　**1.** won't[will not] be　**2.** am going to climb　**3.** Is, going to win

---

REVIEW TEST　　　pp.110-111

1. ③　**2.** ⑤　**3.** ③　**4.** ③　**5.** ⑤　**6.** ⑤　**7.** ②　**8.** ④　**9.** ③　**10.** he isn't　**11.** I am　**12.** ③　**13.** is blowing　**14.** are not going to go　**15.** Are you using　**16.** I am going to talk　**17.** Will it be sunny　**18.** Wendy isn't[is not] wearing a watch.

1　③ -ie로 끝나는 동사는 ie를 y로 고치고 -ing를 붙인다. (lieing → lying)
2　⑤ 〈단모음 + 단자음〉으로 끝나는 동사는 자음을 한 번 더 쓰고 -ing를 붙인다. (begining → beginning)
3　will은 미래를 나타내므로 ③ yesterday는 올 수 없다.
4　일반동사의 현재진행형: be동사 + 동사원형-ing
　　일반동사의 미래형: be going to + 동사원형
5　will의 의문문: Will + 주어 + 동사원형?
　　일반동사의 미래형: will + 동사원형
6　⑤는 are, 나머지는 is
7　② 일반동사 현재진행형의 부정문: be동사 + not + 동사원형-ing (don't eating → aren't[are not] eating)
8　④ 일반동사의 미래형: be going to + 동사원형 (going to wash → is going to wash)
9　③은 일반동사 go의 현재진행형, 나머지는 일반동사의 미래형에 쓰이는 be going to
10　「Is + 주어 + 동사원형-ing?」에 대한 부정의 대답: No, 주어 + isn't.
11　「Are you going to + 동사원형?」에 대한 긍정의 대답: Yes, I am.
12　will의 부정문: won't[will not] + 동사원형
13　일반동사의 현재진행형: be동사 + 동사원형-ing
14　be going to의 부정문: be동사 + not + going to + 동사원형
15　일반동사 현재진행형의 의문문: be동사 + 주어 + 동사원형-ing?
16　일반동사의 미래형: be going to + 동사원형
17　will의 의문문: Will + 주어 + 동사원형?

18　일반동사 현재진행형의 부정문: be동사 + not + 동사원형-ing

CHAPTER
10 비교

UNIT 01　비교급

PRACTICE　　　p.115

STEP 1	**1.** more difficult　**2.** heavier　**3.** cheaper　**4.** harder　**5.** bigger
STEP 2	**1.** louder　**2.** more　**3.** larger　**4.** more slowly　**5.** much faster
STEP 3	**1.** earlier than　**2.** hotter than　**3.** less than　**4.** better than　**5.** more interesting than

---

UNIT 02　최상급

PRACTICE　　　p.117

STEP 1	**1.** most　**2.** nicest　**3.** thinnest　**4.** best　**5.** most interesting　**6.** prettiest　**7.** least　**8.** fastest
STEP 2	**1.** the largest　**2.** wisest　**3.** coldest　**4.** greatest　**5.** most difficult　**6.** most popular
STEP 3	**1.** the worst　**2.** the busiest　**3.** the most exciting　**4.** the most important　**5.** the hottest　**6.** the youngest

---

GRAMMAR FOR WRITING　　　pp.118-119

A　**1.** heavier than　**2.** thicker than　**3.** better than　**4.** more quickly than　**5.** the tallest　**6.** the easiest　**7.** the most popular　**8.** the smartest　**9.** the best　**10.** the biggest

B　**1.** older than　**2.** the youngest　**3.** cheaper than　**4.** more expensive than　**5.** the most expensive

C 1. the shortest 2. more comfortable
   3. the most famous

STEP 2 1. to draw 2. to meet 3. to go
        4. to sell
STEP 3 1. to eat 2. to bake 3. to speak

REVIEW TEST pp.120-121

1. ② 2. ⑤ 3. ② 4. smaller 5. harder 6. ③
7. ④ 8. ② 9. ① 10. the funniest 11. the most
exciting 12. ⑤ 13. ② 14. earlier than
15. better than 16. hotter than 17. the most
delicious dish

1 〈단모음 + 단자음〉으로 끝나는 형용사의 비교급은 자음을 한 번
   더 쓰고 -er을 붙인다.
2 3음절 이상의 형용사는 앞에 most를 붙여 최상급을 만든다.
3 비교급 앞에 much(훨씬)를 써서 비교급을 강조할 수 있다.
4 small의 비교급: smaller
5 hard의 비교급: harder
6 ③ little의 비교급: less (littler → less)
7 ④ difficult의 최상급: most difficult (the difficultest
   → the most difficult)
8 ② 비교급 + than: ~보다 더 …한 (oldest → older)
9 비교급 앞에 much(훨씬)를 써서 비교급을 강조할 수 있다.
10 funny의 최상급: funniest
11 exciting의 최상급: most exciting
12 (A) 비교급 + than: ~보다 더 …한
    (B) famous의 최상급: most famous
13 (A) the + 최상급: 가장 ~한
    (B) interesting의 비교급: more interesting
14 early의 비교급: earlier
15 well의 비교급: better
16 hot의 비교급: hotter
17 delicious의 최상급: most delicious

CHAPTER 11 to부정사

UNIT 01 명사처럼 쓰는 to부정사

PRACTICE p.125

STEP 1 1. To play 2. buy 3. to know
        4. help 5. It 6. like 7. to work

UNIT 02 형용사, 부사처럼 쓰는 to부정사

PRACTICE p.127

STEP 1 1. a message 2. time 3. something
        4. a great way 5. enough time
        6. many places 7. any money
STEP 2 1. ⓐ 2. ⓑ 3. ⓔ 4. ⓒ
STEP 3 1. to ask 2. to hear 3. to wear
        4. to meet

GRAMMAR FOR WRITING pp.128-129

A 1. to exercise 2. to listen 3. to get
   4. to do
B 1. wrong to tell 2. some fruit to make
   3. decided to study 4. happy to hear
   5. went outside to get 6. the books to
   return
C 1. a. wash b. to wash 2. a. help b. to help
   3. a. take b. to take 4. a. travel b. to
   travel 5. a. to drink b. drink
D 1. to buy 2. to enjoy 3. to see

REVIEW TEST pp.130-131

1. ④ 2. ④ 3. ⑤ 4. ② 5. ③ 6. ④ 7. to
8. It 9. ③ 10. ③ 11. ③ 12. to ask a question
13. to hear about his accident 14. to visit
15. to play 16. to buy a jacket 17. time to eat
breakfast

1 to부정사가 형용사처럼 명사나 대명사를 꾸며주며, '~할'이라는
   의미를 나타낸다. 이때 to부정사는 명사나 대명사 뒤에 온다.
2 to부정사가 주어로 쓰일 경우에는 보통 주어 자리에 It을 쓰고
   to부정사를 뒤로 보낸다.
3 ⑤ to부정사의 형태: to + 동사원형 (travels → travel)
4 보기와 ②는 명사처럼 쓰는 to부정사(목적어 역할)
5 보기와 ③은 부사처럼 쓰는 to부정사(감정의 원인)
6 보기와 ④는 부사처럼 쓰는 to부정사(목적)

7	동사 plan의 목적어로 to부정사가 와야 한다.
8	to부정사가 주어로 쓰일 경우에는 보통 주어 자리에 It을 쓰고 to부정사를 뒤로 보낸다.
9	③ to부정사의 형태: to + 동사원형 (to drank → to drink)
10	③ 동사 likes의 목적어로 to부정사가 와야 한다. (listen → to listen)
11	to부정사가 주어로 쓰일 경우에는 보통 주어 자리에 It을 쓰고 to부정사를 뒤로 보낸다.
12	to부정사가 동사의 목적을 나타내며, '~하기 위해'라는 의미를 나타낸다.
13	to부정사가 감정의 원인을 나타내며, '~해서'라는 의미를 나타낸다.
14	to부정사가 보어로 쓰여 주어를 보충 설명한다.
15	to부정사가 동사의 목적어로 쓰여, '~하는 것을'이라는 의미를 나타낸다.
16	to부정사가 동사의 목적을 나타내며, '~하기 위해'라는 의미를 나타낸다.
17	to부정사가 형용사처럼 명사를 꾸며주며, '~할'이라는 의미를 나타낸다. 이때 to부정사는 명사 뒤에 온다.

CHAPTER 12 접속사

UNIT 01 and, but, or

PRACTICE   p.135

STEP 1	1. but 2. or 3. and 4. or 5. but
	6. but 7. and
STEP 2	1. but 2. and 3. or
STEP 3	1. but 2. and 3. or

UNIT 02 when, before, after, because

PRACTICE   p.137

STEP 1	1. because 2. have 3. after
	4. When 5. before
STEP 2	1. ⓔ 2. ⓕ 3. ⓓ 4. ⓒ 5. ⓑ
STEP 3	1. when he heard the news
	2. after the concert is over
	3. because it is raining

GRAMMAR FOR WRITING   pp.138-139

A	1. or 2. but 3. and 4. because 5. after
	6. when 7. before
B	1. when she fell 2. lions and zebras
	3. After I read 4. because the weather was bad 5. left hand or right hand
C	1. because it's too heavy
	2. after he watched the horror movie
	3. when he wears glasses
D	1. but we don't have 2. or soup
	3. and a green salad

REVIEW TEST   pp.140-141

1. ① **2.** ④ **3.** before **4.** because **5.** but **6.** ④
7. ④ **8.** but **9.** or **10.** ④ **11.** ④ **12.** ①
13. ② **14.** math and science **15.** after we went
16. because he got up late

1	내용상 비슷한 것을 연결하는 접속사는 and이다.
2	when: ~할 때
3	before: ~하기 전에
4	because: ~하기 때문에
5	내용상 서로 반대인 것을 연결하는 접속사는 but이다.
6	④ 내용상 비슷한 것들을 연결하고 있기 때문에 and를 쓰며, 세 개 이상의 단어를 연결할 때는 「A, B, and C」의 형태로 쓴다. (and Japan → Japan)
7	④ 원인을 나타내는 접속사 because를 써야 한다. (after → because)
8	내용상 서로 반대인 것을 연결하는 접속사는 but이다.
9	둘 이상의 선택해야 할 것들을 연결하는 접속사는 or이다.
10	④ 원인을 나타내는 접속사 because를 써야 한다.
11	(A) yours와 Jane's 중 선택해야 하기 때문에 or를 쓴다.
	(B) 내용상 비슷한 것들을 연결하고 있기 때문에 and를 쓰며, 세 개 이상의 단어를 연결할 때는 「A, B, and C」의 형태로 쓴다.
12	시간을 나타내는 접속사가 이끄는 절에서는 미래를 나타내더라도 현재시제를 쓴다.
13	when: ~할 때
14	내용상 비슷한 것을 연결하는 접속사는 and이다.
15	after: ~한 후에
16	because: ~하기 때문에

13 의문문, 명령문, 감탄문

UNIT 01 who, what

PRACTICE p.145

STEP 1	1. Who 2. What 3. Whose
	4. Whom
STEP 2	1. Who 2. What 3. Who
STEP 3	1. Whose 2. Who 3. Who(m)

UNIT 02 when, where, why

PRACTICE p.147

STEP 1	1. When 2. Where 3. What
	4. Why
STEP 2	1. ⓔ 2. ⓑ 3. ⓐ 4. ⓒ
STEP 3	1. Where 2. Why 3. When
	4. Where

UNIT 03 how

PRACTICE p.149

STEP 1	1. How much 2. How 3. How far
STEP 2	1. How long 2. How many 3. How often
STEP 3	1. How 2. How 3. How tall

UNIT 04 부가의문문

PRACTICE p.151

STEP 1	1. can 2. she 3. don't 4. weren't
	5. didn't 6. aren't they
STEP 2	1. ⓐ 2. ⓕ 3. ⓒ 4. ⓔ 5. ⓑ
STEP 3	1. do they 2. won't we 3. didn't he
	4. weren't you 5. can he
	6. doesn't it

UNIT 05 명령문, 감탄문

PRACTICE p.153

STEP 1	1. What 2. Finish 3. Don't
STEP 2	1. Be 2. Let's 3. Wear
	4. Let's not 5. Don't
STEP 3	1. How tall 2. What nice teachers
	3. How difficult

GRAMMAR FOR WRITING pp.154-155

A	1. Who 2. Where 3. When 4. Try
	5. Let's stay 6. Press 7. Don't[Do not] enter
B	1. Don't[Do not] walk 2. How far is New York 3. What a great picture
	4. don't drink coffee, do you
	5. was boring, wasn't it
C	1. When 2. Why 3. Where 4. What
	5. How
D	1. How heavy 2. What a hot day
	3. Let's not go out

REVIEW TEST pp.156-157

1. ③ 2. ⑤ 3. ⑤ 4. Where 5. Who 6. ⑤
7. ② 8. does he 9. can't we 10. ③ 11. ③
12. ④ 13. ② 14. What time 15. Let's watch
16. What an interesting story

1 Don't[Do not] + 동사원형: ~하지 마라
2 how로 시작하는 감탄문: How + 형용사/부사 (+ 주어 + 동사)!
3 how much + 셀 수 없는 명사: 얼마나 많은 양의 ~
4 where: 어디에
5 who: 누가
6 ⑤ Don't[Do not] + 동사원형: ~하지 마라 (Not play → Don't[Do not] play)
7 ② 평서문의 주어(His idea)를 가리키는 대명사 it을 쓴다. (he → it)
8 일반동사의 부가의문문: ~, do/does/did (+ not) + 대명사?
9 조동사의 부가의문문: ~, 조동사 (+ not) + 대명사?
10 ③ 취미가 무엇이냐고 물었으므로 '내 취미는 ~이다'라는 답변이 와야 자연스럽다.
11 ③ 다리의 길이가 얼마나 긴지 물었으므로 '다리의 길이는 ~이다'라는 답변이 와야 자연스럽다.
12 (A) 원인, 이유를 묻는 의문사는 why이다.

(B) why로 묻는 질문에 대한 대답에는 주로 because가 사용된다.

13   감탄문은 what이나 how로 시작한다.

    (A) What + a(n) + 형용사 + 명사 (+ 주어 + 동사)!

    (B) How + 형용사/부사 (+ 주어 + 동사)!

14   구체적인 시간을 물을 경우 what time을 쓴다.

15   Let's + 동사원형: ~하자

16   what으로 시작하는 감탄문: What + a(n) + 형용사 + 명사 (+ 주어 + 동사)!

GRAMMAR BASICS

01 단어의 종류 p.2

A
1. after 2. very 3. often 4. oops
5. sometimes 6. make 7. sadly

B
1. 부사 2. 대명사 3. 형용사 4. 부사 5. 형용사
6. 감탄사 7. 동사 8. 전치사 9. 명사 10. 접속사
11. 동사

02 문장의 구성 p.3

A
1. I live in Seoul.
2. She is a teacher.
3. My room is small.
4. Michael likes movies.
5. New York is a big city.
6. You look happy today.
7. The soccer team practices on Mondays.
8. Ms. Jackson sings beautifully.
9. Alice and her husband have a son.
10. The paintings are in London now.

B
1. He feels happy.
2. My sister is a singer.
3. He studies history.
4. John loves her very much.
5. Emily drinks milk every day.
6. Robert sent me an email.
7. My friends call me Annie.
8. He became a famous actor.
9. Ms. Anderson teaches us English.
10. The restaurant became popular.

CHAPTER 01 명사와 관사

UNIT 01 셀 수 있는 명사 pp.4-5

A
1. O 2. X 3. X 4. O 5. X 6. O 7. X
8. O 9. O 10. X

B
1. books 2. roofs 3. classes 4. teeth
5. puppies 6. feet 7. days 8. deer
9. knives 10. men 11. houses 12. stories

C
1. a. watch b. three watches 2. a. mouse
b. four mice 3. a. blackboard b. three
blackboards 4. a. spoon b. five spoons
5. a. lady b. two ladies

WRITING PRACTICE

1. two babies 2. ten boxes 3. carrot
4. three women 5. four trees

UNIT 02 셀 수 없는 명사 pp.6-7

A
1. Love 2. happiness 3. Andy 4. sand
5. money 6. bread 7. France 8. Seoul
9. salt 10. coffee

B
1. advice 2. Tony 3. peace
4. Germany 5. juice 6. Florida
7. two cups of tea 8. four bottles of milk
9. a piece of cheese 10. bread

C
1. slices of bread 2. bowl of soup
3. bottles of wine 4. bottle of cola
5. pieces of cake 6. pieces of paper
7. slices of cheese 8. cups of cocoa

WRITING PRACTICE

1. meat 2. Cambridge 3. health 4. two cups
of coffee 5. ten pieces of paper

A　1. a　2. a　3. an　4. a　5. an　6. a　7. a
　　8. an　9. a　10. an

B　1. the　2. An　3. the　4. a　5. The　6. a
　　7. an　8. The　9. The　10. the

C　1. The flower　2. an hour　3. the violin
　　4. an eraser　5. a keyboard　6. the flute
　　7. The sun　8. the earth

WRITING PRACTICE

1. an apple pie　2. the sugar　3. a dish
4. The clothes　5. the river

REVIEW TEST　　　　　　　　pp.10-11

1. ⑤　2. ①　3. ④　4. ②　5. a week　6. The
world　7. a sofa　8. ③　9. ⑤　10. ⑤　11. ③
12. ④　13. children　14. money　15. slices of
pizza　16. an umbrella　17. The stories
18. three glasses of milk

CHAPTER
02 대명사

A　1. it　2. we　3. he　4. they　5. she　6. they
　　7. it　8. they　9. she　10. we　11. he
　　12. you

B　1. Your　2. She　3. My　4. him　5. theirs
　　6. me　7. Her　8. Greg's　9. its　10. it

C　1. mine　2. her　3. your　4. They　5. his
　　6. ours　7. them　8. him　9. her　10. It

WRITING PRACTICE

1. us　2. Their　3. yours　4. me　5. Jack's

A　1. It　2. This　3. those　4. This　5. It
　　6. That　7. These　8. It

B　1. This　2. Those　3. That　4. These
　　5. That

C　1. It　2. These　3. those　4. That　5. It

WRITING PRACTICE

1. This　2. Those　3. It　4. That　5. These

REVIEW TEST　　　　　　　　pp.16-17

1. ③　2. ③　3. me　4. theirs　5. Her　6. ④
7. ④　8. ②　9. ②　10. ④　11. ③　12. ①　13. ②
14. It　15. them　16. It's[It is] Tuesday
17. I meet him　18. Those bottles

CHAPTER
03 be동사

A　1. are, They're　2. am, I'm　3. is, She's
　　4. are, You're　5. is, It's　6. are, We're　7. is,
　　Sarah's　8. is, Jake's

B　1. are　2. It's　3. am　4. We're　5. is　6. is
　　7. are　8. He　9. are　10. are

C　1. We're[We are]　2. I'm[I am]　3. The
　　children are　4. It's[It is]　5. He's[He is]
　　6. The airport is　7. You're[You are]
　　8. She's[She is]　9. They're[They are]
　　10. Lucy and I are

WRITING PRACTICE

1. I'm[I am]　2. You're[You are]　3. This train is
4. Victoria's[Victoria is]　5. My parents are

be동사의 현재형 2   pp.20-21

A 1. Are 2. Are 3. aren't 4. Is 5. Is
6. I'm not 7. are not 8. is not 9. are not
10. Are

B 1. are not, aren't 2. is not, isn't 3. am not,
I'm not 4. is not, isn't 5. are not, aren't
6. is not, isn't 7. is not, isn't 8. is not, isn't
9. are not, aren't 10. is not, isn't

C 1. Are you, I'm not / we aren't 2. Is it, it is
3. Is Bill, he isn't 4. Is your mother, she is
5. Are they, they aren't

WRITING PRACTICE

1. I'm[I am] not 2. Are you 3. Is it 4. Jane isn't
[is not] / Jane's not 5. Are they

UNIT 03 **be동사의 과거형**   pp.22-23

A 1. were 2. wasn't 3. was 4. were not
5. Was 6. was 7. were 8. were 9. was
10. wasn't

B 1. wasn't 2. wasn't 3. was 4. weren't
5. were 6. was 7. were 8. weren't

C 1. Were you, I wasn't / we weren't 2. Was
the watch, it was 3. Were they, they were
4. Were Jake and Kevin, they weren't
5. Was Chris, he was

WRITING PRACTICE

1. The water wasn't[was not] 2. The rooms
weren't[were not] 3. I was 4. We were 5. Were
your brothers

UNIT 04 **There is/are**   pp.24-25

A 1. are 2. Is 3. are 4. is 5. are 6. was
7. are 8. were 9. was 10. Are

B 1. There are 2. There is 3. There are

C 1. There are 2. There were 3. There was

4. There wasn't[was not] 5. There isn't[is
not] 6. There weren't[were not] 7. There
aren't[are not]

WRITING PRACTICE

1. Is there 2. There was 3. There are 4. There
were 5. There aren't[are not]

REVIEW TEST   pp.26-27

1. ③ 2. ⑤ 3. ② 4. are 5. was 6. isn't 7. ③
8. ③ 9. ② 10. There are 11. There is
12. There was 13. ⑤ 14. ④ 15. ⑤ 16. There
were many trees 17. Was it sunny 18. Are
those cartoons funny 19. This is not my
schoolbag

CHAPTER
04 일반동사 1

UNIT 01 **일반동사의 현재형 1**   pp.28-29

A 1. talks 2. mixes 3. jumps 4. tries
5. passes 6. flies 7. misses 8. writes
9. asks 10. buys 11. sees 12. brushes

B 1. studies 2. makes 3. wear 4. listens
5. clean 6. walk 7. takes 8. does
9. sits 10. read

C 1. a. go b. goes 2. a. know b. knows
3. a. teaches b. teach 4. a. cries b. cry
5. a. have b. has

WRITING PRACTICE

1. rains 2. brushes 3. use 4. fixes 5. eat

UNIT 02 일반동사의 현재형 2　　pp.30-31

A 1. have　2. doesn't　3. Do　4. doesn't
5. don't　6. Do　7. live　8. don't　9. don't
10. doesn't

B 1. doesn't speak　2. don't eat　3. doesn't
want　4. doesn't like　5. don't have
6. doesn't use　7. don't write　8. doesn't
lend　9. don't live　10. don't run

C 1. Does, stay　2. Do, know　3. Does, have
4. Do, use　5. Do, drink

WRITING PRACTICE

1. doesn't[does not] study　2. Do, need　3. don't
[do not] take　4. doesn't[does not] grow
5. Does, start

UNIT 03 일반동사의 과거형 1　　pp.32-33

A 1. loved　2. took　3. cried　4. wanted
5. dropped　6. cut　7. gave　8. taught
9. swam　10. came　11. lost　12. drank

B 1. watched　2. read　3. last week
4. stopped　5. heard　6. did　7. ran　8. had
9. found　10. met

C 1. bought　2. snowed　3. made　4. hit
5. stayed　6. missed　7. went　8. played
9. planned　10. tried

WRITING PRACTICE

1. moved　2. chatted　3. saw　4. slept
5. started

UNIT 04 일반동사의 과거형 2　　pp.34-35

A 1. see　2. didn't　3. pass　4. buy　5. Did
6. didn't　7. do　8. go　9. didn't　10. didn't

B 1. didn't like　2. didn't rain　3. didn't lock
4. didn't have　5. didn't take　6. didn't work
7. didn't enjoy　8. didn't go　9. didn't visit
10. didn't come

C 1. Did, walk　2. Did, fix　3. Did, give　4. Did,
buy　5. Did, get

WRITING PRACTICE

1. didn't[did not] try　2. Did, fall　3. didn't[did
not] drive　4. Did, play　5. didn't[did not] bark

REVIEW TEST　　pp.36-37

1. ④　2. ④　3. ②　4. ③　5. sang　6. doesn't
[does not] live　7. she doesn't　8. we did　9. ④
10. ⑤　11. ②　12. ④　13. ③　14. had
15. doesn't[does not] eat　16. Did, send
17. Does she remember your birthday　18. Jane
did not bring her wallet

CHAPTER 05 형용사와 부사

UNIT 01 형용사　　pp.38-39

A 1. lovely　2. some　3. some　4. any　5. any
6. smells good　7. something new
8. friendly　9. are interesting　10. anything
delicious

B 1. heavy　2. wrong　3. dirty　4. expensive
5. big　6. tired　7. healthy

C 1. some　2. any　3. some　4. some
5. some　6. any　7. some　8. some　9. any
10. any

WRITING PRACTICE

1. was boring　2. wonderful concert　3. brown
eyes　4. something special　5. became famous

A
1. wisely 2. well 3. heavily 4. hard
5. luckily 6. newly 7. clearly 8. warmly
9. quietly 10. beautifully 11. happily
12. strangely

B
1. really 2. very sorry 3. kindly 4. finally
5. easily 6. perfectly 7. late 8. brightly
9. Sadly 10. often goes

C
1. always looks tired 2. never reads fashion magazines 3. My best friend often borrows
4. am sometimes angry at 5. usually leaves his office at

WRITING PRACTICE

1. very dark 2. quickly 3. early 4. is usually clean 5. never uses

REVIEW TEST pp.42-43

1. ③ 2. ① 3. ⑤ 4. ② 5. ① 6. ② 7. any
8. some 9. ⑤ 10. ⑤ 11. ② 12. ②
13. very fast 14. is never afraid 15. easily
16. something strange 17. often calls
18. Interestingly, we found a secret room
19. Rome is an old city

WRITING PRACTICE

1. at school 2. in the bowl 3. in front of the door 4. next to the bookstore 5. behind the curtain

A
1. on 2. at 3. on 4. in 5. after 6. during
7. in 8. for 9. at 10. before

B
1. in 2. on 3. in 4. at 5. on 6. at 7. on
8. in 9. at 10. on

C
1. after 2. on 3. during 4. at

WRITING PRACTICE

1. for an hour 2. before 10:00 p.m 3. after school 4. on Tuesdays 5. during the test

REVIEW TEST pp.48-49

1. ② 2. ① 3. ④ 4. ④ 5. during 6. after
7. on 8. in 9. on 10. at 11. ③ 12. ⑤ 13. ④
14. ③ 15. ⓐ during ⓑ for 16. ⓐ at ⓑ at
17. drank water before the game 18. A movie star sat next to me

---

CHAPTER 06 전치사

A
1. me 2. on 3. us 4. at 5. on 6. in
7. in 8. under 9. on 10. in front of

B
1. behind 2. in 3. at

C
1. a. behind b. in 2. a. in front of b. at
3. a. on b. under

CHAPTER 07 동사의 종류

A
1. ⓑ 2. ⓐ 3. ⓒ 4. ⓑ 5. ⓒ 6. ⓐ 7. ⓑ
8. ⓐ

B
1. jumped 2. came 3. happened 4. drank
5. met 6. kicked 7. knew

C
1. teaches me Chinese 2. gave us these

tickets   **3.** tell us the truth   **4.** lent me an
umbrella   **5.** made us a chocolate cake
6. buys me lunch   **7.** showed me her room
8. sent my friends photos

WRITING PRACTICE

1. arrived safely   **2.** likes pop songs   **3.** have
four children   **4.** made me chicken soup
5. showed us the map

UNIT 02   동사의 종류 2   pp.52-53

A   **1.** feel   **2.** good   **3.** sounds   **4.** looks
5. happy   **6.** sick   **7.** hard   **8.** strange
9. call   **10.** keeps

B   **1.** sounded   **2.** look   **3.** are   **4.** tasted
5. smells   **6.** feels   **7.** looked

C   **1.** called her a hero   **2.** made me angry
3. keeps me awake   **4.** kept the fish fresh
5. call him Captain Park   **6.** found the
internet slow   **7.** made the countries poor
8. keeps her room clean

WRITING PRACTICE

1. felt nervous   **2.** looks healthy   **3.** sounded
boring   **4.** made him rich   **5.** found the bed
comfortable

REVIEW TEST   pp.54-55

1. ④   **2.** ③   **3.** ②   **4.** looked   **5.** heard
6. showed   **7.** ③   **8.** ④   **9.** ②   **10.** ④   **11.** ⑤
12. ②   **13.** smiles   **14.** became dirty
15. painted his house   **16.** lend people money
17. keeps my hands soft

CHAPTER
08 조동사

UNIT 01   **can, may**   pp.56-57

A   **1.** can   **2.** I order   **3.** cook   **4.** Can   **5.** can
read   **6.** I ask   **7.** may leave   **8.** cannot fly
9. find   **10.** can't

B   **1.** can watch   **2.** can see   **3.** can't get
4. can bake   **5.** can't have

C   **1.** May I speak   **2.** Can I sit   **3.** May I see
4. May I answer

WRITING PRACTICE

1. Can[May] I post   **2.** could hear   **3.** Can Emily
eat   **4.** Can[May] I buy   **5.** can[may] enter

UNIT 02   **must, have to**   pp.58-59

A   **1.** has   **2.** have   **3.** do   **4.** must not
5. doesn't   **6.** don't have to   **7.** has   **8.** must
follow   **9.** not write   **10.** have to

B   **1.** must not run   **2.** must listen to   **3.** must
finish   **4.** must not sleep   **5.** must keep
6. must not say   **7.** must not use

C   **1.** don't have to tell   **2.** has to fix   **3.** doesn't
have to work   **4.** don't have to take   **5.** has
to get up

WRITING PRACTICE

1. don't have to wait   **2.** must[has to] take care
of   **3.** doesn't have to call   **4.** must[have to] see
5. must not give

REVIEW TEST   pp.60-61

1. ⑤   **2.** ④   **3.** ④   **4.** ⑤   **5.** ②   **6.** Can   **7.** must
not   **8.** has to   **9.** ②   **10.** ⑤   **11.** ⑤   **12.** ①
13. ⓐ don't have to ⓑ can   **14.** Can[May] I use

15. can sing **16.** doesn't have to do **17.** must [has to] wear

WRITING PRACTICE

1. am not talking **2.** isn't[is not] flying **3.** aren't [are not] packing **4.** Are they climbing **5.** Are you drawing

---

CHAPTER 09 일반동사 2

UNIT 01 일반동사의 현재진행형 1 pp.62-63

A **1.** eating **2.** cutting **3.** playing **4.** drawing **5.** riding **6.** selling **7.** changing **8.** looking **9.** making **10.** getting **11.** swimming **12.** moving

B **1.** is raining **2.** am going **3.** is lying **4.** is traveling **5.** is shopping **6.** are singing **7.** are sitting **8.** are planning **9.** is asking **10.** are putting

C **1.** am tying **2.** is running **3.** are helping **4.** am choosing **5.** is shouting **6.** is crossing **7.** are listening

WRITING PRACTICE

1. am walking **2.** is looking **3.** are hiding **4.** are smiling **5.** is ordering

UNIT 02 일반동사의 현재진행형 2 pp.64-65

A **1.** playing **2.** isn't **3.** visiting **4.** I walking **5.** baking **6.** writing **7.** Is **8.** Are **9.** is not **10.** is

B **1.** isn't[is not] snowing **2.** aren't[are not] waiting **3.** isn't[is not] standing **4.** isn't [not] sleeping **5.** isn't[is not] checking **6.** am not sending

C **1.** Are, writing **2.** Is, jogging **3.** Is, washing **4.** Are, shaking

UNIT 03 일반동사의 미래형 1 pp.66-67

A **1.** be **2.** I'm **3.** meet **4.** to open **5.** take **6.** be **7.** to turn on **8.** is **9.** is going **10.** are

B **1.** will lend **2.** will help **3.** will be **4.** will buy **5.** will start **6.** will pass **7.** will plant

C **1.** am going to call **2.** is going to pay **3.** is going to go **4.** are going to eat **5.** is going to begin **6.** are going to build **7.** is going to watch **8.** are going to exercise **9.** is going to make **10.** are going to arrive

WRITING PRACTICE

1. am going to search **2.** are going to leave **3.** will remember **4.** is going to save **5.** will be

UNIT 04 일반동사의 미래형 2 pp.68-69

A **1.** Will **2.** going **3.** be **4.** will not **5.** study **6.** isn't **7.** they come **8.** Are **9.** not going **10.** are not

B **1.** won't[will not] tell **2.** won't[will not] say **3.** am not going to wait **4.** won't[will not] fail **5.** isn't[is not] going to have **6.** isn't[is not] going to take **7.** won't[will not] wash **8.** aren't[are not] going to wear **9.** aren't[are not] going to go **10.** isn't[is not] going to show

C **1.** Will, like **2.** Will, score **3.** Will, come **4.** Are, going to read **5.** Is, going to leave **6.** Are, going to have **7.** Are, going to watch

WRITING PRACTICE

1. won't[will not] call **2.** Are you going to take **3.** Will he win **4.** am not going to travel **5.** won't[will not] practice

REVIEW TEST
pp.70-71

1. ⑤ 2. ④ 3. ⑤ 4. ② 5. ③ 6. Will you
7. they are 8. ⓐ aren't ⓑ are 9. ② 10. ⑤
11. ④ 12. isn't reading 13. is going to snow
14. Will you make 15. Are they waiting 16. She
will not go 17. Are you going to sell

CHAPTER
10 비교

UNIT 01 비교급
pp.72-73

A 1. wiser 2. longer 3. happier 4. fatter
5. heavier 6. warmer 7. thinner 8. more
famous 9. cleaner 10. less 11. nicer
12. more beautiful

B 1. more 2. larger 3. worse 4. hotter
5. noisier 6. much 7. smaller 8. more
expensive 9. easier 10. more comfortable

C 1. smarter than 2. safer than 3. earlier
than 4. healthier than 5. better than
6. deeper than 7. taller than 8. funnier
than 9. more important than 10. more
delicious than

WRITING PRACTICE

1. lazier than 2. higher than 3. more quickly
than 4. stronger than 5. later than

UNIT 02 최상급
pp.74-75

A 1. funniest 2. fastest 3. largest 4. biggest
5. most 6. wisest 7. least 8. slowest
9. most difficult 10. most wonderful
11. hottest 12. heaviest

B 1. tallest 2. the smallest 3. worst
4. highest 5. most 6. busiest 7. greatest
8. the most 9. laziest 10. most exciting

C 1. the youngest 2. the best 3. the most
boring 4. the shortest

WRITING PRACTICE

1. the luckiest man 2. the smartest student
3. the cheapest tie 4. the kindest boy 5. the
most important chapter

REVIEW TEST
pp.76-77

1. ⑤ 2. ④ 3. ④ 4. ④ 5. ③ 6. thinner
7. more popular 8. worse 9. ④ 10. ③ 11. the
best 12. the hottest 13. ⑤ 14. ④ 15. ②
16. better than 17. younger than 18. the
highest mountain

CHAPTER
11 to부정사

UNIT 01 명사처럼 쓰는 to부정사
pp.78-79

A 1. ⓒ 2. ⓐ 3. ⓑ 4. ⓐ 5. ⓒ 6. ⓑ 7. ⓑ
8. ⓒ

B 1. a. to play b. play 2. a. paint b. to paint
3. a. to buy b. buy 4. a. join b. to join
5. a. finish b. to finish

C 1. to design 2. to lose 3. to leave 4. to
become 5. to touch 6. to see 7. to build

WRITING PRACTICE

1. decided to learn 2. important to keep 3. to
move 4. agreed to take 5. likes to take

형용사, 부사처럼 쓰는 to부정사

pp.80-81

A 1. four bags 2. a lot of emails
   3. some friends 4. money 5. some water
   6. a dress 7. some photos 8. anything

B 1. to get 2. to finish 3. to hear 4. to ride
   5. to see

C 1. to leave his hometown 2. to be healthy
   3. to call Mary 4. to go to the party
   5. to cook dinner

WRITING PRACTICE

1. glad to meet 2. a book to read 3. put on his
shoes to go 4. a passport to travel 5. called
me to ask

REVIEW TEST

pp.82-83

1. ⑤ 2. ④ 3. ④ 4. to 5. lt 6. ① 7. ④
8. ④ 9. ④ 10. ⑤ 11. ② 12. to help sick
people 13. to invite her to my house 14. to
meet Chris 15. to watch TV 16. a story to tell
you 17. wonderful to learn things 18. needs to
be on time

CHAPTER
12 접속사

and, but, or   pp.84-85

A 1. but 2. and 3. or 4. and 5. or 6. but
   7. but 8. or

B 1. a. or b. but 2. a. and b. but 3. a. but
   b. or 4. a. and b. or

C 1. and 2. but 3. but 4. and 5. or

WRITING PRACTICE

1. old but healthy 2. or take a bus 3. and my
mom read 4. but I don't like 5. phone number
or email address

when, before, after, because

pp.86-87

A 1. Because 2. comes 3. because 4. when
   5. after 6. opens 7. When 8. after

B 1. a. after b. when 2. a. because b. Before
   3. a. When b. before 4. a. because b. After

C 1. before it gets too dark 2. because we
   were bored 3. when we came back
   4. after he played the game 5. when I was
   in elementary school

WRITING PRACTICE

1. after I watched 2. because the movie was
funny 3. when my alarm rang 4. because it
was Saturday 5. before you come into

REVIEW TEST

pp.88-89

1. ① 2. ② 3. or 4. After 5. because 6. ③
7. ② 8. and 9. but 10. ⑤ 11. ④ 12. ⑤
13. the kitchen and the bathroom 14. when you
called 15. before he entered 16. because the
bus didn't[did not] come

CHAPTER 13 의문문, 명령문, 감탄문

UNIT 01   who, what   pp.90-91

A   1. Who   2. What   3. Who   4. Whose
5. Whom   6. Who   7. What   8. What
9. Who   10. What

B   1. What   2. Who   3. What   4. Whose
5. Who

C   1. What   2. Who(m)   3. Who   4. Whose
5. What

WRITING PRACTICE

1. Who sang   2. What flower   3. Who was
4. Whose shoes   5. What did you do

UNIT 02   when, where, why   pp.92-93

A   1. When   2. Why   3. Where   4. When
5. Why   6. What time

B   1. When   2. Why   3. When   4. Why
5. Where

C   1. Where   2. When   3. Why   4. Where
5. Why

WRITING PRACTICE

1. When did Peter buy   2. Where were you
3. What time do you go   4. Where did they have
5. Why did you keep

UNIT 03   how   pp.94-95

A   1. How tall   2. How long   3. How   4. How
much   5. How many

B   1. How much   2. How tall   3. How often
4. How far   5. How many

C   1. How much   2. How   3. How long / How
many years   4. How   5. How often

WRITING PRACTICE

1. How long   2. How old   3. How many   4. How
often   5. How

UNIT 04   부가의문문   pp.96-97

A   1. didn't   2. he   3. can   4. weren't
5. can't   6. are   7. will   8. was   9. don't
10. it

B   1. ⓕ   2. ⓒ   3. ⓓ   4. ⓖ   5. ⓔ   6. ⓑ   7. ⓗ

C   1. will you   2. is he   3. didn't he   4. doesn't
she   5. was it   6. weren't you   7. can't we
8. do they   9. can they   10. was it

WRITING PRACTICE

1. was interesting, wasn't it   2. didn't come, did
they   3. will win, won't he   4. spends, doesn't
she   5. can't change, can we

UNIT 05   명령문, 감탄문   pp.98-99

A   1. Let's   2. Be   3. she is   4. How   5. Let's
not   6. What   7. Don't   8. What   9. Do not
10. Let's

B   1. Don't speak   2. Don't swim   3. Stay
4. Let's take   5. Let's order   6. Let's go
7. Let's not sit

C   1. What a brave boy   2. How slowly
3. How great   4. What pretty eyes
5. How kind

WRITING PRACTICE

1. Be   2. How difficult   3. Let's turn on   4. What
a delicious sandwich   5. Don't call me

1. ①   2. ④   3. ⑤   4. What   5. Why   6. ④   7. ②
8. aren't you   9. did they   10. ⑤   11. ③   12. ④
13. How much   14. Let's find   15. Whose cap
16. What a smart robot it is   17. What time does
the game start